D1496152

Prince of the People

Prince of the People

The Life and Times of a
Brazilian Free Man of Colour

EDUARDO SILVA

Translated by Moyra Ashford

VERSO

London · New York

First published by Verso 1993
© Verso 1993
All rights reserved except those pertaining
to the Portuguese-speaking world

Verso
UK: 6 Meard Street, London W1V 3HR
USA: 29 West 35th Street, New York, NY 10001-2291

Verso is the imprint of New Left Books

ISBN 0-86091-417-8

British Library Cataloguing in Publication Data
A catalogue record for this book is available from the British Library

Library of Congress Cataloging-in-Publication Data
A catalogue record for this book is available from the Library of Congress

Typeset in Sabon by Solidus (Bristol) Limited
Printed and bound in Great Britain by
Biddles Ltd, Guildford and King's Lynn

For Graça and Isaura

Contents

Figures

JACOBINA

MORRO
DO
CHAPÉU

N

0   50
km

LENCÓIS

ANDARAI   Paraguaçu

60°W

0°

BRAZIL

SOUTH AMERICA

BAHIA

SALVADOR

PACIFIC OCEAN

Paraguay

Paraguay

ASUNCIÓN

Paraná

São Fransisco

RIO DE JANEIRO

Uruguay   DESTERRO

Paraná

ALEGRETE   URUGUALANA
S.GABRIEL   PORTO ALEGRE

32°S

BUENOS
AIRES

URUGUAY

ATLANTIC OCEAN

ARGENTINA

0   500
km

Preface

This book is an attempt to recover aspects of the daily life, the cultural ambience and the symbolic universe which existed among slaves, ex-slaves (freedmen) and (born) free men of colour in nineteenth-century Brazil, through a case study of the life and ideas of the self-styled Dom Obá II d'Africa (Obá meaning king in Yoruba), a 'street character' who lived in Rio de Janeiro in the final decades of both slavery and empire. To his social superiors Dom Obá was half-crazed; to Rio's slaves, freedmen and free men of colour, he was revered as a royal prince, the Prince of the People. For the historian he represents an unsuspected link between the ruling elites of the day and the common Brazilian people then emerging from the breakdown of traditional society.

In the first four chapters, the book reconstructs the life of Dom Obá as thoroughly as possible from the fragmentary nature of the documentation. The next two chapters (Chapters 5 and 6) are an investigation both of the nature of this relationship with the Brazilian emperor, Dom Pedro II, and of the extent and nature of his leadership within his own kingdom, the 'little Africa' of Rio de Janeiro. Chapter 7 deals with the general scope of Dom Obá's ideas and in particular his thinking on political and social questions, on the process of abolition of slavery and on inter-racial relationships. The last chapter is a discussion of the roots of and the influences on Dom Obá's ideas, his basic suppositions and symbols, and his vision of history.

Introduction

On 2 December 1888, Rio de Janeiro woke up in a festive mood. In a noisy demonstration of gratitude, ordinary people, 'mostly coloured', invaded the Imperial palace in the centre of the city. They were celebrating the 63rd birthday of Emperor Dom Pedro II and his return from Europe, where he had gone for medical treatment. But they were also celebrating – for the first time in the presence of their monarch – the law which had abolished slavery in the country, signed seven months earlier, on 13 May, by Dom Pedro's daughter and regent.

With this confluence of motives, public joy was to break all bounds on that day. 'The popular physiognomy of that monarchistic manifestation was exaggerated in frankness in such a manner that it was necessary for the police to order some less ceremonious citizens to put their shirts on', wrote, with some impatience, a young member of the opposition. One of these citizens, Cândido da Fonseca Galvão, better known as Prince Obá, or Dom Obá II d'Africa, was arrested for presenting himself at the palace with his sublieutenant's uniform festooned with 'belts of far-too-African feathers'. Such a gesture, like nearly everything else that this man did, turned him into a ready target for the 'unoccupied political satirists' of that turbulent time.[1]

A year later, on 2 December 1889, neither empire nor emperor remained. The Republic had been proclaimed seventeen days previously. The atmosphere in the city was no longer one of *festa*. That day, the 'highly popular prince' Dom Obá II d'Africa once again set out from home, wearing his uniform from the Paraguayan War, with its gold braid and epaulettes, swordbelt complete with sword, and hat of regimental plumes. As he went he gathered a considerable crowd, marching in protest in the direction of the Imperial palace. In front of its locked doors, he presented his arms, saluted in his own

1

individual style and, according to all the newspapers the next day, shouted 'Vivas' and 'other exclamations'. The police response was heavy-handed; 'the festive, whistling procession' or, according to another description, 'the joyful and shrill manifestation' was 'rapidly dispersed'.[2]

Considering the slight import afforded this small episode, it was to have drastic consequences. Four days after the protest march, the newly installed provisional government, presided over by a general, stripped the sublieutenant of his military honours for 'habitual bad and disorderly behaviour'.[3] A few months later, on 8 July 1890, Sublieutenant Galvão died 'alone and abandoned in the world', in a rooming house on the Rua Barão de São Félix, in the city's most deprived quarter. Surprisingly, his death made the front page of Rio's newspapers, and nearly every article about him emphasized the prince's 'enormous tribe of followers', or his 'immense popularity', in the city of Rio de Janeiro.[4]

After his death and burial, the prince remained in the popular memory of Rio de Janeiro for many years before finally disappearing. As late as 1918, as Lima Barreto records, it was still possible to come upon 'the last "pretas minas" [African women] who knew Prince Obá', above all in the poorer backstreets, such as the Largo do Moura and the Beco da Batalha.[5] On the other side of the city, in the elegant Confeitaria Colombo and in the Rua do Ouvidor, the bohemian poets would also mention the sublieutenant from time to time in their verses, sometimes with derogatory racial insinuations. Olavo Brás Martins dos Guimarães Bilac (1865–1918), the most famous of Brazil's Parnassian poets, made mention of Obá in a poem written to ridicule the recurrent rumours of a monarchist backlash, or, as it was often termed at the time, a 'sebastianista' ('messianic') counter-coup:

> Surda, a voz dos boatos assevera
> Que grande parte da população,
> Alonga os olhos sôfregos, a espera
>   De Dom Sebastião
>
> Dizem que, de uma longa soledade,
> Que é o ninho escuro da conspiração,
> Ele vira, em busca da cidade
>   De Dom Sebastião.
>
> É o Grão-Pará? o Obá? o Natureza?
> É mulher fraca ou válido barão?
> Ninguem sabe se príncipe ou princesa
>   É Dom Sebastião![6]

[Deaf, the voice of the rumours has it
That much of the population
Narrows their suffering eyes, waiting
    For Dom Sebastian.

They say, that from a distant solitude
That is the dark nest of conspiracy
He will come, seeking the city
    Of Dom Sebastian.

Is he the prince of Grão-Pará? Prince Obá? Prince Natureza?
Is he a frail woman or a valiant baron?
Nobody knows whether prince or princess
    Be Dom Sebastian!]

In a similar vein, Emílio de Menezes, in verses of crude satire, could still classify Professor Hermetério José dos Santos, a black teacher at the Colégio Pedro II, as 'grandson of Obá, the African prince', 'Froebel of nanquin or jet', 'Genial Pestalozzi brushed in tar!'[7]

Who was Dom Obá? What did he represent? Why did he provoke such conflicting reactions? What was he trying to say in 1888 with his African feathers; or later, in 1889, with his swiftly silenced 'Vivas' and 'exclamations'? Why did his words, and even his appearance, touch that society, from the common people to newspaper editors and highly placed state officials, so deeply?

These were the initial questions. The purpose of this book is to make an historical investigation of the life, times and thinking of this man, and, by extension, to contribute to the cultural history of Brazilian society. The setting is the second half of the nineteenth century, an era marked by profound social transformations. It was the time of the abolition of the transatlantic slave trade, the very backbone of the country's economy until then; it was a time of prolonged frontier conflict and the war with Paraguay; of the progressive decline and abolition of African slavery on the domestic front; a time of political crisis, leading eventually to a *coup d'état* and the overthrow of the emperor.

The project of studying a common man as a thinking individual and, at the same time, as a means to the penetration of an elusive popular culture and common mentality is not a new one. On the contrary, such an approach has been magnificently carried out in at least two works published in the 1970s and 1980s. The first, *The Cheese and the Worms*, by Carlo Ginzburg, sets out to study the 'ideas … feelings, fantasies … aspirations' of a Friuli miller, one

Domenico Scandella, as a channel of access to 'the collective mentalities' of sixteenth-century Italy, an 'extremely rich oral tradition', an 'obscure extract, nearly indecipherable, of remote peasant traditions'; the second, *The Great Cat Massacre*, in which Robert Darnton seeks to reveal (with great boldness, considering he is an Anglo-Saxon), 'a fundamental ingredient in artisan culture' in the French *ancien régime* via an old narrative of a massacre of cats carried out with great jocularity by apprentices and workers in a Paris printshop around 1730.[8]

In contrast to Scandella, however – and even to the workers of Rue Saint-Severin in Paris – Sublieutenant Galvão was a well-known personality, almost a celebrity in his time. Moreover, a relatively abundant archive is available: a portrait in oils, painted in 1886; news stories and caricatures in Rio's press; occasional observations of memoir writers, foreign travellers, prominent doctors, police chiefs, politicians, writers, poets, and so on. We also have his own writings, unearthed from archives and, above all, published in the less influential newspapers. Many knew of him because of his participation in 'disorders' such as those of 1888 and 1889; others because they had heard of his articles; yet others because of his frequent visits to the Imperial palace in the Quinta da Boa Vista, and still others (in truth, nearly everyone) because they had seen his regal promenades through the narrow streets of the old city, parading his well-preserved lieutenant's uniform, or, more frequently, sporting an elegant dress coat, top hat, gloves, cane, umbrella and gold pince-nez.

The judgement of his contemporaries could hardly have been harsher. For the German immigrant, Carl von Koseritz, who met him in 1883, Sublieutenant Galvão was nothing more than 'a half-crazed man' whom the emperor was 'patient' enough to receive at the palace and who was given to publishing incomprehensible treatises.[9] For Dr Rodolpho Galvão, in a thesis defended at the Faculdade de Medicina do Rio de Janeiro in 1886, the prince was a classic psychiatric case: 'Everyone knows and has seen passing through the streets of this city ... this original paranoic known as Prince Obá II d'Africa,' he wrote in an attempt to clarify to the examining board the delicate question of systematic delusions of grandeur.

> He is also a megalomaniac who never misses an opportunity to give proof of the systematization of his delirious conceptions, whether in the streets, always conserving princeliness in his manner of behaving and

dressing; whether in the press, where he is constantly exhibiting himself, making his profession of faith and alluding to his regal character.[10]

For Mello Moraes Filho, writing in the 1890s shortly after Dom Obá's death, it was precisely 'alcoholic excesses' which led the prince to megalomania, to the ever-perilous 'delusion of grandeur'. For Moraes Filho, as for many other contemporaries, the sublieutenant was just one more 'typical character' in an 'interminable gallery of street characters' of his time, the Rio de Janeiro of the transition from slavery. In his book, he deals not only with the prince, but also with other notorious characters – who were perhaps the scapegoats of the transition – 'Capitão Nabuco', the strongman of the city; 'Príncipe Natureza', who, like the prince, was seen as a crazy orator; 'Castro Urso', an enormous lottery ticket vendor, held to be a complete simpleton; 'Padre Quelé', 'Bolenga' and many others, renowned for their eccentricities, curious dress or physical deformities.[11] For the writer Hermeto Lima (1872–1947), too, the prince may have been a 'typical character', but he was also a dangerous subject, a case for the police.[12] The journalist, playwright and police chief Vicente Reis (1870–1947) included the prince among the 'most exotic types in the city', but he did not think him dangerous; he described Obá as a 'calm man', 'full of smiles' who 'harmed no-one'.[13]

Within a generation, the prince had become a part of Brazilian folklore. For Arthur Ramos (1903–49), a specialist in black Brazilian culture, he seemed a good example, almost an archetype, of a 'dethroned king or prince of historical or legendary monarchies'. Such kings or princes, according to Ramos's way of thinking – together with the African 'guardian and transmitter of tradition, the old slave who knows the family tales, the bard, the singer of nostalgic songs, the master of ceremonies of popular black games and dramatizations' – ended up permitting the creation of the rich, but neglected, black folklore of Brazil.[14]

By the middle of the twentieth century, almost forgotten, the prince was the subject of an entry in Câmara Cascudo's *Dicionário do Folclore Brasileiro* and a small chapter in a book of *petite histoire*. Both were largely based on the memories of Mello Moraes Filho, which was, on this point, the most accessible and influential text.[15]

As well as being severe, the judgement of the prince's contemporaries was also superficial and did not seem to take account of the other side of the picture. In truth, while affluent society dismissed him as crazy, the prince was revered as a royal prince by a considerable portion of the *carioca* population – slaves, freedmen and free men of colour – who appeared to share his world view, his symbols and ideas. Many paid him a tithe as if he were a true sovereign; they went down on their knees at his solemn passage with exclamations of pride and reverence; they met in the low-class bars to read aloud the articles which he published in both the trashier newspapers and in the mainstream press of the day.[16]

While at the time these were seen as mere *moxinifadas*, that is, incomprehensible rag-bags of ideas, his writings constitute a rare opportunity for taking research into directions which are often little explored because of, among other reasons, lack of adequate documentation. Finally, how is the behaviour of slaves, freedmen and free men in the dramatic moments of disintegration of the slave order to be explained? What did the Brazilian nation think about race relations, the rights and duties of citizenship?

Son of a freed African slave, a first-generation Brazilian, the prince, like his subjects, lived through complex historical and cultural processes. Even today his writings, penned in poorly assimilated Portuguese, peppered with Yoruba and even Latin (see Appendices A, B, C), transmit, as they did at the time, a strangeness, a sensation of socio-cultural barriers, which cannot be disregarded nor disrespected in a work of this type. Penetration of the epoch, and this specific culture, demands a methodological respect for difference. As Lévi-Strauss taught us, basing his practice on Malinowski: 'put yourself in the place of men where they lived, understand their intentions in their principle and their rhythm, perceive an age or a culture as a significant conjunct'.[17] On the same note, Robert Darnton also warns us of the epistemological importance of the residues of indecipherability, which thwart us as we try to penetrate a world of strange meanings. 'When we cannot manage to understand a proverb, a joke, a ritual or a poem' – or, one might add, a prince – 'then we can be certain that we have found something.'[18]

While engaged on research for this book, for the best part of the last eight years, I have been fortunate enough to count on the interest and support of several established historians: Dr Américo Jacobina Lacombe, Dr Francisco de Assis Barbosa, Dr Francisco José Calazans Falcon in Rio de Janeiro and, above all, in London, Professor Leslie Bethell, Professor of Latin American History at the University of London, and a specialist on the Brazilian slave trade and Brazilian slavery, who became not only the supervisor of my PhD thesis but a friend. I must also thank all my colleagues at the Centro de Estudos Históricos at the Fundação Casa de Rui Barbosa in Rio de Janeiro for their interest and critical comments from the very beginning of this project. In particular, I wish to single out Rosa Maria Barboza de Araújo.

I was fortunate in having the opportunity to present parts of this work (and my initial ideas) at a number of academic meetings. In December 1986 at a seminar at the Universidade Federal da Bahia; in June 1988, at an international congress promoted by the Universidade Federal Fluminense and Universidade Federal do Rio de Janeiro, on the occasion of the centenary of the abolition of slavery in Brazil; and in June 1991, at the University of London, as part of the Brazilian studies programme organized by the Institute of Latin American Studies.

On these occasions, as on others, I benefited particularly from the comments of Dr Luís Henrique Dias Tavares of Universidade Federal da Bahia; Sandra and Richard Graham of the University of Texas at Austin; Christopher Abel of University College, London; and Peter Clarke of King's College, London. Dr Robert Levine, of the University of Miami, kindly sent me the manuscript of a forthcoming book on the backlands of Bahia. Babatunde Sofela of the University of Ibadan and course companion at the University of London generously discussed and translated some of the phrases Dom Obá II d'Africa had written in Yoruba.

The research was made possible by the generous assistance of the staff of the following archives and libraries: in Brazil, Arquivo Nacional, Biblioteca Nacional, Arquivo Seletivo do Exército, Arquivo do Instituto Histórico e Geográfico Brasileiro, Museu Histórico Nacional, Arquivo Geral da Secretaria do Patrimônio Histórico e Artístico Nacional, Biblioteca da Academia Nacional de Medicina, Biblioteca e Arquivo Histórico da Fundação Casa de Rui Barbosa, Museu Imperial de Petrópolis, Arquivo Público do Estado da Bahia; in England, the British Library, University of London Library, School of Oriental and African Studies Library and the Library of the Brazilian Embassy. I am especially indebted to Helena Dodd Ferrez and Célia Góes of the Museu Histórico Nacional; to José Gabriel da Costa Pinto of the Arquivo Nacional; Lygia Cunha, of the Biblioteca Nacional, and Vicente Tapajós of Instituto Histórico e Geográfico Brasileiro for sending me materials I would otherwise have missed. Cecília Moreira Soares in Salvador, for a short period, and Pedro Paulo Soares, during his traineeship at the Fundação Casa de Rui Barbosa, helped me in researching archives.

In 1986 and 1987 I was fortunate enough to spend two periods carrying out field studies in Lençóis, in the interior of Bahia. The city no longer possessed anything concrete of the memory of its modest son, Cândido da Fonseca Galvão; the historical documents had been lost or sent to the capital. It did, however, retain much in terms of the architecture, customs, beliefs, sayings and legends of his time. For the warmth of their welcome, their patience in listening to my questions and the generosity of their replies, I must thank virtually the whole city, especially Dona Benedita Pereira da Paixão, still strong and lucid at 75 years of age and still conserving, with all her zeal, the typically Yoruba clay altar left by her great grandmother, a 'legitimate *nagô*' by the name of Cilivera; Sr José Porcino Araújo, the prospector Zé Cangolá, 64 years old, 'son of an ex-captive' and a devotee of Saint George the Warrior. Born in the region near Morro do Chapéu, and driven to the city by drought, Zé Cangolá had known in his youth the 'granddaughters of *nagô*', with their turbans, their African textiles and their characteristic sayings. I also wish to thank Sr Theotônio Oliveira, 96 years old, former diamond buyer and prominent local trader; Ivanice Alcântara de Souza, town councillor and director of the Casa de Cultura Afrânio Peixoto; and, most especially, the collector and guardian of local traditions, Sr Oswaldo Senna Pereira, known respectfully by the whole city as Mestre Oswaldo.

I am indebted to the Conselho Nacional de Desenvolvimento Científico e Tecnológico for the grant which enabled me to complete my studies in London and pursue my training as a historian. Maria Lúcia Lamounier lent me her office at critical moments; my sister Jô and my *compadre* Carlos Règent frequently looked after my affairs in Rio de Janeiro in my absence; Luciano Magnavita drew the map; Graça not only typed the text, but shared all the good and the bad moments along the way.

E.S.
London, April 1992

1

The Illusion of the Mines

Lençóis is like Brazil, all the hinterland of Brazil. Without the illusion offered by the mines, the cupidity and the hope of gain, who of those there on the coastal plains would have come to this place, or would have ventured further, to the depths of this lands without end? Who would have taken account of this that is ours today and was conquered and claimed by them – the miners, the hunters of gold and diamonds?

Afrânio Peixoto, *Bugrinha*, 1922

The Hinterland

Shortly before Brazilian independence in 1822, when the German naturalists Johann von Spix and Karl von Martius crossed the hinterlands of Bahia cataloguing the flora, fauna and geology of the region, they were struck by the spectacle of the Sincorá mountains looming over the 'solitudinous' landscape of 'rugged beauty'. The sierra, with its gentle green slopes, its sudden abrupt escarpments and brilliant white terraces, formed what these scientists described as an 'extremely picturesque' backdrop.[1]

In the foreground, in the valley of the Rio Sincorá, they were delighted by the 'thousands of many-coloured butterflies' fluttering around them and the sparkling stream of clear water running between banks brimming with the 'magnificent' mauve and purple flowers of Melastomaceas, Rhexias and Andromedas.

They had crossed over into Bahia from the neighbouring province of Minas Gerais, following the course of the São Francisco river into the interior. They were struck by the geological formations of mid-west Bahia. Everything they saw reminded them, as they repeatedly noted, of the Tejuco diamond-mining region they had left in Minas

Gerais. They became convinced, and with good reason, that the mountain range known as the Sincorá was no less than the last northern spur of the great Mantiqueira massif, which formed the main source of the mineral wealth of the province from where they had come.[2]

Their hypotheses were clearly seductive; yet if they had insisted in pursuing their research, it might have cost them their lives. It was by then October, the beginning of the driest season of the year, and not even the priest himself in the nearest settlement, also known as Sincorá, 'was able to obtain corn meal'. Their research became of secondary importance. The next day, 'the absolute lack of forage' forced them to make the mountain crossing and then follow the difficult trek to Maracás, the next settlement *en route* for the city and port of Salvador. As they had been warned by the locals, they found nothing for 20 leagues (60 miles) except dry, inhospitable bush (*caatinga*): neither water to drink nor fodder for the animals. The only thing they came across 'in three or four places' were pools of foetid, bitter green water. 'In truth our situation was desperate and we ran imminent risk of remaining with our baggage in this sad solitude until we should die of want.' Their misfortunes reached a crisis one night with the flight of their guide who, like them, feared for the worst possible outcome.

The crossing of the Sincorá mountains a few days previously had already proved to be a difficult enterprise. The famished packmules had eaten a poisonous weed common in the region and 'trembled', 'panted and gasped', falling to their knees on the steepest parts of the trail without the strength to continue. The scientists had then been obliged to carry their specimens to the other side of the mountains themselves. Now in the middle of the *caatinga*, the starving mules, sores on their backs from the packsaddles, 'refused to go a step further'. Two collapsed, dead. The rest, sick and exhausted, had to be abandoned to their fate. 'In this extreme affliction' Spix and Martius were forced to abandon to 'that parched brushland' most of the minerals and animal fossils which they had collected in the course of their painstaking research and concentrate 'merely on saving our lives'.

What in fact saved them was the arrival of another, 'well-organized' mule-train, led by locals, which was providentially following the same route, carrying bales of cotton to be sold in Salvador. Senhor Agostinho Gomes – an 'honoured *fazendeiro*' (plantation owner) from Caetité – 'generously offered us some of his mules ..., gave us part of his stock of corn and, in short, took charge of our journey as far as the coast, where he left us safe and sound'.[3]

Economy and Society

These, then, were the prevailing conditions throughout mid-western Bahia in the time of Spix and Martius, that is, between 1817 and 1820. Apart from some gold-mining settlements dating back to the first half of the eighteenth century, such as Vila do Rio de Contas in the Jacobina district and other smaller hamlets,[4] settlement on the plains of the region, an area covered in scrub bush (serrado), had taken place in the form of enormous plantations (fazendas) situated around the best sources of drinking water, where cattle, horses and donkeys were raised on the tough, drought-resistant native grass. The main product was hide or, less frequently, cotton. Spix and Martius described the Fazenda da Lagoa de Nossa Senhora da Ajuda, which lay between Caetité and Vila do Rio de Contas as 'one of the greatest estates in the hinterland' and counted 'one hundred and sixty slaves'. Fazenda Casa da Telha ('Roof-Tile House Farm' – tiles were a great luxury in the region), also in Rio de Contas, was a 'vast fazenda' with great plantations of cotton in the midst of the caatinga. The owners of these vast estates were almost always absentees, often living in 'incredible splendour' in more civilized regions and entrusting the administration of their affairs, according to Spix and Martius, 'to a mulatto'.[5]

In the drier regions the fazendas were poorer, 'widely scattered' and generally clustered around 'waterholes or filthy reservoirs' known locally as cacimbas, rather than actual springs. The very names of the properties in this area reflect the conditions there: Fazenda do Pau de Espinho (thornwood), Fazenda do Seco (dry farm) and Fazenda do Rio Seco (dry river farm).[6]

In addition to the principal products – gold, leather and cotton destined for the export market – clusters of small farms produced subsistence crops, mainly maize and manioc. On the large fazendas, these subsistence crops were left to the slaves' own initiatives, a system that had existed since the beginning of slavery in Brazil. On the Fazenda da Lagoa de Nossa Senhora da Ajuda, for example, Spix and Martius were able to buy the provisions they needed directly from the slaves who, as they noted, 'cultivated their own small plots on their rest-days'.[7]

Subsistence crops were also produced by a number of small and extremely poor settlements dotted here and there. Such a place was

Arraial de Maracás, a hamlet which, 'half-ruined and very poor, had been abandoned by the majority of its inhabitants', or Vila de Pedra Branca, which was described simply as 'rows of low mud hovels in the middle of which stood a church of the same material' and the 'small and poor' Sincorá, where Spix and Martius were unable to purchase fodder for their animals and where 'not even the priest of the settlement himself was able to obtain corn meal'. The standards of health and living conditions throughout the area appeared to both travellers as 'inferior ... to those of the most isolated folk of the hinterland of Minas' and even 'incredible' in 'a land of such ostentatious riches' as Brazil.[8]

The final element in the social picture was a dangerous, floating population of adventurers known as *valentões* or *jagunços*, who roamed the hinterland, hiring themselves out to do the plantation owners' dirty work. They practised all kinds of atrocities but managed to escape justice by virtue of an intimate knowledge of the terrain and the help of allies. This was undoubtedly the case of the 'gigantic man', certainly a fugitive, who 'wrapped in a horseman's cloak and armed with sword and pistols' swept into the house in which the scientists were staying in Vila de Caetité and with great 'boldness', 'with impetuous arrogance and merry jests' and without so much as a greeting, demanded 'immediate treatment' for his venereal disease.[9]

'Madness, Sheer Madness'

Profoundly impressed by all that they had seen, particularly by the possibility that the Bahian highlands might also prove to be rich in diamonds, the German naturalists reported their findings to one of the region's great landowners, Sergeant-major Francisco José da Rocha Medrado. It was however to take another twenty years before the first successful strike was made in 1841 (at Aroeiras mine, in Chique-chique) by a lieutenant called Malto who had followed the São Francisco river down from Minas Gerais along a similar route to Spix and Martius.[10] New discoveries were to follow, the first in a sequence which is extremely difficult to establish, not least because of the speed of events: Morro do Chapéu (1841), Serra da Chapada Grande, or Aroeiras (1841–2), Serra do Sincorá (1843–4), Santa Isabel do Paraguaçu (1844), as well as Perdizes, Andaraí, Lençóis and other small finds.

In less than six months, the population on the banks of the Rio

Mucugê in the Serra do Sincorá exploded to more than 25,000. In the settlement of Paraguaçu in 1844 it was reported that a *garimpeiro* (prospector) could, in the space of a few hours, find 19 *oitavas*, that is 1,972 carats of diamonds. Rumours of fabulous wealth spread in Salvador and throughout the São Francisco valley and the hinterlands beyond, attracting ever-larger numbers of hopeful prospectors, traders, fugitives and runaways of every kind, particularly from the declining mining regions of Minas Gerais. In a very short time the 'solitudinous landscape' which had so enchanted Spix and Martius had changed out of all recognition.

Places which until then had been lost in the wilderness, inhabited only by a few maize and manioc growers, would acquire, from one hour to the next, a population of 1,800 or 2,000. Depending on the success or failure of their efforts, the prospectors would settle or move on, following the rumours of new finds in a rush which between 1844 and 1848, according to Sílvio Fróes, rivalled those of California and Australia.[11] It was 'madness, sheer madness' in the words of a local observer, who knew some of these pioneers in the early years of the twentieth century 'The most intrepid crossed mountains and jungle in search of streams or rivulets where they would set up their tents and in a few days, if fortune smiled, a great camp would spring up round them ... and so the exploration continued.'[12]

'Woe to You, Lençóis'

The discovery of the *Rio dos Lençóis* diamond fields in 1845 turned the barely inhabited region into the main nucleus of attraction, drawing adventurers of all classes and trades. 'Woe to you, Lençóis! Every down-and-out, every beggar, *jagunço*, horsethief and woman of ill-repute from the hinterland of Brazil has descended upon you,' wrote the novelist Afrânio Peixoto, Lençóis's most famous writer, many years later.[13] Nor, one should add, were these the only migrants. Many freedmen who vegetated on the verge of society in Salvador, the Recôncavo and even in the distant hinterland, saw the diamond fields as an opportunity for integration or even rising within the system. Even the better-off were unable to resist the lure of easy riches. They flooded in from all over the province and, above all, from the declining areas of Minas Gerais. Some arrived in great cavalcades, such as that organized by Commander Antônio Botelho de Andrade, who arrived from Minas with vast quantities of baggage, livestock, slaves, family and dependants.[14]

The almost total absence of law and order during these early days was encapsulated in later years by a saying that was very characteristic of the region: 'There is no such thing as an old woman nor green wood in the mines.'[15] This was a time of adventure and easy wealth, virtually absent of regulation or authority. *Poço Rico* (Rich Well), one of the richest deposits, soon became known as *Poço das Mortes* (Deadmen's Well). The prospectors would dive to the bottom and scrape up the gravel in tin dishes which were auctioned off to the highest bidder as soon as they reached the surface. Such auctions gave rise to many violent disputes: six people were killed and many more wounded in one which, in all its detail, was to remain part of the town lore for many years, giving rise to the change of name.

In view of the wealth of the region, the provincial government soon sought to safeguard the Treasury's interests and establish some form of law and order. Under both the colonial decree of 24 December 1734, and the Imperial law of 25 October 1832, all discoveries of diamonds belonged to the Crown. As early as 1845, the president of the province of Bahia, Barão de Caçapava, classified the illegal extraction of precious stones in the region as 'daylight robbery of the public coffers' and demanded that central government do something about it.[16]

By then the excavations at Sincorá had spread over 'an area of 15 leagues (45 miles) in radius' and the number of prospectors and adventurers of every sort had mushroomed to more than 30,000.

TABLE 1   Value of the Brazilian Currency in US$, 1825–1900

Year	Value of 1 mil-réis in dollars	Value of 1 conto de réis in dollars
1825	1.05	1050.00
1850	0.58	580.00
1875	0.55	550.00
1900	0.19	190.00

The mil-réis was replaced in 1942 by the cruzeiro. One mil-réis is written 1$000; one conto de réis (equals one thousand mil-réis) is written 1:000$000. The signs $ and : are read as follows: 153:247$320 means 153 contos, 247 mil-réis and 320 réis.

Source: Stanley J. Stein, *Vassouras, a Brazilian coffee county, 1850–1900* (Princeton, 1985), p. 293.

The owners of the land – or, according to the provincial president, those who claimed to own land – collected dues which by rights should have gone to the government, and leased small plots for sums which varied, according to their location, from 10$000 to 100$000 a year. Stretches of the river with natural pot-holes, where the diamonds accumulated, were always negotiated separately, and for a special price, some being sold for as much as 5:000$000. Some of the most promising pot-holes were not for sale. There were reports of one, for example, which was supposed to have produced the sum of 16:000$000 in three days' work.[17] The climate of secrecy which reigned for the purpose of misleading the tax inspector has made any more precise evaluation of this early production extremely difficult. Mr Wetherell, the British vice-consul of Bahia, estimated, from 'the opinion of those persons best acquainted with the district' and even some 'speculators', that in the first year, 1845, some 4,000–5,000 carats were dug up every month. In the following year, production rose to between 10,000 and 12,000 carats a month.[18] Between 1852 and 1862, taking the province as a whole, the figures available indicate an average annual production of 5,007 eighths of an ounce (1 eighth of an ounce = 3.6 g). Between 1888 and 1904, it fell to 1,339 eighths of an ounce per year and, between 1904 and 1923, to a mere 300 eighths of an ounce annually.[19]

A fortune lay at arm's reach at the bottom of the fast-flowing streams. There was neither time nor interest in building a solid or enduring infrastructure. Lodgings were simple bivouacs improvised from a piece of the rough bleached calico used for slaves' clothes and a straw roof. From a distance the encampments resembled sheets hung out to dry, and it was this sight, according to the most commonly accepted version, that inspired the name for both the river – Rio dos Lençóis (River of Sheets) – and the settlement which sprang up overnight.[20]

Yet accommodation was not cheap. According to the provincial president in a letter to the Imperial minister of the exchequer, 'each straw hut put up by the inhabitants ... must pay 1:000$000 per month for every braça (1.8 metres) of land occupied ..., there are no lodging houses and these plots are sold for more or less money depending on the demand.' The Barão de Caçapava went on to urge the national government to take prompt action and provide him with support, 'to acquire for the nation's coffers, by whatever means necessary ... all the immense income which some individuals are enjoying, without any right or entitlement'. According to the information he possessed – and the Barão proved to be very well-informed in this respect – the government was losing revenue of more than 200:000$000 per year in the area. If the state had made its presence felt, this sum could have been going into the imperial coffers or into public works in the state of Bahia, 'which sorely needed them'.[21]

It was, however, to take time for the interests of the Treasury, the administration and public order to be imposed on that 'solitudinous country'.[22] With the wealth produced by the diamonds, the cloth and straw shacks gave way to two-storey houses with arched windows of multi-coloured glass. The new houses, solidly built of adobe and tile, soon filled the small valley and extended along both sides of the river in the sloping streets and narrow alleyways which today give the city its unique charm.

On 28 May 1852 the settlement, which until then had formed part of the parish of Santa Isabel do Paraguaçu, was made a District in its own right; on 18 December 1856 it was further upgraded to the status of a Vila – Comercial Vila dos Lençóis – the seat of a new municipality, separate from Santa Isabel; and on 15 July 1857 the *Repartição dos Terrenos Diamantinos* (the Diamond Fields Authority) was transferred from Santa Isabel to the new Vila of Lençóis, reflecting the increasing importance of the area's production. Finally, on 20 May 1864 the town achieved the status of a city, retaining the name of Lençóis. In just nineteen years this tumultuous mining camp had been transformed into the administrative seat of a vast municipality.[23]

'The Court of the Hinterland'

The diamonds brought wealth, influence, titles and culture. Commercial links – with Paris in particular, but also with London and Amsterdam – became increasingly important. Mine-owners and, above all, the *pedristas* – the great diamond merchants – made their fortune and built magnificent mansions protected by bodyguards and *jagunços* (thugs). In Afrânio Peixoto's period romance *Bugrinha*, a novel based on the author's experiences and knowledge of the region, an ex-prospector remembers this golden heyday with nostalgia: 'you could find diamonds by the handful; lying in the virgin gravel wherever you dug. . . . Money flowed like a mountain stream; everyone had *contos* and *contos* of réis. People lit cigars with banknotes and washed their horses with scented soap; you only ever saw silver harness and silk dresses.'[24]

Lençóis embraced civilization with pomp and ostentation. It had become the most important town in mid-west Bahia. Its inhabitants, proud of its newly acquired social and political status, dubbed it the 'Corte do Sertão' (the Court of the Hinterland), an analogy with the distant Rio de Janeiro, seat of the Imperial Court.

The sons of the richest families were sent to study in Salvador, Rio or even Europe. The shops imported the latest women's fashions and Pleyel pianos (some of which still exist) from Paris. Fabrics and luxury items for gentlemen, including indian ink, were imported from England. Comendador Joaquim José Pereira, known as Cata-cury, a rich merchant who lived from 1827 to 1899, had a wife known as Iaiá Douradinha (the Golden Lady) for her blonde hair and extravagant jewels, and sent his sons to study in London. Coronel Ulderico de Magalhães Macedo, another merchant con-nected with some of the richest mines in the region, settled in Paris with his wife, children and slave *áias* (ladies' maids).[25] Again, in Bugrinha, the local colonels frequently boasted that they had more ties with Europe than with Salvador da Bahia, the capital of the province. 'We get everything from there', said a certain *capitão* in reference to Paris, 'and our diamonds go there ... what is Bahia to us?' In another passage, a particular *pedrista* is described as roaming from one place to another, with frequent trips to Europe, 'enjoying the wandering life of a fellow who has been fortunate in business'.[26]

Drought, Famine and Epidemics

Yet problems did exist, despite the wealth and influence which accumulated so rapidly. In 1858 the then Comercial Vila dos Lençóis suffered its first severe epidemic of smallpox, or *bexiga*, as it was known in the region, and the Municipal Council had to make an urgent appeal for vaccine to the provincial president of the time, João Luís Vieira Cansanção de Sinibu.[27] The following year, 1859, the first prolonged and dramatic effects of the great drought which overtook the region began to be felt. The vila, an oasis of plenty in the parched hinterland, was soon invaded from all over the province by hordes of refugees in need of care and work.

In addition, the droughts made it more difficult to wash the gravel in the diamond fields, reducing production and raising the cost of keeping both slaves and the so-called *meia-praças* – free men working as tied labour who were obliged to share the fruits of their labours with a *fornecedor* (provider), or *patrão* (patron) in exchange for a weekly advance for food.[28]

Some of those affected by the 1859 drought were able to find work as *meias-praças*; others had no choice but to labour on the 'work gangs' organized by the Municipal Council. It is from this period that public works such as the Romanesque bridge linking the Praça das Nagôs to the Bairro de São Félix date.[29] In 1860 news of the worsening situation had reached the city and province of Rio de Janeiro, where a public subscription was raised among wealthy landowners and coffee-buyers 'for the benefit of the famine victims in Bahia'.[30] The crisis was to continue until 1862.

By the end of the 1860s, after twenty years of intense exploitation, diamonds were becoming more and more scarce in the gravel beds of the tiny river. At the same time the price of diamonds fell on the international market as a series of events affected both suppliers and clients. First, the South African rush was underway with the discovery of a major diamond field in the Transvaal in 1866. By 1870, the South African Union dominated the international market, bringing an end to the hegemony of Lençóis. And in 1871, the outbreak of the Franco–Prussian War forced a further drop in demand.[31]

In the decade following the 1871 crisis many mine-owners began to abandon the region for the southern parts of the province where they could invest their capital in the growing and selling of cacao, the demand for which promised equally large profits on the international market. The exodus from Lençóis was only mitigated in the 1880s with the exploitation of carbonate, a variety of black diamond which at first had no commercial value but which soared in price with the discovery of its uses in heavy drilling.[32] But the demand was not sufficient to turn back the course of depopulation. This was the destiny of Afrânio Peixoto's family, one of the most influential in the region, who were among those who left, moving to Salobro in the municipality of Canavieiras in the south of the province in 1885. In fact, his novel *Bugrinha* takes place in precisely this era – the mid-1880s – when the diamonds had become scarce but the carbonate still sustained the economy to an extent, bringing some prosperity. It is the story of a socially unacceptable love-affair between a simple but sensitive country girl and a privileged son of the local elite recently returned from his studies in Salvador. For Peixoto, slave-owning Lençóis was nothing more than a microcosm of Brazil, 'always in crisis, never prepared'.[33]

Slave, Freedman, Free Man

This, then, is the briefly sketched background to the first phase – which we could call the phase of political socialization – of the life of that 'free man of colour', Cândido da Fonseca Galvão. His father, an African of the Yoruba nation, was baptized with the name of Benvindo on his arrival as a slave in Salvador. When Benvindo was freed, on an unknown date in the first half of the nineteenth century, he adopted – as many other freedmen did – the surname of his former master, a name that carried great prestige throughout Salvador, Pernambuco and Alagoas.[34]

Shortly afterwards, Benvindo was to take advantage of the recently granted right of freedom of movement and join the Lençóis diamond rush. Evidence would suggest that around 1845 he took part in one of the first influxes from the provincial capital to the hinterlands in search of opportunity and fortune in the Serra do Sincorá.

However, documentary research on this specific point has proved to be particularly fruitless due to the total lack of any corroborating evidence such as birth, marriage or death certificates in any of the archives investigated in Lençóis, Salvador or Rio de Janeiro.

With regard to his son, we know, as all the documents attest, that he was born in Lençóis, and that it was in this city that he played an active part in the recruiting of volunteers for the Paraguayan War in 1865, a role which gave him his first opportunity to display qualities of leadership, as we shall have occasion to see. Although we have been unable to ascertain his exact date of birth, it is probable that he left for the war as a young adult, which would mean that he was born during the 1845 rush and settlement of Lençóis twenty years earlier, or a little later.

The Enlistment Campaign

In 1865 Lençóis, like other communities in the interior and the capital of the province itself, began to live the drama of recruitment and enlistment for the war against Paraguay.

During the empire, as in colonial times, military service was not obligatory. Numbers in the armed forces were maintained principally by forced conscription among the poorest sectors of the population, who were mainly black Africans, Indians and those of mixed blood.[35] Thus, 'in the rank and file of the army, as in the crews of the fleet', wrote Oliveira Lima, 'one only sees blacks and mestizos of various shades'.[36]

On the eve of the war with Paraguay the army regulars – with the exception of those who had fought against Uruguay twenty years earlier – were poorly trained and ill-equipped soldiers, 'who lived in the provinces, guarding and patrolling the hinterland and performing police duties'. The empire's entire army consisted of a mere 'sixteen infantry battalions, five cavalry regiments and some artillery troops'.[37]

Consequently, Brazil went to war in 1865 on a very shaky footing. Swift action was needed: on 7 January the emperor signed Decree 3371, establishing the *Voluntários da Pátria* (National Volunteer Corps) and offered himself as the first volunteer.

In Bahia, which was still recovering from the 1859–62 drought, the effects of the decree were immediate. The province was to contribute more volunteers than any other, as can be seen in Table 2.

By the end of January 1865, the president of the province, *desembargador* Luis Antônio Barbosa de Almeida, had held the first councils to decide the implementation of the enlistment, had published a proclamation in the *Diário da Bahia* and mobilized the detachments of the National Guard stationed in Salvador, converting them 'by order of the government' into a Volunteer Corps. Thus,

TABLE 2   Number of Voluntários da Pátria, by province, 1865

Province		Province	
Bahia	9,164	Paraíba	1,472
Corte	7,128	Piauí	1,420
Pernambuco	5,793	Mato Grosso	1,417
São Paulo	4,824	Sergipe	1,405
Rio de Janiero	4,667	Santa Catarina	1,103
Rio Grande do Sul	3,200	Rio Grande do Norte	814
Maranhão	2,385	Espírito Santo	625
Minas Gerais	2,158	Paraná	613
Pará	2,084	Amazonas	367
Ceará	2,037	Goiás	275
Alagoas	1,591		
Total			54,542

Source: Adapted from Paulo de Queiroz Duarte, op. cit. vol. I, p. 2.

a mere two weeks after the publication of the Imperial Decree, the first Volunteer Corps embarked in Salvador for the front; another two followed in March. This policy was maintained, at the same speed, by Barbosa de Almeida's successors in the provincial presidency: Dr Baltazar de Araújo Aragão Bulcão, Almeida's vice-president, who held the presidency for a brief month and a half, and Bacharel Manoel Pinto de Souza Dantas, who succeeded him on 24 July.

Salvador soon 'resembled a great army encampment or training centre, with soldiers and recruits on every block, in every street and square'. Mobilization went on at a furious pace throughout the province, totalling more than 9,000 men in less than a year.[38]

The movement soon reached the most distant areas of the hinterlands. By the beginning of February, Lençóis had made its first moves to ensure 'that this Municipality will send a great number of volunteers to the army' with the municipal council distributing letters of convocation to 'all persons who wish to offer their services'[39] As in many towns in the interior, the campaign was headed by the most powerful local political chief, Coronel Antônio Gomes Calmon, the commander-in-chief of the Municipality's National Guard, leader of the Conservative party and first Intendent (mayor) of the town.

Coronel Antônio Gomes Calmon's campaign was so successful that it provoked envy and insinuations of darker motives, which were to spread beyond the boundaries of the municipality, appearing in newspapers published in the provincial capital and, shortly after, in Rio de Janeiro, in the paid columns of the Jornal do Commercio. The articles were entitled Negócios dos Lençóis (The Lençóis Affair), a title redolent of scandal. But the author, or authors, never identified themselves, writing under the pseudonyms 'Aristarchus' and 'Justiça' (Justice).

It was thought that the 'affair' was the work of one of the supporters of Antônio Gomes Calmon's local rival, Coronel Felisberto Augusto de Sá, the leader of the Liberal party. Political disputes in small, isolated communities like Lençóis frequently boiled down to personal power struggles between Coronéis and the tense atmosphere reigning during the frantic preparations for war was especially propitious for their exacerbation. It was clearly not a controversy between two schools of political thought: as becomes clear when studying the actions of Conservatives and Liberals during the process of the abolition of slavery, neither party had a clear ideological foundation.[40]

According to 'Aristarchus', on the eve of leaving for the regional capital at the head of his volunteers, the Conservative leader and commander-in-chief of the National Guard, Antônio Gomes Calmon, 'ordered the purely arbitrary arrest' of Tenente Marciano Gonçalves Pereira, the tax-collector for the province. 'Aristarchus' described Tenente Pereira as one of the 'independent' citizens of the municipality who were 'happily not uncommon', and went on to denounce unspecified 'excesses' in the enlistment programme throughout the hinterlands. He also denounced – and this was his main point – the 'numerous illegitimate ambitions' being nurtured under the auspices of patriotic enlistment. 'There is no-one who does not consider himself competent to organize battalions', he wrote, 'when the government guarantees them the opportunity of commandership.' This, said 'Aristarchus', was the case of the municipal commander-in-chief who, 'under this phosphorescence of cheap patriotism', only sought to obtain favours 'at the expense of the government'.[41]

'Justiça' continued in the same vein. He predicted complete failure for enlistment in Lençóis, due to the commander-in-chief's lack of leadership ability and political prestige. According to 'Justiça', the commander's 'subjects' did not trust him, mocked his threats, despised his pretensions and did not want to follow him.[42]

The *Voluntários da Pátria*

In fact, the prevailing means of enlistment did merit the criticism of various contemporaries. Medeiros e Albuquerque, a strong advocate of republican ideas, wrote, 'they are called *voluntários* but were almost always forced conscripts'.[43] In certain circles it was the fashion to refer to these soldiers as 'roped-in volunteers' or 'stick and leash volunteers'.

However, this was not true of the free man Cândido da Fonseca Galvão, nor, certainly, of many others who, like him, had presented themselves at the first opportunity to 'that great conservative and monarchist', Antônio Gomes Calmon.[44] When addressing the emperor many years later, Galvão referred to the episode of the enlistments with great pride.

When the cry of affliction sounded from all corners of the empire and the enthusiastic hearts of the sons of the southern cross became possessed by the most alive and fearless patriotism, they raced clamouring to defend the honour of the homeland so vilely defamed.

In this emergency, he continued, 'the humble subject with whom you are speaking also allowed himself to join in and the living flame, the sacred fire of patriotic love, flowed to his every viscera.'[45] In another text, also addressed to the 'Imperial Master', he explained,

> when our national honour and integrity had been attacked and villified by the despotic ex-government of Paraguay, inspired by the sacrosanct love of Patriotism, I enlisted as a true soldier in the ranks of the valiant troops of the brave Voluntários da Pátria who marched ... in various battles.[46]

Other free men of colour, or ex-slaves, told a somewhat different story. Many, particularly those from the big cities, really were 'roped-in volunteers'. Frequently, they were men who were held to be disorderly exponents of the martial art known as *pernada* (in Rio de Janeiro) and *capoeira de Angola* (in Salvador). This was the case, for example, of another volunteer, also Bahian, who was conscripted at the time of Conselheiro Sinimbu when the people of Salvador demanded 'meat without bones, flour without chaff and good thick bacon'. History does not record his name, but he cannot have been a bad recruit, or at least, a bad marching companion. 'He was a tall and muscular creole who walked with a rollicking swing and sported a pointed turban above a wide shiny forehead,' wrote Dionísio Cerqueira in his reminiscences of the war. 'He was very clean – it was a pleasure to see the shine on his beltbuckle and buttons. He was famed for the cigarettes he made, which he sold to the officers. He greatly loved to sing.'[47]

For many, however, the war offered the chance of ceasing to be cheap labour. From colonial times slaves had enlisted under false names as a way of gaining their freedom or, at least, a better life. While campaigns involved hardships and offered poor prospects of promotion, they were a means for escaped slaves to legitimize their status.

The law also offered freedom to those slaves who took the place of their masters or their masters' sons in the army; the arrangement suited both parties and in the Paraguayan War many took advantage of it. Likewise, many free men and freedmen saw joining the army as a proof of personal bravery and a step towards integration into mainstream society. In this respect Galvão and his companions were typical. They had many historical precedents, the most illustrious of whom was Henrique Dias, the 'black captain', who fought the Dutch in the seventeenth century.

Voluntário Galvão did not enlist alone but as the leader of a group of fellow freedmen he had persuaded along with him. 'I succeeded in bringing 30 Brazilian citizens, my neighbours, their breasts overflowing with enthusiasm and love for their homeland,' he wrote to the emperor. Feeding and outfitting these citizens had used up all his 'minuscule resources'.[48] These 'minuscule resources' may have been the hard-earned savings of a free man of colour or – as appears more probable in this particular region – the result of a *bamburrio*, the local expression, still in use today, for a lucky strike in the diamond fields.

Besides the slaves and free blacks, the fervent atmosphere of the time was also to infect the sons of the highest elites. The declaration of war was the first truly national issue since the Declaration of Independence 43 years earlier. The same thinking that spurred *Voluntário* Galvão into action in the interior of Bahia also inspired the dreams of the well-born, many of whom were assiduous readers of the romantic heroic novels fashionable at the time such as Gonçalves Dias's *Timbiras*, Basílio da Gama's *Uruguai* and José de Alencar's *Guarany*.[49] For these young men, nationalist feeling had been further stirred by affront at the British interference which had brought about the abolition of the slave trade in 1850 and by subsequent disputes such as the so-called 'Christie Affair' in 1863 when the British ambassador to Brazil, William Christie, ordered the seizure of several Brazilian vessels, outside Rio de Janeiro, to show British willingness to use force if necessary against the slave trade. Many of those who were to go to war three years later – such as Antônio Tiburcio Ferreira de Souza and Dionísio Cerqueira – took part in marches and rallies in Rio de Janeiro, parading through the Largo do Paço and Rua Direita shouting nationalist slogans against what they perceived as the interference of Great Britain in the internal affairs of the proud nation in the process of formation.[50]

Dionísio Cerqueira, a product of the Bahian elite, was in his second year at the Escola Central in Rio. As he watched his friends from the Escola Militar da Praia Vermelha set off for war in their gleaming uniforms, he felt an immense pang. He wrote, 'when I saw … all those dear companions in marching order proudly bearing the carbines with which they would defend the fatherland, I found them admirable and, to confess my sin, was so jealous that I could no longer bear to open a book.' He was 17 years old and overcome with an irresistible 'magic force' (to use his words) which was impelling him towards the theatre of operations in the south. On 2 January 1865, five days before the decree which created the *Voluntários da Pátria*, he presented himself at Campo de Santana Barracks in top hat, waistcoat and tails as an 'army volunteer'. A well-born youth, raised 'with the habits of comfort and in the midst of plenty', Dionísio left for the war as a simple foot soldier, whose pay plus bonuses never reached more than 'half a *pataca* and five réis a day' (that is, the minuscule amount of 165 réis). The only thing that saved him during the hard years he spent at the front was the monthly allowance of £2 sterling, which his father had the foresight to send him.[51]

During the campaign, which he saw through to the end, Dionísio found himself in the company of many other boys from backgrounds similar to his. In the corps from Bahia he often encountered 'colleagues and friends of my childhood', various cousins, including José Joaquim, the brother of Dom Antônio de Macedo Costa, archbishop of Bahia. In the corps from the Court he encountered old comrades from the Escola Central. He also made new acquaintances from all over the country, all of them young men like himself between 17 and 20 years of age. As he tried to explain: 'We adored our fatherland and hoped that in its victory we would find our portion of glory.'[52]

We can only imagine what was going through the minds of the young men of Lençóis who marched through the streets of the town on 1 May 1865. From the windows of the Municipal Hall, emotional orators leant out to hail them; Galvão was promoted to sergeant and the whole contingent of 230 volunteers set off for the provincial capital.

The Battlefields

The son of poor parents, Sire, ... This obscure and humble subject
of your Imperial Majesty stifled a heartfelt sigh in a breast choked
with longing and paid heed to the voice of honour which
demanded sacrifice for the fatherland. He bathed the hand of his
dear Father with tears, imprinting it with tender and expressive
kisses and courageously hastened from there to the glorious fields
of strife, ready to seal the liberty and dignity of the Empire of the
Southern Cross with his blood!
Cândido da Fonseca Galvão, 21 March 1872

In Salvador on 24 May 1865 the young recruits from Lençóis were
formally inducted into the III Volunteer Corps, under the command
of Lieutenant-Colonel Domingos Mundim Pestana of the National
Guard, veteran of the Bahian battle for independence against the
Portuguese and author of a treatise on military ordinance highly
regarded in its day.[1]

The '3rd Volunteers', as Cândido da Fonseca Galvão was frequently
to refer to them, were officially designated the 24th Volunteer Corps
by the Repartição de Ajudância-General in Rio de Janeiro. The core of
the corps was the 230 young men from Lençóis, the remaining 16 came
from the neighbouring municipality of Santa Isabel do Paraguaçu and
the police corps of Salvador itself – a total of 246 men.[2]

Although the uniforms of the various volunteer corps were not
standardized, they could be identified, according to Dionísio Cerqueira, 'by the glorious device of gilded bronze which they wore on
the sleeves of their tunics'.[3]

The 24th Volunteers were a *zuavo* battalion, wearing a uniform
adapted from the zouave regiments of the French African Army. The
Bahian *zuavos* attracted attention in the theatre of war not just for
their eyecatching uniform but also for the fact that even the officers

were blacks. The Conde d'Eu, Princess Isabel's husband, called them 'the most beautiful troop in the Brazilian army' and praised the bravery of their officers.[4]

Dionísio Cerqueira also remarked on the troops' uniform and its ethnic composition. The ensemble could not, in fact, have failed to be interesting: brilliant red Cossack breeches, white, calf-length gaiters and a royal blue, gold-trimmed jacket cut in a wide V neckline. The ensemble was finished off with a fez, a back-pack, a forage sack on a baldrick, a wooden canteen, a sword bayonet and a *Minié* rifle (see Figure 1).

Salvador was a hive of activity, its streets teemed with recruits from all parts of the hinterland. It was a city in the grip of tension; as the preparations for war gathered pace, disputes broke out within the ruling elite and discontent among the soldiers occasionally

FIGURE 1   Uniform of the 'Zouaves of Bahia', 1865–70

erupted into insubordination. The provincial capital became the sounding box for political disputes born in the hinterland, such as the one that had broken out in Lençóis between Colonels Sá and Calmon.

The contingent of volunteers from Santa Isabel do Paraguaçu, for example, had been raised by Lieutenant-Colonel Landulfo da Rocha Medrado of the National Guard. On arrival in Salvador on 29 May 1865, he was stripped of his command by the order of the acting vice-president of the providence, Dr Baltazar de Araújo Bulcão.[5] Dionísio Cerqueira recounts another story, that of one of his cousins, João Evangelista de Castro Tanajura, a major in the National Guard who, having raised a corps of volunteers from the hinterland at his own cost, 'died of a cerebral fever caused, it is certain, by the bitter deception of seeing his battalion given over to the command of another, who had political influence in the ruling party'.[6]

These battles for personal power had direct repercussions on the morale of the troops. The situation which greeted the young men from Lençóis, including Sergeant Galvão, was therefore tense. For example, the troops from Santa Isabel did not acquiesce readily in the provincial vice-president's decision to dispense with their commander. They mutinied and ended up being confined to a cavalry barracks while several of their officers were arrested and held under armed guard.[7]

This and other occurrences such as desertions, disputes within the command structure, disorderly behaviour among the troops and breakdowns in civil order were common. 'Each day brings conflict, whether among the troops or the civilians, and police action, when it does occur, is always ineffectual, if not completely useless,' reported the *Jornal do Commercio* in Rio.[8]

With its fighting force already complete, the 3rd Company of Zouaves moved its quarters from the *Quartel da Palma* to the *Arsenal da Marinha*. As a result of one of the power plays of the period, the corps was now without a sublieutenant, the incumbent having also been dismissed by the order of the acting vice-president. 'In consequence, this post is now vacant, and it has become necessary to fill it,' wrote the commander, requesting a remedy and noting that of the entire corps, only the two sergeants, Almeida and Galvão would be 'at all suitable for the post under discussion'.[9]

The appointment was soon ratified.

The Vice-President of the Province, by virtue of the powers vested in him under paragraph 5, article 6. of the Law of 3/10/1834, herewith

nominates citizen Cândido da Fonseca Galvão to the post of sublieutenant of the 3rd Bahian Company of Zouaves.[10]

Early in June, the corps marched to the archbishop's palace, where
they were blessed. On the 17th they left for the south on the English
steamship *Saladin*. The president of the province addressed them,
inciting them to war with reminders 'of the unjustifiable aggressions'
suffered by the empire. 'Then, march!' he declaimed, 'and ... you
will gather the laurels which the justice of our cause and your own
valour assures.'[11] The area commander, Joaquim Antônio da Silva
Carvalho, also delivered an impassioned speech, stressing the value
of discipline:

> Comrades of the 3rd Bahian Company of Zouaves! I have laboured to
> meld and organize you, instruct and discipline you; in short I have done
> for you exactly what I did for the 1st and 2nd Companies of your highly
> honoured name. Now, to complete my gratifying and honourable task,
> I have come to witness your embarkation, to offer you the enthusiastic
> yet tender embrace of a brother.
>   Listen to these words. and, should anything that I have done for you
> merit it, reward me with gallant and orderly comportment on the
> battlefield. I wish for nothing more than to witness your glory and
> victory for the fatherland, this is my only goal. Brave men of the 3rd
> Company of Bahian Zouaves! God is with you; you have a courageous
> and honourable commander who will lead you as a chief on the field
> of battle and treat you as a loving father in your sufferings. Go, and
> with a spirit equal to your patriotism, strive and win! The sweet sorrow
> of our parting today will soon be repaid by the joy of your triumphant
> return.[12]

The soldiers' cheers for the Church, the emperor, the constitution,
the army and the volunteers were echoed by the small crowd, which
had gathered to watch the embarkation, and the ship put out to sea. Six
days later it steamed into Guanabara Bay, to the heart of the Brazilian
empire. Here the troop disembarked and marched under the command of Mundin Pestana to the *Campo da Aclamação* (now the *Praça
da República*), where they were to be quartered.[13] This was the newly
appointed sublieutenant Cândido da Fonseca Galvão's first experience of the Imperial capital. The experience was, in fact, very brief,
even though many of the city's inhabitants were unable to ignore the
sight of 'a black of gigantic stature, of martial mien and respectable
gaze' who, full of pride, marched at the head of the battalion.[14] On the
morning of 3 July the 24th and 28th Volunteer Corps from Rio Grande
do Norte embarked at the Arsenal da Marinha for Rio Grande do

Sul.[15] The emperor, Pedro II, the minister of war and a huge crowd were present on the occasion. His Imperial Majesty reviewed the troops and inspected the soldiers' berths on board the steamships *Jaquaribe, Brasil* and *Falcão*.[16] This was Galvão's first encounter with the emperor, 'the Brazilians' God' as he usually referred to him. Three days later the troops landed in Desterro in the province of Santa Catarina, and on 23 August joined up with the army on active service in Rio Grande do Sul.

Sublieutenant Galvão was to see Pedro II once more during the war, on the occasion of a staged march to Vila de Uruguaiana. The emperor was making the same journey, following the course of the war in person; on 3 September 1865 the two columns met. The 24th Volunteer Corps, together with the 19th, 31st and 4th Battalion of Foot Artillery, which formed the 1st Brigade of the 3rd Division under Colonel Joaquim José Gonçalves Fontes, had camped close to the town of São Gabriel. The entire brigade was lined up and inspected by the royal party and then performed manoeuvres under the directions of the General Marquês de Caxias and General Silva Cabral. The following day there were further exercises under a fierce sun until noon followed by an inspection of the cantonments and the mobile hospital.

A month later, on 6 October the brigade, now commanded by Colonel Alexandre Gomes de Argolo Ferrão, arrived at the Arroio Inhanduí in the vicinity of Alegrete, where they were met by the Conde d'Eu. The count was returning from Uruguaiana where, two weeks earlier, at the side of his father-in-law, the emperor, he had witnessed the town's surrender. Argolo Ferrão told the count that he was satisfied with the progress of the march which, despite all the difficulties encountered, was covering 15 miles a day. The Conde also spoke to the black officers of the Bahian Zouaves – doubtless including Sublieutenant Galvão – and praised them highly. In the count's opinion they were all very good officers, 'entirely equal to every detail of their duties and proud of their battalion'.[17]

The troops arrived in the town of Uruguaiana, by then under allied control, on 11 October. From there they crossed the River Uruguay at Passo de los Libres and marched towards Mercedes at the rearguard of the Uruguayan army, led by Venâncio Flores. In Correntes, on Argentinian territory, they waded across the Mirinai river at Passo das Eguas and, bearing due north, finally joined up with General Osório's army at its camp at Lagoa Brava on 2 January 1866.

In February a troop reorganization put the 24th Volunteers under the command of the 13th Infantry Brigade, in its turn part of the 4th

Division under Brigadier Guilherme Xavier de Souza. The whole Division consisted of 47 officers, including Sublieutenant Galvão, and 588 soldiers.

In April the brigade was ordered to Porto Corrales on the southern bank of the Paraná river. On the 16th a naval vessel ferried them to the left bank of the Paraguay river, which was still in enemy territory. In May the allied armies (Uruguayan, Brazilian and Argentinian) forded the Estero Bellaco (a muddy bottomed river, which could only be crossed at a few points known as *passos*) and camped in deep order in the region of Tuiuti, facing the Paraguayan defence lines.

The 4th Division approached from the left, crossing some marshes and camped to the centre and left of the allied position at the junction of the Passo da Pátria-Humaitá road.[18]

'Lord God, Have Mercy on Us'

This ended nine months of heavy marching from Porto Alegre, against intense cold, torrential rains, epidemics, lack of equipment, late salaries and rations, which consisted almost exclusively of barbecued fatty beef and dry manioc flour. Dionísio Cerqueira – the young student who had volunteered in the city of Rio de Janeiro, subsequently promoted to sublieutenant – provides the best available account of the atmosphere in the camp. Aware not only of the concerns of the great commanders but also of those of the ordinary soldiers, his account of the war is a document of immense value for both Brazil's military and social history.[19]

The region was bounded by two great rivers, the Estero Bellaco and the Rojas, and scattered with lakes – the Tuiuti, Piriz and other smaller ones – marshy tracts, woods and clearings.

On 23 May, 'all felt the imminence of a major encounter between the two armies, with all the forces gathered'. The commanders inspected their companies' weapons and ordered all troops to prepare for battle the following day, allowing no exceptions, 'not even the members of the baggage train or the officers' batmen'. At 8 o'clock that night, the tattoo sounded and all the corps formed to recite the rosary before the flag. They then said the prayer of the Brazilian soldier, dedicated to Nossa Senhora da Conceição, to the accompaniment of the bands of the forty battalions present.

It was autumn. The temperature had dropped and the night was humid. The prayer was followed by the call to kneel, greatly moving Dionísio as he saw 'all those simple, rough and faithful men' on their knees 'with their muscular hands clasped to their broad chests' to intone 'full of contrition and faith, "Lord God have mercy on us"'.

The service ended with the last post, played by the cornet-major of the 7th Volunteer Corps from São Paulo, who was greatly admired by all for the haunting vibration resounding through every note. 'He played the call like an anthem of farewell,' remembered Dionísio with emotion some forty years later, 'and ended slowly and softly with great sadness, until it died away with a distant moan, melting into the silence of the night.'[20]

The Battle of Tuiuti

On the following day, 24 May, it was the stirring sounds of the *assembly*, *advance*, *accelerate* and *charge* that called the cavalry, infantry and artillery into action. Both sides demonstrated more *bravura* than technique during the battle – five hours of desperate fighting at close quarters on swampy ground.[21]

When the ceasefire sounded, Dionísio was finally able to take stock of himself: his shirt (the only one he possessed) had a tear in the right shoulder from a glancing bullet; his sword had broken in half and the soles of his boots had been lost in the mud of the marshes.[22]

The battle toll was horrific. George Thompson, an English engineer serving under the Paraguayan leader, Francisco Solano López, secretly returned to the battlefield a few days later. 'The thickets and the clearings between were full of bodies,' he reported.

> The corpses were not decomposing but becoming mummified. The skin stretched over the bones was yellow and extremely dry. The field was covered in shells, cartridges and projectiles of every description, the trees riddled with rifle bullets in many places.[23]

This was the greatest battle to take place in South America. The 30,200-strong Paraguayan army faced an allied force of 32,400 (21,000 Brazilians, 9,700 Argentines and 1,700 Uruguayans). Each army – with the exception of the Brazilian force, which was led by General Manoel Luís Osório – was commanded by its respective head of state, the *caudillos* of the region: Solano López, *el Supremo* of Paraguay, Bartolomé Mitre, the commander-in-chief of the allied forces and head of the government of the Argentinian Confederation, and Venâncio Flores, president of the Eastern Republic of Uruguay.

The Paraguayans suffered losses of 13,000 killed and wounded,

TABLE 3   Losses in the Battle of Tuiuti, 24 May 1866

Soldiers	Dead	Wounded	Total
Paraguay	6,000	7,000	13,000
Allies	996	2,935	3,931
Brazil	737	2,292	3,029
Argentina	126	480	606
Uruguay	133	163	296

Source: Murad, op. cit., p. 23.

the allies, 3,931. (For a breakdown of these figures by nationality, see Table 3.)

Of the Brazilian forces, 62 officers and 675 other ranks died, resulting together with the wounded in more than 3,000 men *hors de combat*. The losses were particularly severe among 'the valiant band of the gallant Volunteers', to quote Sublieutenant Galvão. In his corps alone, the 24th, 152 men were lost, 44 of them dead. Although victorious, the allied forces were exhausted and unable to take any immediate advantage of their victory. They were to remain in the same place for nearly two years more, engaging in minor skirmishing and suffering from the unhealthiness of the terrain and devastating cholera epidemics.

During the time the 24th Volunteer fought a battle on 16 July at Punta Naró, when they faced the fire of 'four small cannon' and deep trenches dug under the direct supervision of George Thompson, suffering more than 69 dead and wounded. Two days later they were once again in combat at Isla Carapá, where 2 officers and 3 soldiers were killed, and another 18 soldiers wounded.[24]

Very little is known about individual roles in combats such as these, yet Dionísio Cerqueira, a temperate and critical observer, refers to the Zouaves as a whole as 'strong and brave men'. In another passage he makes a specific reference to the 24th, remarking on General Deodoro's training which, 'in a short time' had transformed the corps 'into one of the best in the army'.[25] Melo Moraes Filho, another contemporary, refers to statements by the volunteers themselves about Sublieutenant Galvão in the years following the war. 'His companions say', he wrote, 'that the Prince's faith in his office was pure and praiseworthy', and that 'in all the battles fought against the armies of the dictator López he was always in the vanguard fighting with tenacity and courage.'[26]

Sublieutenant Galvão himself, when referring to the period, swore that he had marched 'always with a view to sustaining the glory of my Sovereign Monarch and also that of my dear fatherland'. And, in his characteristic style,

> My will to be brave and bold was not fired by love of the leprous gold which is the cause of every disgrace to those unhappy souls who are guided by bad principles ... but by the thought, ever in my mind, that when I returned from these battlefields, I wanted to see my monarch covered in glory, and draped in the trophies of the tyrant who had dared to throw down the gauntlet.[27]

Nevertheless, on 31 August 1866 the sublieutenant was invalided out of the campaign, wounded in his right hand. Barely two weeks later, the 24th Corps was itself disbanded and the few soldiers remaining in its seriously depleted ranks transferred to other units.

Although the outcome of the war was practically decided, it continued to drag on as a siege campaign until Asunción was taken and, finally, the death of Solano López on the banks of the Aquidabã, impaled by a lance wielded by another Bahian volunteer, known as Chico Diabo.[28]

The Legacy

The importance of the Paraguayan campaign in the social, cultural and political history of Brazil cannot be exaggerated. The great battles, particularly Tuiuti, redefined the symbols of valour for the nascent sense of national identity. It was Brazil's period of heroes and of tradition. It was the time of Caxias, patron of the army; of Osório, patron of the cavalry; of Mallet, patron of the artillery, and of Sampaio, patron of the infantry, the branch in which Galvão served.

The idea of Brazil as a nation gained a solidity unimagined outside certain elite circles. Both during and after the war the armed separatist movements, which had characterized the first half of the century, not only ceased completely but disappeared from the political horizon.

The war brought Brazilians from nearly every province into close and prolonged contact with others from regions which until then they had scarcely heard of. To the simple men of Rio Grande do Sul – the *guascas* – the term 'Bahian' signified a Brazilian from any other province. As the Bahian Dionísio noted, 'for them, Brazil was divided into two parts: the first, which was very large and bred good horses, they called the *província*, the second, which was very small and inhabited by folk who didn't know how to ride a horse, *Bahia*.'[29]

The war also brought men from every social class into contact with each other. They were together for the first time, partners in the same undertaking: from the slaves granted freedom in return for their service and free men of colour such as Cândido da Fonseca Galvão to the sons of the elite such as Dionísio Cerqueira. Colour and class were obviously major barriers between these two Brazilians, although both were proud of being Bahian, Brazilian, volunteers and, at least at Tuiuti, sublieutenants.

Such contact was difficult, as may be seen from the various testimonies, but of great significance. Dionísio, who in Rio de Janeiro in 1865 still presented himself as 'an army volunteer' in top hat, waistcoat and tails, recognized the difficulties of relating to his new comrades, recruits 'from all the lowest levels of society'. The differences were very great and, he confessed, it was only the fact that he was possessed by 'the enthusiasm of faith' that enabled him to support what at the time appeared humiliating.[30]

Having spent ten months on campaign as a simple soldier before being promoted to sublieutenant, he had the opportunity to observe the behaviour of these men at close quarters.[31] His *Reminiscences* of the war are, in this sense, a sort of ethnographic study of the soldiers of the time. Early on, during the marches, Dionísio noted that despite the obvious lack of training, they were willing and constantly good-humoured even in the worst moments 'far from everything that . . . they loved in the world'.[32] He observed the 'abnegation' and 'stoicism' not only of the soldiers, but also of the women who, with red clothes tied around their heads, had followed their men from the hinterland to the battlefields. Women of the people who with unswerving courage and from necessity would give birth in the makeshift camps and resume the march the following morning, in their thin rags using the cloth of their tent as a saddle-pad and the tent poles lashed to their backs.[33]

From the earliest skirmishes Dionísio found himself deeply impressed by the 'good and generous hearts' of these rough people, who on hearing the ceasefire at the end of each encounter 'no longer seemed the same fierce warriors' of a few minutes earlier but 'carefully and full of charity' went out to help the enemy wounded. Some, as Dionísio witnessed, even went so far as to share their meagre supplies of tobacco and cigarette papers with them,[34] or to quench the desperate thirst of those who had lost blood with water from their canteens.[35] He also records the reciprocity of the Paraguayan soldiers, such as the unknown soldier who, after a hotly contested fight, carried a wounded Brazilian on his back along the road until he could leave him in his own camp.[36]

The war was a time of authority and hierarchy as well as of comradeship, of the fear of dying and the joy of victory, shared by blacks, whites and those of mixed race under the same banner. The sort of acts described above greatly moved Dionísio and others like him. Many returned from the war disaffected with the society in which they lived and converted to abolition of slavery. Seventeen years later, a manifesto of the Club Militar addressed to the Princess Regent asked for permission to dispense with the onerous duty 'of capturing poor negroes who flee slavery, whether they are tired of suffering its horrors, or because the light of liberty has warmed their hearts and illuminated their souls'.[37]

After victory the empire would never be the same again. The prestige of uniform grew as never before; the heroes of the day were all soldiers, as was shown by the life stories of more than 183 Brazilians born between 1850 and 1900, collected by Gilberto Freyre in the middle of the twentieth century. After the war the most popular games for small boys throughout the empire were soldiers and the battle of Tuiuti. For many years children's imaginations were populated with classical warriors such as Hannibal, Alexander the Great, Napoleon Bonaparte and Nelson and, above all, with national army leaders such as Caxias, Porto-Alegre, Osório, Barroso and Tamandaré.

This was only one aspect of a wider social phenomenon which was not, as may be seen, restricted to childhood. Many of Freyre's subjects attributed this interest to the influence of 'their background and their masters', as did Claudio da Costa Ribeiro, who was born in 1873 in Recife; to the influence of their own fathers, such as the case of Padre Matias Freire, born in 1882 in Mamanguape in Paraíba; to the influence and even collaboration of an 'old veteran soldier' such as Demóstenes Ipiranga, born in 1880, claimed; or even to hearing about it, as did Leopoldo Lins, born in the Pernambuco hinterlands in 1857.[38]

The Republic was declared by a military junta nineteen years after victory. Both the new president, Marshall Deodoro da Fonseca, The Founder, and his vice-president and consolidator of the regime, Floriano Peixoto, The Iron Marshall, were veterans of the Paraguayan campaign.

========= 3 =========

The Homecoming

Attend, Senhor, in your Imperial munificence, the just call of this
soldier, one who heard, in time, the plangent cries of the suffering
fatherland.... He merely asks for the honours of the rank in
which he served, and the corresponding pension.

Cândido da Fonseca Galvão to the emperor, 1872

Wounded in the right hand – or, as he himself termed it, 'the victim
of a cruel infirmity' – Cândido da Fonseca Galvão retired from active
service on 31 August 1866.[1] After being disembarked in Rio de
Janeiro, he was ordered back to his native province. It was during
this journey that the difficult process of re-adaptation to civilian life
began.

'With the return of the victorious regiments from the River Plate',
wrote Oliveira Lima, 'it would appear that the government of Rio de
Janeiro, for its part, feared that any excess of militaristic fervour
would incite popular demonstrations.' In particular, the return of the
volunteers was seen as a potential threat to peace and public order.
The main policy, therefore, was to 'dispense with all pomp, disperse
the units, disguise the standards and silence the music' and, as
rapidly as possible, proceed towards disarmament and general
demobilization.[2]

Despite the fact that Brazil had emerged from the war victorious,
the situation was precarious. The country plunged into a long
succession of social and political crises which, nineteen years later,
were to culminate in the proclamation of the Republic. Contemporaries saw these crises as isolated 'questions'; that is, as
separate conjunctural manifestations which, one after the other,
created a period of great political unrest. For land- and slave-owners,
the very pillars of the monarchy, it was the *abolition question* that

37

permeated and coloured the entire period; for the Catholic hierarchy, it was the *religious question*; for the army, the *military question*; for the urban classes, a confusing battery of questions ranging from the cost of living to the ideologies of progress.

Back in Bahia

Like many other returnees, Galvão's first objective was to obtain some social recognition for his efforts and merits. He tried all the established channels, making a point of addressing himself directly to the emperor:

> I come to you today as a supplicant who has not received any of the benefits awarded to those who, like himself, offered their services in the defence of the beloved Homeland; I come to humbly implore Your Majesty to grant this subject the honorary title of his rank and award a commemorative Campaign Medal.[3]

This petition, however, became embroiled in bureaucratic difficulties and had a difficult path, due to the fact that the Adjutant General's Office required, under Order of the Day no. 52, an affidavit (*fé de ofício*) 'detailing the relevant services rendered during the Paraguayan Campaign'.[4]

This document could not be produced, according to the applicant, 'because the house in which he had resided in the town of Lençóis ... had caught fire and burnt to the ground with all its contents'. Without proof of his service in the campaign, the bureaucracy was unable to assess the justice of his case, although it duly recognized his right to the general campaign medal.[5]

The impasse was finally resolved a year later by Order of the Day no. 880, issued on 30 September 1872: 'By the decree of the 25th of the current month, the honours of the rank of army sublieutenant is granted to the former commissioned sublieutenant of the 3rd Company of Bahian Zouaves, Cândido da Fonseca Galvão, in recognition of his services during the war against Paraguay.'[6]

Galvão was still not entirely satisfied. He was still 'unable to resume his occupations as a result of illness which he had acquired in the Field ... of War' and, the following year, applied for a pension.[7]

Dissatisfaction appears to have marked this period of Galvão's life, as it did the lives of many other returnees. One of the secondary consequences of the war, according to some, was precisely the emergence of the figure of the 'disgruntled veteran' in Brazilian society.[8]

In June 1876, 'having been released from the *Asilo de Inválidos da Pátria*, where ... he had received the means of subsistence for himself and his family', Galvão applied to the minister and secretary of state for war, Duque de Caxias, to be enrolled in the *Companhia de Inválidos da Província da Bahia*. Whether it was the justice of his case or possibly that the minister really did know of and prize Galvão's services during the war, the fact is that the request was granted immediately.[9]

Yet on the following day the ensign made two further demands. First, as a champion of the crown in peace as in war, he asked for the 'special grace' of wearing his dress uniform or 'great dress' on holy days and imperial feast days. Second, he asked for a three-month advance on his allowance, due to his return to Bahia and his financial straits, to be repaid from later instalments.[10]

In addition to his dissatisfaction the ensign appears to have been somewhat confused. In 1880 he addressed a complaint to the senate, asking for the restitution of the 20$000 per month 'which, on leaving for Paraguay, he had signed over to his father and which this worthy had never received'.[11] On investigation the complaint was disallowed as the *Repartição Fiscal* (paymaster's office) has receipts signed by his father, Benvindo da Fonseca Galvão, from July 1865 until February 1866.[12]

The sublieutenant was certainly not alone in his pretensions. The volunteer Agostinho Petra de Bittencourt, who had been a battalion musician during the Paraguayan war, believed himself to be the heir to a fabulous fortune deposited in the National Treasury. He bombarded the ministry of war in particular with endless demands in respect of the post he had occupied – whether this was as a musician, first class, which the ministry's records showed, or a music master, as he claimed to have been. Never satisfied, Agostinho, according to Lima Barreto, 'petitioned without let or respite' for year after year and was still doing so at the beginning of the twentieth century. In one month alone he submitted more than ten appeals, all on the same issue.

Another who haunted the ministry in pursuit of his rights was honorary Lieutenant José Dias de Oliveira, described as a stout man of advanced age 'with a long and abundant beard'. Lieutenant Oliveira, always gesticulating wildly and shouting in a hoarse voice, defended his rights to the rank of major by the use of arithmetic. Before the war he had been a police lieutenant in Paraná and, on the strength of this, was made an honorary lieutenant in the army. In Oliveira's mind, two lieutenancies added up to the rank of one major.

Cases such as these and 'others more significant, if less picturesque' served to convince the civil servant Afonso Henriques de Lima Barreto that if the empire, faced with imminent war, 'had not told the volunteers, in so many words, that when they returned they would never have to work again, it had certainly promised them great things, because all whom I have come across were possessed of an unshakeable conviction of the State's debt to them'. Lima Barreto believed that this sentiment had been increased 'a hundredfold' and 'deformed' after victory by the simple natures of men who had recently been freed from slavery or who were still living in conditions little short of it.[13]

It was not just the homecoming that was difficult. Once home, everyday life seemed compounded with more difficulties and complications. It was in this immediate post-war period that the first allusions to Sublieutenant Galvão's alcohol abuse and even mental illness appear. As early as May 1876, the commandant of the *Quartel do Asilo de Inválidos da Pátria* reported that

> this officer, having for a long period been given to the vice of intemperance, has latterly entered so frequently into this state that, on top of the fact that even in his natural state, he is not very convenient, in drunkenness he becomes even more insolent and unbearable. He respects no man's person, nor attempts to discriminate in choosing the target of his grosseries and injurious expressions.

It was precisely for drunkenness that Galvão had been imprisoned in the barracks a few days previously. Instead of reforming his behaviour, he went about declaring that 'prison for me has the importance that I give it'. Such conduct, in the eyes of his commandant, could only be attributed 'to madness' and 'to his state of inebriation', a truly 'insupportable' combination.[14]

Early in 1877, his habitual drunkenness and insubordination 'to the point of refusing to obey his superiors' led a court of inquiry to recommend his expulsion from the Volunteers Asylum.[15]

The Road to Rio

Galvão, like so many of his contemporaries in the 1870s and subsequent decades, would soon leave Salvador in search of better working and living conditions in the Imperial capital. By that time, the prosperity of the south-east, with its coffee plantations and the political prestige of the Court, already contrasted sharply with the apathy, recession and general impoverishment of the north-east.

To understand better the voluntary migration undertaken by free men of colour such as Cândido da Fonseca Galvão, it is first necessary to describe, at least in general terms, the earlier movement which paved the way for voluntary migration, lending it a more profound historical significance. This was the forced migration of labour – the so-called *interprovincial slave traffic* – a translocation which provides an accurate index of the profound changes taking place in the society, economy and politics of the empire.

The following sections of this chapter offer a wider view of this process, beginning with the regional economic imbalances of the nineteenth century and the consequent internal redistribution of the slave workforce; the impact of this process on the living conditions and aspirations of the slave, freed and freeborn coloured populations of Salvador; and, finally, the options open to members of these groups from the 1870s onwards. Zouave Sublieutenant Cândido da Fonseca Galvão set off on the road to Rio de Janeiro in pursuit of an individual goal, but in doing so he was part of an historical process.

Regional Imbalances and the Labour Market

The crisis became clearly perceptible in Bahia in the wake of the sugar industry's most brilliant phase of expansion, which lasted through the second half of the eighteenth century until the beginning of the 1820s. After that the traditional crops of the north-east – sugar, tobacco and cotton – fell into decline, as they gradually became less and less able to respond satisfactorily to the rigours of the international market.

The economic crisis coincided with the wearying struggle for independence, which lasted for almost a year from 1822 to 1823. On top of this, there was an absolutely unprecedented sequence of uprisings, rebellions and conspiracies – for this or any other province – among the free population as well as the slaves.

With the suppression of the African slave traffic in 1850, Salvador, a traditional entrepôt and internal redistribution point for slaves, did not merely lose the opportunity to purchase slaves from the exterior as did other provinces. It also, and perhaps most importantly, lost a lucrative trade in exports (tobacco, '*cachaça*' – white rum and snuff), and re-exports (European manufactures) to Africa.

The slave traffic, as is known, could not exist unilaterally. On the contrary, it presupposed the construction of methods of reciprocity and exchange, of an entire trade system. From the Brazilian viewpoint at least, slaves were the central object of this trade and its most valuable component. Consequently, for each slave shipment arriving in Brazil, several shipments of traditional products and even European manufactures had to be sent to Africa in payment.[16] At its peak, at the end of the eighteenth century and the beginning of the nineteenth, this two-way traffic supported more than 164 commercial houses in Salvador's *Cidade Baixa* (the lower city, or port region, which stretched from the Praia da Preguiça to the environs of the Mercado do Ouro).

With the decline from 1820 onwards, nineteenth-century Bahia was to be further afflicted by outbreaks of disease. In 1850, the poor sanitary conditions prevailing in the city led to the first great yellow fever epidemic. Initially transmitted by the crew of a ship sailing under the US flag, it resulted in more than 3,000 deaths.

The fever returned again in 1852 with even more devastating results. In 1855 it was the turn of cholera, which struck with catastrophic effect, killing some 7,900 people in Salvador alone and more than 18,000 in the towns of the 'sorrowful belt' surrounding the city – Santo Amaro da Purificação, Cachoeira de São Félix, Maragogipe, Nazaré das Farinhas, São Francisco do Conde – causing serious disruption to sugar production.

In economic terms, this long series of crises was to reach its apex at the beginning of the 1870s. Sugar production, the mainstay of the Bahian economy since the sixteenth century, fell from 53,884,090 kg in 1871 to 29,599,068 kg in 1873. During the same period, coffee exports (a new crop in the province) fell from 5,112,240 sacks to 3,405,420, while production of another traditional crop, cotton, fell from 6,679,851 *arrobas* (1 *arroba* = 14.7 kg) to 1,574,410.

In contrast to the declining traditional economies of the northeast, the coffee-based economy of the south-east was expanding fast, stimulated by demand from the urban markets in Europe and the United States. Coffee's increasing importance was officially recognized in 1822 when a branch of the coffee bush was incorporated into the arms of the newly independent nation.

The Paraíba valley, running through the provinces of Rio de Janeiro, São Paulo and Minas Gerais, 'valley of slavery and great plantations' in the words of a French scholar who visited it in the

1880s,[17] became the main artery of the new national economy. In 1868 the south-eastern regions of Brazil grew half the coffee drunk in the world, while the north-east faced fierce competition from various other major producers to place its principal product, sugar, on the international market.

Market forces were thus to force a relocation of the nation's social, political and economic axes. This geographical shift was reflected perfectly in the distribution of patents of nobility, particularly those of the baronage. Approximately 30 per cent of the titles bestowed by the empire after 1840 were conferred on landowners, commission agents and bankers linked to the coffee trade.[18]

In 1872–3 the coffee harvest totalled 115,285 *contos* of réis, while the combined revenue from sugar and cotton came to less than 49,000 *contos*.

Such marked differences in export values were reflected domestically in the earnings of each region and, consequently, in the cost of labour. Since the colonial period these regional variations, following Brazil's various export cycles, had always resulted in a flow of slaves from one region to another through the direct mechanism of cash sales.

To cite one example of this phenomenon, a serious drought in Ceará and the other north-eastern provinces in 1847 led to massive sales of slaves to the coffee regions, particularly those of Rio de Janeiro. With the end of the African slave trade in 1850, it was natural that the more prosperous regions of Rio de Janeiro, São Paulo and Minas Gerais should take advantage of the reigning economic logic of the domestic slave market, which forced the less successful and ruined slave-owners to sell their slaves, both locally and further afield, including other, distant provinces.

The Domestic Slave Trade

The years from 1850 to 1885, when the transfer of slaves from one province to another was finally prohibited, saw a rapid concentration of slave labour in the coffee-growing municipalities surrounding the Imperial capital. This process – profoundly destabilizing to the slave order – was felt most deeply in the north-eastern provinces, which lost the majority of their slaves. In truth, with the abolition of the African traffic in 1850, the 'new African coast' for the coffee belt was the rest of Brazil, from far north to far south, but particularly the north-east.[19]

This forced migration, achieved through buying and selling, fluctuated according to specific economic circumstances, whether on the side of demand (periods of greater or lesser expansion in the slave cultivation of coffee) or supply (periods of stagnation or temporary recovery in the north-east or, for example, in the jerked – pressed and sun-dried – beef industry of Rio Grande do Sul).

During the 1870s and 1880s the droughts in the north-east and the expansion of coffee cultivation into the western regions of São Paulo took these transfers to unprecedented levels. Two further contributory factors were the passing of the Rio Branco Law on 28 September 1871, and the growth of support for abolition, particularly in Rio de Janeiro, in the years that followed. The Rio Branco Law declared 'free all children born to slaves', liberated the 'escravos da nação (the slaves that belonged directly to the emperor) and set up an 'emancipation fund' for the rest.

Estimates suggest that transfers of slaves to the coffee plantations totalled 300,000–400,000 individuals over a 35-year period.[20]

The domestic slave trade, both legal and clandestine, was calculated by contemporary observers to have funnelled an average of 5,500 slaves per year into the province of Rio de Janeiro between 1852 and 1859.[21] In São Paulo province, the slave population multiplied from 80,000 in 1866 to 200,000 in 1875. In 1877 the coffee provinces – Rio, São Paulo and Minas – accounted for more than half the slaves in the empire.

The level of sales in Bahia remained exceptionally high for almost the entire period. The available data, although limited to legally registered transactions, is a useful indicator of the general dynamic of the process. Between 1853 and 1855 the province officially shipped 3,477 slaves to Rio de Janeiro alone. In 1854, exit tax was paid on 1,835 slaves sold out of the province, of whom 1,392 were destined for Rio de Janeiro. The figures remained high into the following decade, with 2,047 slaves sold in 1860 and 1,771 in 1861.

At this point the revitalization of the Bahian cotton industry taking advantage of the disorganization of market during the American Civil War caused a sharp drop in the numbers of slaves sold out of the province. Between 1862 and 1866 sales outside the province fell to an average of only 347 a year. But by the beginning of the 1870s, when the return to cotton production in the southern United States precipitated a new crisis in Bahia, the sales of slaves again soared: to 1,063 in 1870–71 and 1,459 in 1873–4.[22]

Profitability and Prices

Behind this process, in Bahia as in the other provinces which exported slaves, lay the income-generating differential of slave labour and the consequent difference in a slave's market value, depending on whether he was employed in the declining and stagnating regions or in the expanding regions linked to the external market.

In 1854, according to the calculation of Deputado Geral João Maurício Wanderley, the future Barão de Cotegipe, a good slave in the dry hinterland of Bahia could provide his master with a return of no more than 30 or 40 mil-réis a year. His market value in the province was around 700 or 800 mil-réis.[23]

If the same slave were to be transferred to Rio de Janeiro, Minas or São Paulo, then, after a short period of adaptation and training, he would be able to work up to 2,000 coffee bushes, producing around 25 sacks of beans a year in the best plantations.[24] Valuing each sack at the 1854 price of around 16$640, this slave – who could produce no more than 40 mil-réis in the interior of Bahia – would, in the south-east produce up to 416 mil-réis a year. Extrapolating this calculation over decades (the average price of a sack of coffee multiplied by 25), this same slave would produce around 602 mil-réis a year in 1861–70, 762 mil-réis in 1871–80 and 697 mil-réis in 1881–90.[25]

This huge difference in income-generating potential was clearly reflected in slave market prices. The average price for a slave, male or female, between the ages of 20 and 25, more than doubled in the prosperous coffee municipality of Vassouras, Rio de Janeiro, between 1852 and 1854, rising from 630$000 to 1,350$000.[26] In 1862 the *Monte Alegre* plantation in the prosperous parish of Pati do Alferes in the same municipality could muster a workforce of 196 slaves – males and females of all ages – worth an average of more than 2,200$000 each, rising to 2,500$000 for the most valuable. On other estates belonging to the same landowner, the best slaves were valued at between 2,000$000 and 2,200$000.[27]

However, prices on the sugar plantations of the north-east during the same period fell by at least half. In Salvador in 1862 a male slave in his prime would fetch anything between 1,261$000 (1859–60 average) and 1,165$000 (1865–6 average). A female slave was worth even less – between 1,004$000 and 887$000. An adult slave costing around 543$000 at the time of the prohibition of the African traffic, would, by 1887, have cost somewhere between 784$000

(1875–6 average) and 800$000 (1879–80 average). On the eve of abolition in 1887, this price had dropped to no more than 468$000 for a man and 365$000 for a woman.[28]

In the mountain uplands of Rio de Janeiro, the pioneering region of coffee expansion, prices soared out of all comparison with the north-east between 1850 and 1877, when they attained the impressive average of 1,925$000 for men and women in the prime of life. Even on the brink of the 1888 abolition, which would be total and without compensation, slaves were still fetching as much as 850$000 in the region.[29]

The earnings differential between the north and south extended to the urban milieu, where the profits of the coffee boom were spent. Some of the less scrupulous merchants – by the moral judgement of their own period – went so far as to buy pretty young girls from the north-east for the purpose of prostituting them in the streets of Rio de Janeiro. Wet nurses were also considered to be good business in the capital. To give some idea of the figures involved, it was calculated in 1881 that a wet nurse bought in the north-east for between 400 and 600 mil-réis could earn her master 900 mil-réis for 18 months' hire in Rio de Janeiro. When her milk dried up the woman could then be sold in the capital for 1,500$000.[30]

Freedom in Salvador

The African and mixed race population of Salvador underwent profound and dramatic social changes during the period under consideration. First, the slave population rapidly declined from around 300,000 in the mid-1860s to 165,403 in 1872; 132,822 in 1884; and 76,838 in 1887.

This sharp fall, which reached 42.1 per cent between 1884 and 1887, cannot be attributed solely to the leeching affect of the interprovincial slave trade, but is also linked to another, parallel process, which augmented the free population.

This might, to a certain degree, be seen as a positive aspect of the difficulties confronting Bahian society throughout the nineteenth century. Crises in the export sector, together with prolonged political problems – often aggravated by periodic droughts – reduced the demand for labour and forced the badly indebted owners to emancipate at least part of their workforce, whose price had fallen in real terms.

Thus the same process which had encouraged the transfer of

slaves to other, more prosperous provinces also appears to have facilitated an opportunity of freedom for at least some slaves: those who had managed to accumulate enough savings in better times and those who were able to perform well within the crisis itself. In the light of this, Kátia Mattoso has been able to document a significant increase in the number of manumittances granted in Bahia between 1779 and 1850.[31] This evidence is supported by a further study by Mattoso, Klein and Engerman. Using a much larger sample over the period 1819–88, it shows a particularly high rate of manumittance between 1840 and 1880, representing some 5–6 per cent of the entire slave population of Salvador.[32]

Pressured by their economic difficulties, an increasing number of masters in Salvador resorted to hiring out their slaves *ao ganho*, selling their skills or services to others for cash. Most of these earnings would be handed over to the owners. But this was a form of exploitation which offered the slave greater freedom of movement and initiative, enabling many to accumulate the capital or establish the social ties needed to purchase their own liberty.

From the 1820s onwards, the free and freed population of the capital had increased with each crisis in the export sector and each period of drought which drove considerable numbers of free men to leave their small communities in the interior in search of work in the provincial capital or the surrounding area of Recôncavo.

By the middle of the century this growing population of free poor who had no place in the market was causing unease. The response to this took the form of a decree in 1850 promulgated by the provincial president, Francisco Gonçalves Martins, the future Viscount of São Lourenço, restricting the trade of stevedore exclusively to freeborn Brazilians. As a result, some 750 Africans were prevented from working on the loading and unloading of cargo, despite being freedmen. This was probably the first political measure taken against slave labour in the province, and also against African workers, even those who had already obtained their freedom through their own efforts.[33] Twenty years later, in 1870, Francisco Gonçalves Martins, again provincial president, set up the *Companhia União e Indústria* to employ only freeborn porters. Many coloured Brazilians found work in the *União e Indústria*, including many veterans of the Paraguayan War.[34]

By 1874 this process, which included transfers and manumittances, had gone so far that no less than 87.2 per cent of Bahia's total population (or 1,120,846 out of 1,286,249 individuals) were no longer or had never been slaves.

See Conrad, Destruction
p. 284

Voluntary Migration

Nevertheless, in this same period (post-1870), the conjunction of factors favouring a slave's buying his or her freedom appears to have gone into decline. In Salvador the total number of manumittances granted annually, which had grown steadily since 1819, began to fall steeply from 1870 until abolition was finally achieved in 1888.[35] The deepening economic crisis and the general impoverishment made it more difficult to find the means to purchase freedom, just as it created terrible problems of survival for those who were already free or freed.[36]

The life of the poor blacks, whether slaves, ex-slaves or free men, in overcrowded Salvador was far from easy. With the intermittent drought, which reached its peaks in 1868, 1871 and 1877–80, great numbers of workers flooded into the capital from the hinterland.

The serial collapse of Salvador's banks in the 1873 crisis increased the difficulty of obtaining work and threatened the traditional areas of activity for the self-employed in Salvador. In this situation a growing number of freedmen, free men of colour and slaves found themselves competing for the same limited places in the crowded tenements and for the same work in the streets of the city. The provincial capital appeared to be glutted with casual labour and errand boys, petty street hawkers and small tradesmen (paviours, carpenters, smiths, cobblers, barbers, seamstresses and sweetmakers), who had the most traditional means of self-employment.

Many, both freeborn and ex-slaves, were tempted to migrate in search of a better life. Many – principally Africans, but also creoles (blacks born in Brazil) and even some mulattos – became totally disillusioned with what they called 'the land of the whiteman' and thought of returning to Africa.[37] Others saw Brazil as their own country. For this second group, the Imperial capital, flowing with the money generated by the coffee trade, arose as the new Mecca for their hopes. The very interprovincial trade in slaves – migration forced by sale – together with the social and political prestige of Rio de Janeiro, clearly showed the route to be followed. This voluntary migration – the 'opção Brasil' – would exert a decisive impact on the culture and ethos of the city of Rio de Janeiro.

These influxes of free men of colour and ex-slaves came to the Imperial capital in search of the means to make a living or even a measure of social legitimacy. Although it is a theme that still wants for both quantitative and qualitative research, there are some notable cases to be found, above all through study of the popular music of the period. Hilário Jovino Ferreira, for example, was born in Pernambuco, raised in Salvador and landed in Rio on 17 June 1872. Freeborn or freed man (this is uncertain) Lalau de Ouro, as he became known in the city, was one of the central figures – together with Tia Bebiana de Iansã, another respected Bahian – in organizing one of the first carnival *ranchos* in the city. The traditional *ranchos* were processions which formed part of the Christmas cycle of popular festivities, commemorating the birth of Jesus and the coming of the Magi. In Rio de Janeiro, under the influence of the Bahians, this religious festival was gradually transformed into a secular celebration, the 'carnival *ranchos*' (which already existed at the time of Dom Obá II d'Africa) and, from 1928 onwards, into the famous 'samba schools'.

It was another Bahian, Getúlio Marinho, who helped create the choreography which is so characteristic of today's samba parades – the *mestre-sala*, with his sweeping courtly gestures as he guides the *porta-bandeira*, the crinolined standard-bearer, through her paces.

Hilária Batista de Almeida, the well-known Tia Ciata de Oxum, was also born in Salvador, in 1854, probably the daughter of enfranchised parents, arrived in Rio de Janeiro in 1876 at the age of 22. The year after her arrival, Cândido da Fonseca Galvão came to Rio as part of the same wave of migration which continued after them.

Not just the processional form of the parade, but the samba itself, as a musical form, was born in this community. The great Bahian matriarchs such as Tia Ciata, Tia Amélia do Aragão (mother of the composer Donga), Tia Presciliana de Santo Amaro (mother of the composer and primitive painter João da Baiana), Tia Veridiana (mother of the composer Chico da Baiana) and others, would promote in Rio de Janeiro the sessions of *candomblé* (a voodoo-like rite) and *batuque* (literally, banging; a song and dance), which, from the 1870s would give birth to the new musical form. It was the Tias (literally, Aunts), particularly Tia Ciata at the beginning of the twentieth century, who hosted in their homes meetings of the '*bambas*', or leading lights of popular music – men such as the composers Sinhô, Donga, João de Baiana and Heitor dos Prazeres; the composer and musician Pixinguinha; the poet and songwriter Catulo da Paixão Cearense and many others. The first samba to be recorded, probably in 1911, was 'In the House of the Bahian', a *partido alto* (an improvised samba with call and response) by an unknown composer.[38]

The Rio de Janeiro in which this group of north-easterners,

recently freed from slavery, found themselves and their specific methods of survival and obtaining a place in society will be the theme of the next chapter.

4

Life in Rio de Janeiro

Bahia will never fail to recognize that Bahians launch themselves
in Rio. . . . Which is to say . . . that it is in Rio that everyone comes
to receive the stamp of greatness.

Dom Obá II d'Africa, 1885

When the French occupied Lisbon, the Portuguese royal family and
all the state apparatus moved to Rio de Janeiro in 1808. On 16
December 1815, the city of Rio was decreed the capital of the United
Kingdom of Portugal, Brazil and the Algarve. Dona Maria I, the
'mad queen', died in the city in 1816 and Dom João VI was crowned
King of Portugal there, at the Largo do Paço on 6 February 1818.

From 1808 on, the city was to become the privileged main stage
of Brazilian history, the space and the symbol of the national unity
that was then in the process of being created. Its inhabitants were
able to observe the play of the politics of the day from its port, from
the Largo do Paço, the Largo do Rocio, from Quinta da Boa Vista.
They were also often able to become participants, through protest
movements or simply by being public opinion.

On 26 April 1821, the city watched the departure of the king,
Dom João IV, for Portugal. On 11 January the following year, its
citizens heard his son, the Prince Regent, backed by the coffee barons
and their armed retainers, openly defy the court in Lisbon and
declare 'I stay'.[1]

After Dom Pedro I's 'cry of Ipiranga', 'Independence or death',
delivered on the outskirts of São Paulo, it was once again the people
of the city of Rio de Janeiro who, on 12 October 1822, acclaimed
him the first emperor of Brazil in a noisy but solemn manifestation
at the Campo de Santana. It was in the Municipal Chambers that the
political constitution of the empire was sworn in, on 25 March

51

1824. In the same room, on a 16 November, 65 years later, the provisional government of the Republic was sworn in. The Republic had been proclaimed the previous day, once again in the former Campo de Santana. After 1822 this square had been known as the Campo da Aclamação; it would be renamed once again, as the Praça da República.

From 1823 onwards, the city saw the play of national politics disrupt its streets and palaces. It was the mirror of the emerging national identity, the place of projection.

Everyone was aware of the importance and political prestige of the city, especially during the reign of Dom Pedro II. 'Bahia will never fail to recognize that Bahians launch themselves in Rio,' said Sublieutenant Zuavo Cândido da Fonseca Galvão, echoing the words of a prominent politician of the day. 'Which is to say', he continued, 'that it is in Rio that everyone comes to receive the stamp of greatness.'[2]

It was on Rio's streets that the campaign for the abolition of slavery and the republican movement were born. Throughout the 1880s, the city endowed these two issues with due importance and true national projection.

On 1 January 1880, the sublieutenant had barely arrived in the city when he was to witness an infuriated mob overturn street cars, tear up tram rails and defy the massed ranks of police. Incited by middle-class journalists of republican ideals such as Lopes Trovão and Ferreira de Meneses, the people were protesting against a recent increase in taxes. The last straw had been a 20 réis (1 'vintém', or tuppence) fare increase in the street cars which were then the principal form of city transport.

The crowds who, in one way or another, supported these protest movements in the 1880s, especially those who came out in support of the abolition of slavery, would be impressive even today. Although the number of people directly involved in the abolitionist campaign (mainly civil servants, lawyers, businessmen and army officers) never exceeded more than 300, popular support for the idea mounted steadily. Abolitionist celebrations at the beginning of the decade managed to mobilize crowds of up to 2,000 people. By 1887 they reached around 5,000.[3]

Such was the power of disruption of these protests, both from the people in the street and from the elites, that article 3 of the first constitution of the new Republic, drawn up in 1891, already envisaged the transfer of the capital to the centre of the country, where it would be safe from agitators and insubordinate mobs. In

1908, President Campos Sales complained about 'the agitated multitudes that bring tumult to the streets of the capital', and as late as 1925, President Artur Bernardes in a presidential address spoke of the nefarious influences of the 'tumultuous and agitated life' of the population of Rio de Janeiro on the conduct of affairs of state.[4]

The centre of national politics from 1822 onwards, the city became, by extension, the *Corte* (Court), with a capital 'C'. It was there that Cândido da Fonseca Galvão came to live and defend his ideas; a period of ten years in all, starting with the Tuppenny Revolt. The Corte, and more specifically, the social sphere where the Zouave sublieutenant, migrant from Bahia and self-avowed 'black prince' circulated, are the subjects of this chapter.

The Imperial 'Court'

In the second half of the century, the Imperial capital went through a phase of great transformations and improvements. After ceding to foreign pressure and abolishing the slave trade, the Court was infected with a vogue for capitalism and entrepreneurial activity.

Large volumes of capital, which until then had been tied up in the slave trade – one of, if not *the* major undertaking in the country – suddenly become available and flooded on to the market in search of investment opportunities.[5]

Shortly after abolition, the Eusébio de Queiróz law legislated limited companies. By 1851, there were already eleven limited capital companies in existence, seven of which had subscribed capital.[6] In the first ten years, between 1850 and 1860, this unprecedented activity resulted in the establishment of 62 industrial companies, 23 insurance companies, 20 steamship companies, 14 banks, 8 mining companies, 8 railroads, 4 land settlement companies, 3 savings banks, 3 transport companies and 2 gas companies.[7]

It was a period of fast-moving modernization. The Dom Pedro II Railroad (which later became the Central do Brasil) was started on 11 June 1853; the first 48 kilometre-long stretch, linking the Corte to Queimados was inaugurated in 1858. In 1861, trains were running to more distant suburbs, as far as Cascadura, making two journeys a day, one into work, one back home again.

The very first railroad in the country, linking Porto da Estrela to Raiz da Serra behind Guanabara Bay, had been inaugurated on 10 April 1854. The first overhead telegraph wire, linking the Corte to

Petrópolis on the top of the Serra do Mar, the mountain ridge behind Rio, dates from 1857.

In 1854, the dim, foul-smelling fish-oil street lamps in the city were replaced by modern gas lighting. Three years later, the first contract for a sewage service was signed. Rio was becoming civilized. From 1868 onwards, agile, mule-drawn street-cars (later converted to electricity) began to substitute the slow, rocky 'gôndolas', which carried up to twelve passengers and had also been pulled by mules. The change was welcomed unanimously in the city. After 1870, the new streetcars also replaced the uncomfortable, horse-drawn 'maxambombas', which covered the route from the São Francisco de Paula Square to Caju and Cancela in the then distant district of São Cristóvão.[8]

From 1850 onwards, the coffee farmers in the Rio hinterland beyond the Serra do Mar were able to obtain generous credit from their commissaries at Corte, both for buying slaves in the north-east (as has been seen earlier) and for enlarging their plantations, improving their productive installations, erecting palaces and importing dinner services from France.[9]

One must not, though, lose sight of the precise historical dimension of these improvements. Everything seems very small if compared with other standards, particularly European ones. From this point of view, from the time that Sublieutenant Galvão arrived in Rio until his death, the city was still an old colonial burgh with narrow, dirty streets, poorly maintained houses, peeling hoardings, pot-holed pavements and dusty shops, exactly as a French journalist, correspondent of *Journal des Debats*, saw it in 1889 when he arrived to cover the newly proclaimed Republic.[10]

The city and the society of those days can be understood more clearly through the censuses carried out in 1870 and 1872, shortly before the arrival of Sublieutenant Galvão; in 1890, the year of his death; and, as counterpoint, the 1906 census.

One of the first characteristics to consider is the burgeoning population and its damaging effects on working conditions and living standards. In effect, in the 20 years from 1870 to 1890, the city population more than doubled, increasing from 235,281 to 522,651 inhabitants. The trend was to be long-lasting: from 1890 until 1906, the city grew at an average annual rate of 3.5 per cent, reaching 800,000 in 1906.[11]

In contrast to the overall population, the slave population at the Corte, as in the majority of Brazilian cities, fell rapidly from 1850 onwards as a result of the demand for labour from the neighbouring coffee-growing municipalities. In 1849 there were 78,855 slaves in the city out of a total population of 205,906 inhabitants; by 1874 the slave population had fallen to 47,084; by 1884, to 32,103; by 1885, to 29,909 and, finally, on the eve of total abolition, to a mere 7,488.[12] In the specific case of Rio de Janeiro, the transfer of slaves to the coffee *fazendas* continued despite the Saraiva-Cotegipe Law of 28 September 1885, the Sexagenarians Law, which, in response to demands from the north and north-east, had included in its article 3, paragraph 19, the prohibition of traffic between provinces. The only exception was when the slave-owner himself moved from one province to another. The following year, in response to counter-pressure from coffee-growers, the Imperial capital was classified (for the purpose of transferring slaves) as an integral part of the Province of Rio de Janeiro, which permitted sales to continue until 1888.

The biggest city in Brazil, the nerve-centre of national politics, Rio progressed towards a greater specialization of work and, above all, the growth of state bureaucracy, during the 1880s. The contingent of civil servants more than doubled between 1872 and 1890, rising from 2,351 employees to 5,074. The number of lawyers trebled, from 242 to 761; doctors more than doubled, from 394 to 965; and employees in commerce – shops and traders – rose from 23,481 to 48,048.[13]

At the same time, the numbers of those 'with no declared profession' rose substantially, reflecting the final crisis of the slave system. From representing 30 per cent of the total population in 1870, the proportion rose to 37 per cent in 1872 and to no less than 44 per cent in 1890. Among those with 'no profession' (except for a short period) was Sublieutenant Cândido da Fonseca Galvão.

This economically and socially marginalized sector of the population, composed above all by blacks and the brown-skinned, *pardos*, both natives of the city and migrants to the city, constituted, by sheer force of numbers, a type of parallel city, half way between the imprecise limits of the legal and the illegal. In this city of Rio de Janeiro, in Sublieutenant Galvão's words, who was always extremely careful in his choice of words, 'every living being seeks means, either licit ... or illicit in view of the nature of finding the means to acquire daily bread for himself and his family.'[14]

Living from hand to mouth – licitly or illicitly – this underworld made its presence felt throughout the city, and was particularly visible to contemporaries, both natives of the city and foreign travellers, in the form of growing prostitution, which was responsible for the ill-repute of many streets in the centre of the city. More widespread were the beggars and the so-called 'chicken thieves' (petty thieves) and gangs of *capoeiristas* (those who knew the martial art *capoeira*).

The numbers are impressive. Around 60 per cent of the slave population in 1872 had no professional qualification. In 1890, the 'with no declared profession' totalled no fewer than 48,100 individuals, almost exactly the same numbers as the 48,661 employed in manufacturing industry or the 48,048 employed in commerce. This latter included the host of street traders who plied their wares throughout the city, from the centre to the outskirts, carrying enormous baskets or wooden trays on their heads. The most numerous professional group, both during the slave period and after, continued to be domestic servants. In 1890 they numbered 74,785.[15]

Whites, Browns and Blacks

For the immense majority of people, eking out a living and surviving the poor conditions at work was extremely difficult. The available data appear to show that the death rate exceeded the birth rate. Between 1889 and 1891, for example, 13,169 births were registered, as against 17,574 deaths.[16]

The first epidemic of yellow fever swept through the city in 1850: it had come from Bahia as a by-product of the domestic slave traffic. Nine years later smallpox arrived. But yellow fever, above all, was the scourge of the city, claiming 59,069 victims by the end of the century.

The burgeoning population growth rate, which reached an annual average of 5.2 per cent between 1872 and 1890, can be largely explained by the surge of domestic migration which accompanied the slow dismantling of the slave order and also by the arrival of foreign immigrants. The scale of this influx was such that in 1890 only half Rio's population had been born in the city. The other half was made up of Brazilians from other provinces (Rio de Janeiro Province, Bahia, Minas Gerais, Pernambuco and even São Paulo), who represented 26 per cent of the population, and foreigners, who accounted for 24 per cent.

The Brazilians who came from other provinces were mainly '*homens livres de cor*' (free men of colour) such as Sublieutenant Galvão; and *libertos* (freedmen) and, even before 1888, escaped slaves. All were seeking better work opportunities and a better life in the big city, far from the oppressive life in the country and the provincial cities. All, as Galvão said, were trying to 'launch themselves' in the city of Rio de Janeiro, and also 'promoting the means to acquire daily bread' for themselves and their families.

Blacks and *pardos* (mixed race) represented 44.79 per cent of the population in 1872 and 37.2 per cent in 1890. According to the available data, the proportion of blacks fell from 24.13 per cent in 1872 to 12.34 per cent in 1890. In the same period, the proportion of browns rose from 20.66 per cent to 24.94 per cent.

These figures should be treated with some caution and not be seen as a scientifically precise form of racial classification. We may suspect a relative exaggeration in the numbers of whites, who rose to 62.7 per cent of the population in 1890, at the cost of the number of blacks and browns. This is probably due to the lack of explicit criteria for defining the colour category in any of the censuses mentioned here. The same is true in the categories of profession and literacy. In the specific case of colour, the absence of fixed guidelines is fully in accord with the Brazilian system of classification which is recognizedly multi- and not just bi-racial, allowing a large range of nuances between whites and browns. These often varied in accordance with the social status of the person concerned. It is also worth remembering that it was precisely at this time that the 'ideology of whitening' first emerged. It was, in part, a corollary of the very system of classification. Indeed, in 1906 the category of colour was simply omitted from the census.[17]

Education continued to be, as it was in colonial times, a privilege of the few. In 1872, 63.82 per cent of the population was illiterate. Even in his creole Portuguese, with his colourfully idiosyncratic syntax and vocabulary, Sublieutenant Galvão was in a minority – the 36.18 per cent of the population who, at the time of his death, knew how to read and write in the city of Rio de Janeiro. By 1906, the illiterate still represented 40.2 per cent of the population.[18]

In absolute numbers, foreigners increased from 78,676 in 1870 to 124,352 in 1890. But their relative proportion fell from 33 per cent to 24 per cent over the same period.[19] While numerically inferior, the immigrants – especially the Portuguese and Italians – took the best jobs, whether in the trade and retail sector or in the emerging factories. In 1872, only 6,123 Brazilians worked in trade, as against 17,358 foreigners. Four years later, 2,631 Brazilians and 9,264 foreigners applied for industrial and professional licences.[20]

The resentments which accumulated from then onwards against the immigrant population and above all against the Portuguese immigrants who controlled the corner shops and cheap rented accommodation would, in the early days of the Republican government, soon after the death of Dom Obá II d'Africa, explode into a radical wave of anti-Portuguese sentiment, the so-called *carioca* Jacobinism.[21]

Rooming Houses

The population explosion aggravated all the old problems of habitation, food supply and public health. With inadequate public transport, the working class – employed, underemployed or unemployed – had little option other than to live in cramped surroundings in the centre of the city, near their work or actually in the workplace. Rented accommodation fell into one of the following categories: the so-called *'estalagens'* ('mews' – tiny, often one-room houses in terraces either side of a single entranceway), *'casas de cômodos'* and *'casas de habitação'* (rooming houses), *'hospedarias'* (cheap hostels) and, at the very bottom of the market, the *'cortiços'* (overcrowded, crumbling houses subdivided into tiny rooms).

In 1886, the United States Consul, Christopher C. Andrews, calculated that a head of family who earned between US$4 and US$30 a week in accordance with his trade, would have to pay between US$5 and US$8 a month to live in a 'mews' and between US$3.5 and US$4.50 month to live in a *cortiço*.[22] In 1890 no less than a quarter of the population – around 130,000 people – lived like this, above all in the *cortiços*.

The housing question was serious, long-lasting and particularly affected the bottom rungs of society. From within this world in 1886, Cândido da Fonseca Galvão wrote in outrage about an old African woman, sightless with age and penniless, who put her own daughter out to prostitution in order to pay for the house where they lived in the Rua da Alfândega in the city centre.[23]

Prince Obá himself had personal experience of the problem, judging by his constant changes of address. Hermeto Lima, it seems, saw him living in an attic in Rua Uruguaina, above the Externato Gama school and the Azevedo bookshop.[24] In May 1886, when his last child was born, he lived in what the newspapers of the time described, ironically, as 'The Royal Palace of Engenho Novo', a district further from the centre.[25] His wife, Dona Raiza-me Abiodum, died at this address on 24 November 1887.[26] A few months later, the prince moved to the Largo do Benfica, beyond São

Cristóvão, due, he said, to the 'displeasure' that he suffered with widowhood.[27]

But nor did he stay long in this far-off district, where rent was cheaper. When he died, in July 1890, it was 'in the house or his residence', back in the centre of the city on the Rua Barão de São Félix.[28] Three moves, therefore, between May 1886 and July 1890, or an average of one every 16 months.

The housing problem was long-standing in Rio de Janeiro and affected even the middle reaches of society. In the preceding decade, for example, the *carioca* Quintino Bocaiúva, journalist of the opposition and advocate of the Republic, moved seven times in 12 years, averaging 20.57 months at each address.[29]

The Rua Barão de São Félix was not a very salubrious address, as we shall see. João do Rio, a journalist who wrote memorable reports revealing this subworld to *carioca* readers, described the inside of one of these 'Africans' houses' in 1904. His description could have fitted the life of Alferes de Zuavos, or his contemporaries, fourteen years earlier. 'They retain the outward appearance of an earlier age,' wrote the journalist. His description is probably a unique ethnographic document:

> They almost always have sombre slats over the windows and house the head of the household plus another five, six or more people. In the sitting room there is broken, dirty furniture, mats, benches; on top of the tables, covered dishes, bowls of water, straw hats, herbs, oil cloth pouches holding the *opelé* [sacred cowrie shells and other items used for divining the will of the Yoruba traditional gods or *orixás*]; on the walls, drums, strange clothing, bits of glass; and in the backyard, nearly always turtles, black hens, cockerels and goats.[30]

It is clear that it is not just a residence in the western sense of the term but a space with two purposes, sacred and profane, a place to live and pray. There were prosaic daily utensils: 'broken, dirty furniture, mats, benches' and 'bowls of water, straw hats'. And there were also the objects used in Afro-Brazilian rituals: herbs, drums, 'strange clothing'. In the yard, both the animals used for subsistence and those for sacrifice in the rituals. The prince was described in newspaper reports of the time as living among parrots and songbirds.[31]

Little Africa

The concentration of blacks in the streets around the port, stretching from the ill-reputed Valongo, the place where slaves disembarked and sold from the eighteenth century onwards, as far as Formosa Beach and Saco do Alferes and, behind, as far as the 'new city over the swamp'. Heitor dos Prazeres, a samba composer and naive painter in vogue today, one of the most illustrious natives of that region, referred to it, years later, as 'little Africa'. This very exact and expressive description has been taken on by the more recent historiography of the city to show the social and cultural Afro-Brazilian unity found in these quarters and, indeed, throughout Brazil.[32]

The community in the districts of Santana, Cidade Nova, Santo Cristo, Saúde and Gamboa – the Little Africa of Rio de Janeiro – organized itself around earning its living in the capital, first of the empire, then of the Republic, through the common Afro-Brazilian heritage of work, *festas* and religion.

Under slavery, the sexual division of labour established the aptitudes of each sex and laid down the direction to be followed by each. The men, more valued as slaves, were at a disadvantage in freedom. Some found work through their traditional skills as builders, carpenters, barbers, and so on. But the great majority, with no specialized training but in good health, worked as stevedores or porters in the streets, or as street-sellers or simply as odd-job men, always at hand for whatever needed doing. Some resorted to tricks and small cons, giving birth to the legend of the *'malandro carioca'* (the Rio street urchin).

For women, the job market seems to have been a little better. This gave rise to the tradition of the 'Bahian aunts', the strong matriarchs who organized this underclass community. Many, as we have seen, found work as domestic servants (cooks, or 'all work' cleaning women). Many also worked at home, taking in washing, ironing or sewing. Others, who had a little capital and a gift for leadership, organized relatively prosperous cottage industries, making and selling Bahian specialities, or even setting up small businesses known as *'quitandas'*. Tia (Aunt) Ciata de Oxum made Bahia specialities and sold them from a tray at the corner of Rua 7 de Setembro and Rua Uruguaiana. She also set up a stall at the Festa da Penha. Later on, she started hiring out authentic Bahian costumes for the theatrical companies and for carnival. The business prospered to an extent that she took on other employees besides her family.[33]

Tia Carmen – or Dona Carmen da Praça Onze, as she became known – also made and sold Bahian specialities such as '*cocada-puxa*' (chewy sweet coconut), '*queijadinha*' (coconut cup-cakes) and '*bolinho de estudante*' (tapioca roll) – in the streets of Rio de Janeiro. Born in Salvador in 1879, daughter of a freedwoman who sold her sweetmeats on Itapoã beach and the Bonfim festival – Dona Carmen moved to Rio with her mother at the age of 14 in 1893.[34]

Tia Bebiana employed several young girls besides her own family, in her home, making shoes. Tia Preciliana de Santo Amaro, daughter of ex-slaves Fernando de Aruanda, from the Jeje nation, and Maria Joana, a Nagô, managed to open a small shop selling religious artefacts in the Rua do Sabão. Tia Gracinda, the wife of the *Pai-de-Santo* Assumano Mina do Brasil, at one time owned a bar known as Gruta Baiana.[35]

The boys sold sweets in the streets; the girls stayed at home, shut off from the world, helping their mothers and learning their cooking secrets. Some girls sold their bodies and youth. Josefa da Lapa, also known as Josefa Rica, started off selling food in the street and ended up running a brothel in Lapa.[36]

Until 1888 both men and women had to compete with slave labour. A few gained a reputation for their sorcery and were able to make a living from this. They included the African Quimbambochê, Assumano Mina do Brazil, João Alabá, and others. João Alabá presided over *nagô candomblé* at 174 Rua Barão de São Félix where Josefa Rica and the respectable Tias Ciata de Oxum, Perciliana and many others used to go regularly. Tia Ciata was the Iya Kekere, or 'the little mother', the second highest dignatory in the *candomblé* hierarchy, responsible for the initiation of novices and for the '*iaôs*' or 'daughters of saints' who had already been initiated.[37] The devotees of *candomblé* were known as '*tias*' (aunts), '*mães-de-santo*' (mother of the holy), '*pais-de-santo*' (father of the holy), '*irmãs-de-santo*' (sister of the holy), '*mães-pequenas*' (little mothers) and the houses of worship became known as 'centres'. This was not by chance: they were the points within this sub-culture around which society could organize itself in the transition from slavery to a free labour market, through family ties and religious kinship. It was in the centres that their mystic origins, social ties, hierarchies and hopes could be fostered.

Despite what might appear at first glance when studying the movements towards homogenization, this pan-African population did not make up a cohesive unit. Although they shared a similar social standing – and, indeed, because of this – the inhabitants of

Little Africa also preserved the old discord of Africa itself: divided upon questions of different origins, customs and religions.

At the beginning of the twentieth century one can already distinguish, in Little Africa, and in the city as a whole, different ethnic groups or 'nations', such as Ijexá, Ebá, Aboum, Hausa, Itaqua, Cambindas, Oyó, Nagô, and so on. Fierce religious and philosophical rivalries raged between the Muslims and those who worshipped the '*orixás*'. It was not easy to live in that mini-Africa, where the Muslims did not get on with the 'people of the saint', whom they called, pejoratively, '*auauado-chum*' and where, in turn, 'the people of the saint looked down on the creatures who did not eat pork, calling them *malês*'. Some took a superior attitude to the 'daughters of the holy' of the '*macumbas*' and to certain other blacks. Antônio, João do Rio's informant, told him, Looking at the Cambinda blacks you can understand why it was the African who was the slave to the white man.'[38]

Despite these internal divisions – as the reporter noted – the inhabitants of this Little Africa, in contrast to the rest of the city, were all related, in that they shared a common language (Yoruba or the creole Portuguese of Alferes Galvão), 'more or less identical outward customs' and sorcery.[39]

The followers of the *orixás*, always more numerous than the Muslims, were nearly always more open to concepts of integration and to syncretism with Catholicism, the official religion of the Empire.

The *festas* held for the *orixás*, such as those at the wooden shack in Tia Ciata's backyard in Praça Onze, were frequently preceded by a Catholic mass, especially on the day of Our Lady of the Conception. Statues of the Virgin with the infant Jesus in her lap dominated the church of Nossa Senhora do Rosário dos Pretos (Our Lady of the Rosary of the Blacks) and the church of the Hospício. The Virgin had long been identified with the seductive Oxum, divinity of the River Osun in the country of Yoruba. Oxum was the *Iyaloode*, the most important woman in the city; queen of all the rivers and freshwaters, without which man cannot exist; goddess of female fertility, all-embracing mother, who is still worshipped in Cuba, Brazil and Africa today with the same plea for her favours: 'ore yeye ô!'[40]

Another 'daughter' of Oxum, Dona Carmen Teixeira da Conceição, 'still lucid, talkative, vain and devoted to carnival' lived to be more than 100. As recently as 1987, Dona Carmen, who, like so many of the Afro-Brazilian *tias*, was also a devout Catholic, watched the inauguration of the monument to Zumbi de Palmares in Praça Onze and boasted of being 'the oldest member of the Saint George sisterhood' in all the city of Rio de Janeiro.[41]

The Street

In 1890, Sublieutenant Galvão lived in the Rua Barão de São Félix in a type of dwelling not specified by the documents. This street was notorious as a region of over-populated '*cortiços*' ('beehives'), the refuges of '*capoeiras*', prostitutes and sorcerers. Galvão lived at number 26. A little higher up, in number 132, was the *Cabeça de Porco* (Pig's Head), probably the largest, and undoubtedly the most notorious of Rio's '*cortiços*'. A little further up still, at number 174, was João Alabá's *candomblé*.

Besides the *pai-de-santo* João Alabá and Sublieutenant Galvão, the *cortiços* of Barão de São Félix housed many other Bahian migrants at the end of the empire and beginning of the Republic. The average rooming house in those days consisted of some ten rooms, each housing one family. Because of its size and final destiny, the 'Pig's Head' was unique and deserves to be studied in more detail.

The 'Pig's Head' was certainly one of the sources which Aluísio Azevedo drew on when writing O *Cortiço*, considered to be one of the milestones in urban Brazilian literature.[42] 'Cabeça de Porco' came to be used, throughout Brazil, as a synonym for the worst sort of rooming house and is still in use today.

The expansion of this *cortiço* (which can be traced through the payments of the 'urban tithe', the building tax, at the Town Hall) seems to indicate the existence of a nucleus which was originally composed, as in the majority of '*cortiços*' of a large, old, two-storey house, divided and subdivided into tiny rooms. Other smaller rooms had been built in the backyard and these too expanded continually. In 1878, according to the urban tithe registers, the principal building was divided into 89 rooms, while the space at the back contained five one-storey rooms and two stables. In Sublieutenant Galvão's day, in 1890, there were 104 rooms in the main house and 21 ground-floor rooms. Even the attic was occupied.

The descriptions of it at the end of the period suggest that the original nucleus of the house had overflowed into a labyrinth of passages, where rooms for human habitation were jumbled together with chicken coops, storerooms, barber's shops, cobblers, and so on, all housing between 2,000 and 4,000 people.

Three years after the death of Cândido da Fonseca Galvão in
1893, 'the Pig's Head' was demolished by order of the local council.
The operation, a veritable military manoeuvre, involved three
hundred workers from the Public Works Authority, the police
infantry, the cavalry, firemen and was supervised by the chief of
police and the mayor, Barata Ribeiro, himself. A few yards from
there, on the hill, Morro da Providência, a shanty-town mushroomed, built partly from the building materials taken from the
'Pig's Head' demolition. Four years later, with the return of the
soldiers from Canudos in the interior of Bahia, it gained the name
'favela' after a plant in the hinterland.[43]

'Thorns and Hardships'

In addition to the housing problem which we had just examined, we
can piece together more of how Sublieutenant Galvão lived in the
capital, and, through him, the living conditions of other migrants,
both Bahians and others, who had recently emerged from slavery.
The newspaper O Paiz, for example, mentions that after the 'festive'
demonstration of support for the deposed emperor in December
1889, Dom Obá had sat down to a lunch consisting of 'the delights
of a modest feijoada with a glass of paraty to top it off'.[44] We know
from the Gazeta de Notícias that the prince died 'unattended by a
doctor'. Finally, according to the Diário de Notícias, he was given a
'pauper's burial' which was, none the less, well attended.[45]

The problem of food supply goes back several decades. From the
end of the eighteenth century until the first half of the nineteenth
century – both previous to and during the expansion of coffee
plantations in Rio de Janeiro – fazendeiros, smallholders and
shareholders would produce foodstuffs not only for their family and
slaves, but also to supply the market of the Corte.

Self-sufficiency was advocated as ideal by the first farming manual
to reflect the real experience of the coffee expansion economy rather
than being a mere compilation or translation of a foreign work.
'Every farmer', wrote Baron of Pati do Alferes in 1847,

> should plant basic foodstuffs sufficient for his own use in order not to
> have to buy in provisions for his own consumption: he will then be free,
> and his servants will be well fed and satisfied, because when one buys
> food in, there is never abundance and the slaves will always suffer to a
> greater or lesser degree.

This ideal, however, suffered such dramatic changes in the second half of the century that in subsequent editions, published in 1863 and 1878, the Baron's son, who revised and updated the work, chose to omit this passage. It no longer made any sense at a time when subsistence farming had been abandoned in order to concentrate all available resources of land and slaves on the coffee monoculture.[46]

Several contemporary authors have provided detailed analyses of the more general causes of this process and the consequences for both urban and city life. From the mid-century onwards, as virgin land was gradually incorporated and slave labour became scarce, coffee, an export crop, gradually took over the best land to the detriment of foodcrops. As the area of land used for planting subsistence products decreased, the farmers who had previously produced surpluses and sold them to the Corte, themselves became consumers.

With the rise in coffee prices, the small farm, which had traditionally produced foodcrops, also started planting coffee. The shortage of labour affected these small farms even more than the big estates. Sharecroppers with few resources of their own, and little capacity for resistance, saw the best land taken over by the coffee plantations. In many cases these extended, literally, to their front doors. The shortage of labour resulted in higher prices, the need to import food and speculation by the leading merchants in the Corte.[47]

In the 1850s, the price of food staples consumed by the working classes more than doubled in Rio de Janeiro. Between 1850–1 and 1858–9, the price of an *arroba* (14.7 kg) of rice rose from 1$520 to 3$300; sugar, from 1$700 to 3$750; salt beef, from 2$720 to 5$500. An *alqueire* (36.27 litres) of beans, the most popular food, more than doubled from 2$300 to 4$980. These are wholesale prices; goods were far dearer at the corner shop.[48]

By the 1880s, the shortages and poor quality of food was already a long-standing problem in the Imperial capital. The supply of fresh meat, for example, continued to be insufficient despite the complaints which had been made since the 1860s and despite the opening of the municipal slaughterhouse in Santa Cruz in 1881. Based on available data, we can presume that most people would not have had meat to eat every day as the average daily consumption of fresh meat over the decade was as low as 11 g per inhabitant.[49]

A Very Modest *Feijoada*

A more reliable source for the analysis of what the poor ate during
the last decade of the monarchy can be found in that 'modest
feijoada' eaten by the prince on 2 December 1889. The *feijoada* is
the best-known dish in Brazilian cuisine and is especially central to
the cooking of Rio de Janeiro. In its 'modest' version, it probably
consisted of black beans with salt beef, rice and manioc flour. The
fuller version, known as 'complete *feijoada*', would have also
included salted or smoked pork, various types of sausage, pork
crackling, fried kale and sliced oranges.

Mr Ricketts, the British Consul in Rio, may not have been an
aficionado of *feijoada*, but he does seem to have understood its
importance in the life of slaves, freedmen and free men. Salt beef and
black beans 'cooked into a soup forms the staple article of food of
the masses of this country', he told the Foreign Office in 1885. In an
earlier report, dated 1880, Mr Ricketts probably had the Caribbean
colonies in mind when he reported that 'this dried meat ... cooked
with the black bean in Brazilian-fashion forms a most nutritive and
sustaining diet, and might be used with advantage in many countries
where the high price of fresh meat takes away from the poor the
power of purchasing it'.[50]

Besides the ingredients used in *feijoada* – beans, rice, salt beef and
manioc flour – the poor ate wheat bread with their morning coffee
and, on Sundays and special occasions, dried cod, a much appreciated inheritance from the Portuguese.

Some salt beef came from the '*saladeros*' of Rio Grande do Sul,
but most was imported from Argentina, Uruguay and the United
States. Rio de Janeiro consumed (and redistributed to the interior) an
average of 25,842,230 kg of dried beef annually between 1880 and
1885. The beans – the heart of the *feijoada* – were also imported. In
1880, 29,337 sacks were unloaded at Rio's port. Nearly all the rice
was imported from India and England. In 1879 the city imported
145,800 sacks of rice, rising to 194,898 the following year when the
prices varied from 8$300 to 11$000 per bag. During the years
1881–2 and 1883–4, an average of 214,761 sacks arrived in the city
each year. In 1884–5, 173,988 sacks were imported at prices from
8$500 réis to 10$000 réis per sack. Maize – another staple for slaves,
freedmen and free men of colour, whether in the city or the country
– came from Rio da Prata, the United States and Liverpool. Some
96,500 sacks were imported in 1879 and 103,507 the following
year, with the price ranging from 3$500 to 5$800 a sack.

Wheat flour came from Argentina, Uruguay, Chile, Italy, Austria and other countries, but principally from the United States, which accounted for three-quarters of the world market. In 1879, 406,500 barrels were imported, in 1880, 388,076 barrels; each of these fetched between 16 and 24 mil-réis. In 1881–2 and 1883–4, annual flour imports averaged 37,550,120 kg. In summary, as Mr Ricketts calculated, taking an average consumption of 1 lb per head per day, Rio's total imports of rice, flour, maize and beans in 1880 was only enough to feed a population of 300,000 people for 375 days.[51]

Only the side dishes – manioc flour, kale and the sugar cane rum *paraty* – were likely to have been produced locally. The local custom was to start or finish the meal with a draught of *paraty*. In this particular case, it was, as the newspaper says, taken as a digestive, 'a chalice of *paraty* to top it off'.[52]

Besides taking labour from the plantations, the war effort, lasting until 1870, also put a strain on the cost of living, both in the country and in the city of Rio de Janeiro. New taxes were levied, principally by increases in customs duties. The problems worsened, above all during the 1880s, when Brazil's economy was hard hit by the low prices of its export goods – not only the traditional sugar, cotton and tobacco, but also the 'king coffee'. What had formerly been a virtual Brazilian monopoly was being challenged from other producers; Brazil's share of world coffee production fell from 49.5 per cent in 1855 to 45.9 per cent in 1878.[53]

Domestically, the country was going through the critical years of the eradication of slave labour, a time of great agitation in Rio de Janeiro with the campaigns for abolition and the Republic. As the whole financial life of the country had previously revolved around the price of slave labour, loans granted to farmers were still based more on the guarantee of their workforce than on their collateral in land, infrastructure and coffee plantations. It was a time of great pressure and political campaigns for 'hands', 'credit for farm production' and railways to reduce the cost of transport between plantations and port. The principal demand by the landowners during the whole process of abolition and after the onset of the Republic, was compensation for the capital they lost with their slaves.[54]

The 1880s was also a decade of sharp financial fluctuations. The fall in the value of exports and, consequently, in import capacity, had a negative impact on public revenue. Faced with chronic deficits, the Treasury resorted to foreign loans, such as those contracted in

London in 1883, 1886 and 1888; to the inflationary issue of banknotes; and to tax increases in an attempt to balance the public accounts.

Given the economic, social and political importance of the *fazendeiros*, in whose ranks were to be found the most illustrious members of both political parties, the political proposition of protecting export crops – the principal source of revenue and the motor of the economy – seemed perfectly natural. Taxes on coffee, sugar and maté tea exports were reduced from 9 per cent to 7 per cent in 1882. At the same time, both Liberal and Conservative cabinets made changes in import tariffs throughout the period in order to protect the farming sector, encourage the emerging industrial sector and, above all, increase tax revenue and balance the public sector books: the Liberals, taking office in 1878, introduced the Afonso Celso and Saraiva taxes; the Conservatives, from 1885, the Cotegipe and João Alfredo taxes (the taxes being named after the prime ministers who introduced them).[55]

The Tuppenny Revolt

Inflation and fiscal policy based on imports and non-agricultural activities (such as the new taxes of 1879 on commercial licences, buildings, civil servants' salaries, and so on) particularly affected the urban population, above all the poorest, such as the residents of Little Africa.

It was not by chance that the 1880s began with a violent street demonstration precisely against the introduction of a particularly unpalatable new tax of 10 per cent on the streetcar fares. The protest became known as the 'Revolta do Vintém', or 'Tuppenny revolt', after the amount of the increase – $020, colloquially 'um vintém'.[56] The tax was first announced on 13 December 1879, as part of a long series of new taxes or increases in existing taxes which the Liberal cabinet, led by the Viscount de Ouro Preto, introduced in an attempt to make up the budget deficit. From that moment onwards, mass demonstrations were held in the city, led by middle-class journalists who whipped up local discontent at the crippling cost of living for their own ends. Above all it was the journalists on the *Gazeta de Notícias* who espoused abolition and/or republicanism, men like Lopes Trovão and José do Patrocínio. Trovão, a radical republican, spurred the population of Rio de Janeiro to action against the constituted authorities. 'Only through a revolution', he wrote, 'will the people be able to force the public authorities to carry out its civic duties.'[57]

Besides the republican radicals, the Conservatives also saw an opportunity in the general discontent to bring down the Liberal cabinet, which had been in power since 1878. On 1 January 1880, the day on which the new tax was due to come into effect, the poor took to the streets of the city centre in a violent demonstration and began to rip out iron tram rails, overturn street cars and put them to the torch. Troops fired into the crowds: eyewitnesses described the city as having been transformed into a battlefield. The official death toll was 3 dead and 28 injured. After the battle, even eminent Liberals, such as Joaquim Nabuco and Francisco Otaviano, came out in opposition to their party leadership and openly criticized both the taxes and the force used in putting down the revolt. Under fire from friends and enemies alike, the Ouro Preto cabinet fell. Once again the divisions between local and national politics had become blurred in the streets of Rio de Janeiro, when the ordinary people, the republicans, abolitionists, conservatives and liberals – each in pursuit of their own objectives – managed to bring down the government.[58]

While the newspapers of the day recorded only the part played by the middle-class leaders such as the journalists Lopes Trovão, José Ferreira de Meneses, José do Patrocínio and Carlos de Carvalho, one can say that this street demonstration, the 'celebrated tuppennies', as the prince called it, had launched the most active period of Dom Obá II d'Africa's political militancy. From that moment on, he was, without doubt, the best-known local character in the city. Following the example of other illustrious Conservatives – official members of the party – the sublieutenant had fought on that day, not for the 'revolution', like Lopes Trovão, but, on the opposite flank, against the hardships of living, which he considered were damaging to the institutions of the day. From then on – as he succinctly described it years later – the prince was on the warpath, 'in defence of the Monarchy' and 'against certain members of the politics of the past'.[59]

Taxes and More Taxes

Despite the revolt and the growing dissatisfaction at the hardships, the cost of living continued to increase over the rest of the decade. One kilo of best quality salt beef (returning again to that modest *feijoada* enjoyed by Sublieutenant Galvão) leapt from $520 to $800 in the years between the Tuppenny revolt and 1886.[60] Many, in the years that followed the revolt, began to see the implications of a pro-export fiscal policy as being prejudicial to the less favoured urban classes while others benefited from it.

'What an age are we living, so full of thorns and hardships for those on one side, the side of the poor who most need plenty,' said Dom Obá II d'Africa who had developed *sui generis* ideas of social justice. He went on, undaunted: 'it is the other side, the nobles, who should work for nothing because they are the richest.'[61]

The discontent was enormous. In Little Africa, the population sought to explain their plight: some blamed the taxes, others, the 'greed for money', yet others thought the cause lay in chronic unemployment or the decadence of political customs. Dom Obá, for one, in an article written in 1883, launched a fierce attack on those who, he claimed, 'vexfully usurped the blood of poverty with taxes and more taxes'. Continuing he said:

> it is the poor who die of hunger, with no work, many who are employed lose their jobs and become desperate with hunger, and the nation continues to fall apart, as we see every day – murders, all manner of thievery, all species of intrigue, all for greed and the love of money.[62]

The Faithful Vassal

Ask our Monarch if there is a Brazilian in Brazil who is more
closely related to the African nation than I.

Dom Obá II d'Africa, 1887

The daily struggle for existence which Dom Obá II d'Africa had in
common with so many north-eastern migrants in the Imperial capital
and which he described so vividly as 'thorns and hardships' was,
however, only one strand of his life. Sublieutenant Galvão did not
limit his sphere of action to the ghettos of Little Africa. This chapter
and the next will examine his role in the political life of Rio de
Janeiro in more detail: his motives; his access to the official world;
the role he played as a link between this world and his other one,
Little Africa; his links with his constituency and the style of
leadership that he exercised. On the one hand, we have the Faithful
Vassal of Dom Pedro II; on the other, the Street King of Rio de
Janeiro. We will take one at a time.

Dom Obá II's access to the palace and to the emperor himself is
a well-documented fact. It figures both in the documentation of the
time and in the anecdotes of the ubiquitous Court gossips. In his *O
Império em chinelos* ('The Empire in Slippers') published in 1957, R.
Magalhães Júnior recounts a telling incident. This may well have
been based on oral tradition – a tradition that still thrives in Brazil
today and that is signposted by expressions such as *conta-se* ('it is
said') and *segundo corre* ('it went around').

'It went around' that the military guard of the Imperial Palace at
Quinta da Boa Vista once failed to salute Prince Dom Obá II
d'Africa with due military ceremony. The prince – and sublieutenant
– understood that he had a right to the correct formalities. According
to Magalhães Júnior, Dom Obá 'demanded, at the top of his voice,

that they perform the neglected military honours' and ended up being threatened with imprisonment. The succeeding uproar, at the main entrance to the palace, was so great that the emperor decided to intervene, summoning the officer responsible.

'When Dom Obá comes here it would be better to salute,' said Dom Pedro II.

'But Your Majesty, he doesn't merit it, he is crazy, a madman,' replied the officer.

'Which is precisely why you should not thwart him,' came the reply, bringing the matter to a close. 'He will then be satisfied and we will not have to suffer such irritation.'[1]

Mello Moraes Filho, a contemporary of the prince, witnessed the counterpoint of this episode. A sentry once greeted the prince with a particularly elaborate military flourish. The prince then, 'in an excess of emotion, drew a 2$000 or 5$000 note from his pocket and handed it to the soldier, before proceeding to mount the steps with admirable majesty.'[2]

Dom Obá never missed the public audiences held at Quinta da Boa Vista on Saturdays. He also appeared, even on solemn occasions, at Dom Pedro II's city palace, the Paço da Cidade. Whether he was wearing his sublieutenant's uniform or was decked out in smart civilian dress, Dom Obá was always 'one of the first to pay obeisance'. Although many contemporaries claimed that his presence was an embarrassment, the emperor, in respect of his past services and military office, 'ordered that he be allowed freedom of access, despite the protests and the ridicule that this provoked'.[3]

At least once, on a state occasion, he was allowed access to the balcony of the Paço da Cidade and proceeded to wave to the crowds below. On another occasion, he caused great embarrassment in the throne room when he broke royal protocol and presented himself at the forefront of the diplomatic corps as if he were a foreign ambassador serving in Rio de Janeiro.

> Dressed splendidly, puffed with pride and dragging his sword in his wake, he bowed reverently to kiss the hands of the Emperor and Empress; he approached the Princess and greeted her with a respectful bow; he then tossed a truly intimate and cordial goodbye to the Count d'Eu, who was sitting behind.

As he withdrew backwards, ceremoniously retracing his steps, the prince tripped on his own sword and, as he fell, his boot came crashing down on the foot of the Nuncio who, according to Mello Moraes, angrily hissed something between his teeth.[4]

This vivid picture can, in more concrete terms, be counterbalanced by an examination of His Imperial Majesty's visitors' book at Paço da Quinta da Boa Vista between 1882 and 1885. What it registers is significant. Dom Obá was present at every single one of the audiences held by the emperor from 17 June 1882 (when the register began) until 13 December 1884, a total of 125 visits. On fourteen of these he was the first to arrive at the palace. On 29 July 1882 and 1 November 1884 he was, for no apparent reason, the only visitor. Dom Obá signed, in his own hand, 'Príncipe Obá 2 d'Africa Alfes. Galvão'. On one or two occasions, when it seems that the officer in charge of the registers signed him in, it read only 'Alferes Galvão', without his assumed royal title.[5]

Such compliments to the emperor, which regularly took place at Quinta da Boa Vista, constituted a privileged political forum. They were a point of personal contact between the emperor and the rest of society. The registers available, which run from 17 June 1882 to 13 December 1884, allow a summary of the most important political and social questions of the time. As one turns the pages of names of those present at the *beija-mão* ('hand kissing'), as these sessions were known, one sees the nobles of the land: the coffee barons, counts and viscounts; eminent politicians – ministers of state, presidents of provinces, senators, general deputies, counsellors; diplomats such as the Consul General of the United States Thomas Adamson, and other foreign representatives; leading civilian and military personalities such as *Marechal* Deodoro da Fonseca, *Marechal* Floriano Peixoto, Dr Afonso Penna, Dr Nilo Peçanha, *Conselheiro* Rui Barbosa, *Marechal* Hermes da Fonseca, *Almirante* Custódio José de Mello, *Almirante* Eduardo Wandelkolk, Dr Francisco Pereira Passos and others; distinguished artists and intellectuals such as the photographer Marc Ferrez, the painter Victor Meireles and the writer Machado de Assis. The most diverse currents of political thinking, including the positivists, the republicans and the abolitionists such as Benjamin Constant Botelho de Magalhães, Quintino Bocaiúva and José Carlos do Patrocínio. Whites, blacks and those of mixed race; representatives of employees and professional associations that ranged from the state school Parents and Teachers Association to the Sociedade Propagadora das Belas Artes, the students from the Faculdade de Medicina do Rio de Janeiro, Sociedade Acadêmica Deus, Cristo e Caridade, the Associação Promotora da Instrução, the Club de Engenharia, the Associação Industrial, the Associação dos Empregados no Comércio do Rio de Janeiro; representatives of opposition journalists and doctors (such as that made up of Moncorvo Filho, Silva Araújo, Moura Brazil and Carlos Ramos); and many others besides.[6]

How did this political arena, attended by such a wide spectrum of society, work? I will analyse this in the next section, looking at the documentation available and, in particular, at the audience that took place on 13 October 1883, which has specific significance for our purposes.

The Hand Kissing

On Saturday, 13 October 1883, it had been raining for three days and the roads to São Cristóvão from the city centre were almost impassable. In the small audience chamber at the Imperial palace, just over twenty people waited for the emperor. As the visitors' book shows, this was fewer than half the number who would be present on a typical day.[7]

As was the custom, the visitors had begun to arrive in the late afternoon, a little before 6 pm, and had entered through the main door – which was normally used only by ministers and highly placed civil servants – to take their places. One or two of the visitors might have paused, if the light permitted that day, to look at the paintings on display in the gallery leading off the audience chamber. Once again, the first person to sign the visitors' book had been Dom Obá II d'Africa. Next to the sublieutenant, in his privileged place in the front row, sat Major Morin. A veteran French mercenary who had served Dom Pedro I, Morin was 86 years old and still sported the white-collared uniform of the early years of Independence. Despite his age, he was also one of the regulars and would be there every Saturday, come rain or shine.

Besides Sublieutenant Galvão, there were several other veterans of the Paraguayan War sitting in rows further back: Lieutenant-Colonel Cunha Mattos, who had been taken prisoner by Solano Lopes during the war, Honorary Lieutenant Pedro Augusto da Cunha, Lieutenant-Colonel Ferreira Lima and Sea Captain Marques Guimarães. There were nobles, such as the Baron of Palmeiras and Conselheiro Paula Souza; intellectuals, such as Victor Meirelles, a painter in oils, the bibliographer Sacramento Blake; and a commission of teachers from the Imperial Instituto dos Meninos Cegos (the Imperial Institute for Blind Boys).[8]

The most numerous group that day, and also the one that attracted most attention, was that of the owners of *Companhia*

Comércio e Imigração Chinesa, the China Trade and Immigration Company, who were solemnly accompanying Mandarin Tong Kingsing (as his name appears on the register) and his Californian secretary, a certain G. A. Butley. Mr Butley and Sublieutenant Galvão were the only blacks in the Imperial audience chamber that day. The prince, according to the eyewitness von Koseritz, was dressed 'in fine black clothes and wore a gold pince-nez with blue glass'; Mr Butley, according to the same source, appeared to be 'a true gentleman' besides being 'covered with diamonds'.[9]

Tong Kingsing drew more eyes than anyone else. He wore 'a Chinese silk robe', his 'curious beret ... bore the blue insignia of the mandarins' and he sported 'a good-length pigtail, artistically plaited'. The mandarin had arrived only three days previously and was already the talk of the town. On the day that he landed, hopeful coffee barons and 'the cream of society' threw open Madame Haritoff's 'fairy tale reception rooms' for a crowded salon and ball at which French champagne was served.

For many at the ball, Asian immigration in the form of semi-slavery seemed a viable solution to the 'question of labour' on their estates. A crisis, which had begun in 1850 with the outlawing of the slave trade from Africa, had become particularly acute from 1870 onwards with the process of progressive abolition which followed the Paraguayan War.

Another person who had braved the road to São Cristóvão that day, despite the rain and, as he noted, the fact that the 13th 'is considered to be an unlucky date', was the German Carl von Koseritz, accompanied by his eldest daughter, Carolina. Koseritz came from Dassau, arriving in Brazil in 1851 when he was 21. He was also a mercenary in the service of Dom Pedro II. Like Major Morin, Koseritz had ended up staying and putting down roots. Like him, more than 130,000 Europeans – notably Portuguese, Germans and Swiss – had arrived in Brazil during the 1850s.[10] From 1883 until abolition five years later, the Germans constituted the most populous foreign colony in the empire, totalling some 22,000 in the state of Rio Grande do Sul alone.[11]

A man of spirit and initiative, founder, managing editor and principal journalist of *Koseritz Deutsche Zeitung*, a German-language newspaper which had been circulating for 19 years in the provinces of Rio Grande do Sul, Paraná and Santa Catarina, Koseritz was one of the leaders of the prosperous German community. This was his fourth visit to the Imperial hand kissing since May. According to the registers he had been present on 5 May, 9 June, 11

August, and, finally, on that rainy October afternoon. He always
signed his name Carlos (not Carl) von Koseritz, perhaps in an effort
to show that he was an equal, integrated and participating citizen of
his adopted land.[12]

His daughter, who was born in Brazil, also had a Portuguese
name, Carolina von Koseritz. Carolina spoke Portuguese well, wrote
short stories and translated from the German. Her most recent work,
the translation of the *Requiem*, by Dranmor, a much appreciated
poet of the time, had just been published in Rio de Janeiro, with a
preface by Sílvio Romero. Koseritz had brought two copies that
afternoon, which he was to present to the Brazilian emperor and
empress.[13]

Many Brazilian projects were present in that waiting room. In
contrast to the Chinese mandarin and the owners of the China Trade
and Immigration Company (who were doubtless backed by the
coffee barons), Koseritz represented interests which were more
concerned with the domestic market, with the smallholder and the
industries in his colony in the south. During his previous visit on 11
August, he had presented the emperor with a memento from the
population of Pelotas, which like Rio de Janeiro had also been
adversely affected by recent tariff policies. Today, on 13 October, he
would deliver another memento, from the factory-owner Adolf
Voight, also a prominent member of the Rio Grande do Sul colony.
Herr Voight had sent it, together with 'some samples of toilet soap'.
At the two opportunities, Koseritz was apparently not disappointed.
Although he had not achieved anything concrete, His Majesty had
received him with 'the habitual accessibility' and 'promised to study
[the tariff question] carefully'. The emperor had described the matter
as being 'very complicated and important' and, finally, 'shown his
interest in the progress of Rio Grande's industry'.[14]

As for the labour question, Koseritz's thinking was at odds with
that of the owners of the China Trade and Immigration Company.
There, in the waiting room, observing the Chinese pigtail, the
German reflected that 'all those supporters of yellow immigration
should be made to use a similar appendage, in order to distinguish
them more easily from the other sons of men, which would be very
practical'. For him, Chinese immigration was nothing more than
'traffic in human flesh'. On this point, he was severely critical of the
masters of land and slaves who had traditionally dominated the
country; neither the system of labour nor the structure of landownership, based on the large estate, pleased him. Kozeritz, like many of
his contemporaries, envisaged another sort of empire.

'These coffee barons are indeed the pig-tailed ones of Brazil,' wrote Koseritz on that 13 October when he arrived back at the hotel in Santa Teresa, where he usually stayed. The question seemed to him to be one on which no compromise was possible:

> We declare war on the big landowner and will try to lead to victory the system of small properties with the introduction of agriculture colonies. The coffee barons want to continue to lead their lives of vagabonds which is why they seek new slaves, yellow-coloured ones, to substitute their former black ones.[15]

We know that Koseritz broached these sensitive matters at the 13 October hand kissing. It is probable that he took this opportunity to bring the subject up because he wanted to get his word in before the important meeting scheduled for the following day, Sunday, 14 October 1883.

For Koseritz, as for other Germans in the south of the empire, 14 October would be busy and eventful. In its morning edition the Rio de Janeiro newspaper *Jornal do Commercio* had finally acknowledged the existence of the meeting that day and printed a sympathetic article outlining its objectives; the *Diário do Brasil*, besides a favourable article, also carried, in its entirety, the court edict convening the meeting. Koseritz was cheered; earlier he had suspected that Rio's newspapers were hand in glove with the coffee barons due to the 'active publicity' that they had given, a few days earlier, to the arrival of the Chinese mandarin and the ball held in his honour.[16]

At 11.30, the reception room of the Liceu de Artes e Oficios in the centre of the city was packed to bursting point, with people spilling out into the corridors. Judging by the public who had attended, the coffee barons were far from being a homogeneous group of 'pig-tailed ones' as Koseritz had imagined. Or, at least, the expression 'coffee barons', applied in a generic sense, did not do full justice to the elites of the day. Gathered in the reception rooms there were landowners and nobles, capitalists, industrialists, traders, politicians and intellectuals. Among the well-known personalities were the Viscount of Barbacena, a senator of the empire; Leão Veloso, a former minister of state; the general deputy Taunay, *Comendador* Bellegarde, *Comendador* Malvino Reis, engineer André Rebouças and the elderly senator Nicolau Pereira de Campos Vergueiro, one of the most prominent of the São Paulo coffee barons. In 1847, he had been responsible for the first large-scale experiments in attracting European immigrants as sharecroppers on the large coffee estates.

Although this system had managed to attract more than 130,000 Europeans to the country between 1850 and 1860, it was, like the others that had been tried, already turning into disillusion, both for the landowners – who were accustomed to treating their workers as chattels – and for the colonists, who were unused both to the climate and to the plantation system and ended up 'fleeing' to the cities or to other estates where they found work as managers or security personnel. In São Paulo, the system was to result in a round of strikes and revolts against the land barons, something that was unprecedented in the Empire.[17]

From the end of the African traffic in 1850 the labour problem had dragged on without solution, getting worse at every step. The question was the explicit motive for that extremely well-attended and tense public meeting on 14 October 1883. Koseritz, one of the event's organizers, opened the session, on time, with a long speech defending the need for immediate action

> because on one hand we have the abolition of slavery and the disappearance of the current system of agriculture, but, on the other hand, after the arrival of the Chinese envoy, we are threatened with a coolie immigration, which is no more nor less than another type of slavery,

yellow and temporary, but still slavery. He went on to extol the success of German immigration in Rio Grande do Sul, a system which revolved around the small property; he openly criticized the 'indifference of the government' and the 'influential circles in the capital'; and cited statistics on neighbouring Argentina, which had made great progress with European immigration while Brazilians remained inactive. Finally, to long applause, he proposed the setting up of a large immigration agency and detailed the success that could be achieved, especially if it were organized in collaboration with the Berlin Central Committee.[18]

When the floor was declared open for debate, Nicolau Vergueiro, speaking with the authority of his respectable experience on the subject, openly challenged Koseritz's proposal that such an association could solve the problem of immigration in the country. First, he said, far-reaching reforms of a political nature were called for, such as 'the great naturalization', civil marriage and the end of established state religion.

Koseritz, fearing for the outcome of the meeting after this unscheduled but loudly applauded speech, took the platform again and 'in a long and heated discourse' pointed out that these very reforms were also 'cornerstones' of his own programme. It was precisely for this reason, he explained, that it was necessary to found a strong, representative agency 'if possible with thousands of members' to 'conquer the press' and 'apply pressure to the government and the legislative bodies'.

Dr Taunay, who had been proposed as secretary, delivered a 'brilliant speech' openly opposing Chinese immigration. As he talked, a petition was passed round those present. More radical factions showed their hand. Dr Enes de Sousa, for example, not only supported the proposed measures against the Chinese but also launched a direct attack on the coffee barons, proposing that a land tax be imposed.

Not surprisingly, the land barons at the meeting hardly welcomed the idea. While there appeared to be a general consensus on the need to promote immigration, not all in that crowded room agreed with Dr Taunay's petition or with Dr Enes de Sousa's proposed tax. A man by the name of Azevedo, for example, advocated a totally different position – that in such a situation, Brazil could not allow itself the luxury of 'rejecting any immigrant, and should open its doors to all the nations of the world'.

Eventually, though, the setting up of the Brazilian Immigration Society was unanimously approved and an inaugural session fixed for two weeks' time, to be held 'before His Majesty the Emperor'. The statutes' commission was headed by members of the local elites – the president was the Viscount of Barbacena; secretary, Deputy Taunay – but also included representatives from the German colony: Carl von Koseritz, Hermann Blumenau and Hugo A. Gruber.[19]

This digression helps us understand the atmosphere of the previous day, 13 October, in the Imperial Palace of Quinta da Boa Vista. For Koseritz, the presence of a Chinese mandarin in the audience chamber was not a happy occurrence. It was instead proof of the social forces levelled against him, a 'singular coincidence ... exactly at the moment when we are appealing for the foundation of a large agency with the object of looking after German and Italian immigration'.[20]

Besides Tong Kingsing and the owners of the China Trade and Immigration Company, whose proposals were identified with the interests of the most reactionary of the coffee barons, those who were only concerned with the question of labour on their farms, and the acclimatized immigrant *Carlos* von Koseritz, representative of the German colony in Rio Grande do Sul and spokesman for those who were, on the following day, to found the Brazilian Immigration

Society, there was also another current of thought in the palace on
that rainy Saturday.

The representative of Little Africa in Rio de Janeiro, of the
'brown-skinned and blacks' who lived precariously on the margins
of society as self-employed odd-jobbers – there, as we know, was
Dom Obá II d'Africa. This population, of whom the great majority
were neither slave, nor master, nor waged worker, were either
virtually invisible or only noticed by their contemporaries, whether
Brazilians or foreigners, for the problems which they caused. It is
true to say that their 'inexistence' was one of the primary pre-
suppositions, both of those who advocated the Koseritz solution and
those who favoured the Kingsing solution. 'We do not have a free
population,' wrote a coffee baron in a discourse on European
colonization four years after the abolition of the slave trade.[21] 'Brazil
does not have a people,' said a prescient Frenchman, a resident
professor at Rio de Janeiro's *Escola Politécnica* and long-term
resident of Brazil, in a 1881 study of the question of labour in the
country.[22]

Yet, nevertheless, there was the prince, in the waiting room,
carrying out his usual Saturday ritual. Koseritz observed him thus:

> He treats everyone haughtily, as befits a powerful prince; he advances
> regally to the front row, not once glancing sideways, and takes his place
> alongside Major Morin. With a superior smile, he then surveys the rest,
> greets the palace staff casually and strikes a dignified pose to await the
> arrival of the Emperor.

When the emperor arrived, however, 'all his pride melts like butter
in the sun ... he bends his knees like a miserable vassal and, still on
his knees, kisses the hand of the Emperor ...'[23]

Like von Koseritz and Tong-Kingsing, the prince was also thinking
about 'the labour question'. In the following pages we will examine
in more detail the currents of opinion surrounding a subject which,
from the time of the abolition of the African slave trade, had become
the great intellectual and political debate of the age.

The Audience Chamber

In Rio de Janeiro, a region where coffee production based on slave
labour was beginning to decline, it had not taken long for the
plantation owners to become convinced of the difficulties of
transition. They came to this conclusion not through the lack of

trying other solutions, but precisely because they had tried them. Indeed, ever since the African trade began to come under serious pressure from abroad, the coffee barons had attempted to introduce European or Asian colonists into the old province of Rio de Janeiro and other coffee regions. But once the immigrants discovered the reality of working on the plantations, alongside the slaves, they bitterly regretted the contracts they had signed before embarking, when they knew nothing about the reality of the country they were going to. The Europeans found the toil particularly unacceptable. The majority – such as the Swiss in 1825 and the Azoreans in 1837 – ended up fleeing the work fronts.[24]

Yet escape, even for the immigrants, was a risky undertaking. They could be imprisoned and mistreated and returned to the plantations to work out their contracts. In practice, however, society seemed totally ineffective in the control of these escapes. Many of the colonists had skills which made them socially desirable; furthermore they were white and theoretically free. Indeed, with the exception of those plantation owners who were directly affected, nobody really felt responsible, or even interested, in ensuring that the contracts were honoured. Unlike the slaves, the colonists did not have masters and this fact greatly facilitated the establishment of complicity throughout all parts of society. And again, unlike the slaves, these fugitives, lost in anonymity in the capital of the empire, were always able to improve their lot as employees in trade or as specialized artisans; or, counting on the complicity of the plantation owners themselves, moving to other estates where they worked as overseers or administrators in the management or disciplinary staff. Many of the coffee barons no doubt were convinced that the foreigners needed a certain period of adaptation to the land and, as one wrote at the time, only 'after abandoning their primitive masters would they subject themselves to a third or fourth master whom they would then serve well'.[25]

This applied to the workers engaged on contract, 'bound by ties', as was the expression. The voluntary immigrants (who until 1850 came mainly from Portugal, with smaller numbers from Switzerland and Germany) were even less likely to submit themselves to the work and climate of the plantations. Free and not bound by any contract, they found work mainly as artisans, shop staff or traders in the cities. In the case of the Portuguese, they also worked as foremen on the estates, but would never wield a hoe or scythe on the land. In the second half of the nineteenth century, the city of Rio de Janeiro was to house a considerable colony of Germans and Swiss. Dranmor, for example, the pseudonym of Fernand Schmid, the poet whom Carolina von Koseritz had translated and offered to the emperor on that rainy Saturday in 1883, was another immigrant to the Brazilian empire. He was born in Berne, Switzerland, in 1823 and arrived in Rio de Janeiro while still a youth. His whole career was spent in the city, first as a shop worker and after 1870, as the owner and writer of the *Deutsch Brasilianische Warte*, a newspaper for the German and Swiss colonies. Finally, he became Consul General for the Austrian Empire, with accreditation at Court.[26]

As a result of all this experience, the Baron of Pati do Alferes, in the most prestigious farm manual of its time, stressed that:

> [we] go on board ship to pay the fares of the colonists, but these hardly ever compensate their master [sic], and usually disappear or flee without completing their contracts ... because they find ... someone who ... offers them a piece of land to work on or someone who seduces them away with promises of better wages.

This statement, published for the first time in 1847, was one of the parts left in its entirety in the posthumous editions of the manual published in 1863 and 1878, both of which were very carefully revised and brought up to date.[27]

Ten years after publication, the author himself, Baron of Pati do Alferes, emphatically echoed the same opinion. 'In the space of ten years various estate owners have given up this solution,' he told the Baron of Muritiba, senator, state counsellor and representative of the early Central Colonization Association, who had raised the question of inviting European colonists as sharecroppers or salaried labourers. He continued: 'not a single one has been happy, because the colonists have either deserted, or refused to subject themselves to him, or have ended up becoming insolent, and their tendency to insubordination and intolerance cause them to make absurd demands'.[28]

After 1850, as slaves became increasingly expensive, the baron, his sons and many plantation owners in Rio de Janeiro province none the less gradually reached the conclusion, forced on them by reality, that replacing slaves with European workers was not viable whether under the system of *parceria* (sharecropping), *locação de serviços* (contract workers) or *assalariamento* (salaried workers). It was not so much the difficulty of attracting the colonists to Brazil, but to attract them as labour for the export plantations and keep them there. Despite successive efforts, both in Rio and in São Paulo, the plantation owners soon found that the immigrant, like the Brazilian free worker, failed to provide a regular source of labour for the plantations. The slaves themselves, once freed – or by the time they were in the second generation – abandoned the plantations as soon as they could in order to set up as independent rural smallholders (when they had managed to acquire a few acres of land) or to become self-employed in the cities, as we have seen in the case of Little Africa in Rio de Janeiro.

Nor did the immigrants, whether voluntary or contracted, remain in the coffee-growing region in sufficient numbers. Those who did stay were those who had managed to obtain the guarantee of liberty, security and, above all, of property – that dreamed-of 'little piece of land' which would turn them into independent producers. By 1855, therefore, it had become clear that despite the rising costs,

> the big plantation can only be sustained by those farmers who have enough slaves to work their land, and the great landowners may as well give up hope of having colonists to work their plantations as they once had slaves ... the colonist will settle on the land that suits him and till the land himself, in imitation of the free men of the country ... working for himself and by himself.[29]

Thus, the coffee barons found themselves locked into a socio-economic structure which was recognizably in crisis. 'The provinces of the North today constitute the only source of the workers needed by the coffee plantation in order to meet the always increasing needs of service,' a Rio de Janeiro farmer commented, as early as 1854. In summary, after 1850, at the same time that slave labour was in rapid expansion in the coffee provinces, the slave system itself, so deeply entrenched since the earliest days of colonization, was to lose the secret of its own reproduction. The domestic trade in slaves could not last for ever. 'Sooner or later, with more or less delay', added the same farmer,

> this torrent of forced migration will have to wear itself out through lack of input. Besides this, the price of these slaves is ruinous. It does not even appear to us to be possible for the work of a slave to be productive enough to cover all the expenses of looking after his health and strength and the interest on the capital invested in him; because of this profits have to be large because the slave represents capital which, from one moment to the next, disappears.[30]

Given the weight of the export sector within the economic, social, political and demographic structure of the empire, a number of barons and men of ideas soon convinced themselves that the problem was not simply, as many understood it, a straightforward 'question of labour' on the plantations but also involved the ethnic and cultural make-up of the emerging nation. In 1854 the 'farmer, lawyer and capitalist' Luís Peixoto de Lacerda Werneck – without doubt one of the most educated of the coffee barons in the province of Rio de Janeiro – openly criticized the experiments with contracted European and Asian workers. According to him, settlement which was 'bound by ties ... only offers the prospect of disgrace for the country'. He favoured, on the contrary, 'spontaneous colonization' from Europe, attracting settlers with the offer of access to small properties where they could produce foodstuffs. Not only would they not be in direct competition with the big slave-based export monoculture, but they would complement it. He thought that 'spontaneous settlement' in Rio de Janeiro should be concentrated on land which had already been over-farmed, located near the capital, leaving the new, fertile lands and the available slaves for export agriculture. 'One must attract the attention of whole classes in Europe who are unhappy there, who want to make a living but cannot find work and end up begging from door to door as the cripple begs for his bread,' he concluded.[31]

Impressed by the development and expansion taking place in Europe and North America, and influenced by the scientific prejudices of the era, many coffee barons had from the very beginning reacted against the idea of linking Brazil to an entire culture – Chinese or Asian – which they considered to be inferior and destined for extinction. The same plantation owner wrote in 1854:

> The Chinese race, stationary, of a dubious civilization, inert to progress, has to cede its place and be exterminated and destroyed by the nations originating in Europe and America which, obeying a providential mission, are marching ahead in the imposition of ideas, armed with the sword of the gospel and the torch of civilization, conquering and possessing the world with their ideas.

It was thus no longer a 'question of labour' but of the very future of a country emerging from its traditional slave-based order. 'No, without doubt, the Chinese are not men of this century, they are not the builders of civilization,' he continued, hopeful that the Chinese 'will not become the perdition of the Brazilian race, which is already mixed with the deformity of the indigenous race and the African'. On the contrary, what Brazil needed was 'a lively, bold, population, full of the ardour of work, industrious and the friend of progress', in short, 'the European race, active, tireless, laborious'.[32]

In the succeeding decades – above all after the royal speech of 22 May 1867, when the emperor himself first brought the political issue of emancipation before the Chamber of Deputies and the Senate – these questions would take a more dramatic course. In the following year the journalist Quintino Bocaiúva – in common agreement with the then minister of agriculture, Counsellor Dantas – published a controversial pamphlet entitled *A Crise da Lavoura* ('The Plantation Crisis'), in which he recommended, as an emergency measure, the 'importation' of Asian colonists – Indian and Chinese coolies – as low-cost 'work machines' in substitution for the slaves. After the royal speech, Bocaiúva became convinced that it was necessary to promote both types of immigration: the ad hoc immigration of European workers and the contracted labour of Asians. In the first category, which he described as 'the labour that brings civilization', he included North Americans who were unhappy with the victory of the North and the abolition decreed by Abraham Lincoln. The second category, the 'labour that tills the soil' was necessary to solve the crisis in the export plantation.[33]

After two decades of frustrated experiments it became clear that white immigration – whether European or North American – would never be a 'nursery of workhands to substitute those whom we lack'. Quintino, did in fact end up taking part, together with the Cuban capitalist Bernardo Caymari, representative of the United States and Brazil Mail Steamship Co., in an attempt to attract US workers to the empire. 'This emigration', he affirmed during a stay in New York from 1866 to 1867,

> cannot and should not be of this nature. Its origin, its character and its resources warrant higher ambitions and more noble aspirations. It is first and foremost the exodus of a class, an expatriation with a social and political basis and cannot, in any way, be considered in the same light as those transmigrations stimulated by misery and a surfeit of population in any given territory.[34]

Despite the prejudices that held the 'Asian race to be incapable and weak for farm labour', the coolies did represent 'labour for a miserable salary'. In the English, French and Spanish dominions of the Caribbean and Guyana, as well as in California and the Republics of Peru and New Granada, they had begun to constitute the post-abolition labour-base.[35]

So why not resort to this source of labour? With the failure of white colonization or immigration on the coffee plantations, this export monoculture, the linchpin of the national economy, was, with emancipation imminent, running the political risk of also ending up without slaves. Many, above all in the longer-established regions where the productivity of the coffee plantations was falling fast, began to look at the question exclusively from the economic point of view. 'The question is one of price,' wrote Quintino Bocaiúva, demonstrating the need for cheap labour to replace the slaves in order to maintain exports as the dynamic centre of the national economy.[36] In 1868, given the shortage of free labour, the average salary, both in the country and in the town, was around 25$000 per month, while an Asian labourer would not cost more than 14$000 a month throughout the duration of his contract, which was normally for seven years.[37]

Although he favoured the abolition of slavery and 'subdivision of the big plantations' in principle, Quintino was also aware of the economic, social and political realities of the country. He thought that any radical restructuring of landownership or the system of labour was improbable 'for a long time to come', and concluded, 'in such a case, what type of colonization, if it is not what I have suggested, will do for the indiscriminate work in which the two forces [slave labour and free labour] balance and assist each other?' In short, he was recommending 'the promotion of the development of the rural property ... without altering its form and essence.'[38]

While such ideas found ardent support among the coffee barons, in the press, in parliament and in the ministry itself, they came up against barriers which were difficult to overcome. Not everyone, though, seemed worried about maintaining the 'form and essence' of the slave plantation. Starting with the emperor himself, as Quintino suggested when he referred, discouraged, to the many 'crosses' he had to bear due to the famous 'lápis fatídico' (the 'fateful pencil' wielded by Dom Pedro II when despatching decrees).[39]

For many, the question went further than the simple 'question of labour' for the plantations, as some barons wanted it. The newspaper A Vida Fluminense, for example, published a satirical cartoon showing the Brazilians of the future – in the year 1900 – using, not their customary Western-style clothing, but Chinese trousers and fans. In the same vein, Nicolau Joaquim Moreira, president of the prestigious Sociedade Auxiliadora de Indústria Nacional (Society of Assistance to National Industry), spoke out in open opposition to the ideas of Quintino Bocaiúva in a speech he made on 16 August 1870. Appealing to 'the most significant laws of ethical anthropology', Dr Moreira expressed his concern at 'the future mongolization of Brazil', opposed 'the crossings between disparate races', and, summing up, could see no 'advantage whatsoever in substituting the African element with the demoralized Chinese'. He held that the Chinese would end up as near-slaves in Brazil, as had been demonstrated by the Cuban experience.[40]

He advocated European immigration, 'the fertilizing flow of free and intelligent immigration'. For him, the country's problem lay not so much in 'the deficiency of hands' as in slavery itself and the never-changing methods of plantation management.[41]

At the beginning of the 1880s, the decade that was to define the question, Joaquim Nabuco, with the support of the British abolition-ists, also opposed the importation of coolies. The question was brought up once again during the Sinibu Cabinet. 'I think with you', he wrote, in English, to Charles H. Allen, secretary of the influential British and Anti-Slavery Society, 'that any labour contract celebrated in China will soon degenerate into a slavery bond for the contracted, in whatever country he may choose to settle.' He also opposed 'the idea of sustaining artificially the large proprietorships with the Asiatic, instead of the decaying African stay [sic].'[42]

This intellectual and political debate – which extended from 'the lack of hands for the plantation' to the shouts of warning against the ethno-social characteristics of the country which was emerging with the transition from slavery – thus dragged on from the end of the 1840s until that rainy 13 October 1883 when, in the palace audience chamber, we found, side by side, the mandarin Tong Kingsing, the German Carl von Koseritz and the 'African' Cândido da Fonseca Galvão.

For the next few years, such problems were to be discussed not only in parliament and the press, but also in the streets. Dom Obá II d'Africa, at least, had definitive ideas on the subject. Like the Baron of Pati do Alferes, Luís Peixoto de Lacerda Werneck, Quintino Bocaiúva and many others, the prince also doubted whether European or American workers would come to substitute the workgangs of slaves on the big plantations. 'Don't believe in the white colonists,' he warned in one of his newspaper articles,

> it makes no difference which nation they come from – we have exuberant proof that every time that they disembark here, they only work and submit themselves until they have paid back their fares and then they become shop workers, traders or find themselves any other sort of work, anything, just as long as they don't have to wield an axe to cut down the trees in the forest, or a hoe to plant and weed or a scythe to clear the undergrowth.[43]

Like Quintino, Tong-Kingsing, the owners of the China Trade and Immigration Company and so many others, the prince had also thought about the 'salvation' of the plantation on which the economy of the empire depended. Like the others, he advocated the 'form' but unlike them, he opposed the 'essence'.

'I would not be cooperating if I stood by and allowed tobacco and coffee, the two supports of the crown, to diminish for lack of free labour,' he wrote. But his idea was not of European workers, whom he knew would not come, or Asian workers, whom he did not even mention, but of 'free workers who could come from my domains in Africa, as I am the only heir of this legacy in Brazil'.[44]

For the prince, free blacks meant Brazilian citizens. 'Only thus will our forests become resplendent with the arduous labour of African colonization which patriates itself in our shores,' he said, in support of this immigration, which would benefit not only the Brazilian plantations but would also be 'for the good of the uneducated peoples of Africa'. On this last definition he echoed the dominant concepts of the time.[45]

Like everybody else, the prince also sought the backing of the emperor for his proposal. For some time he had been pressing the emperor to appoint him ambassador for the Brazilian empire on the *Costa d'Africa* (West Coast), and in doing so, provided ammunition for the political satirists of the age.[46] But the prince had an answer to the critical, unpleasantly racist jibes. In November 1886 he wrote, 'They say that it would be a shame and disgrace for Obá to be nominated for Guinea in order to bring free workers to the forests of Brazil. And was it not a disgrace for the prince to go to Paraguay with the Zouaves to eat bullets?'[47]

It was thus that the prince, Dom Pedro II's faithful vassal, brought up not only these but other related matters at the Saturday hand kissing sessions. 'Ask our Monarch', he wrote in another of his articles, 'whether in Brazil, there is any other Brazilian who has better relations with the African Nation than I, in order to merit the support and the Trust that will easily make the immigrants of that nation come here.'[48]

Although it may seem strange, it was not in any way a new idea. It had come up many times since the end of the slave trade in 1850, and always met with the formal disapproval of the British. Although the theme warrants more detailed study, we know that at least one bill for the importation of 'free Africans' was put before the provincial Legislative Assembly of Pernambuco in 1857. According to research carried out by Leslie Bethell, the British government, represented by Lord Clarendon, 'made it clear, as they had done on more than one occasion in the past, that such a move would be regarded, and treated, as a covert renewal of the slave trade'.[49] Judging by his writings, the prince was unaware of these long-standing diplomatic obstacles.

Prince of the Streets

'With God, a little is much; without God, much is nothing.'
Brazilian proverb, quoted in Dom Obá II d'Africa, 1885

The existence of the channels of communication between a street prince and the Emperor of Brazil can be explained, initially, by the Paraguayan War. Contemporaries saw the prince, who always wore his military uniform on formal occasions, as a consequence of the war, just like the many other 'new developments' (*novidades*) which had become a feature of life in the post-war capital of the empire, from the abolitionist movement in parliament and on the streets to the republican club, republican newspaper and republican party, the street revolt against the 'vintém' tax and the emergence of soldiers in political life. The prince may have been the least important of the new developments, but he was, historically, one of them. Mello Moraes thought that such communication was possible due to a certain moral recognition on Dom Pedro's part, 'despite the protests and the ridicule that this provoked ... perhaps because [the emperor] took his services to the homeland into account and made consideration for the honours of his rank.'[1] Carl von Koseritz, on the other hand, while recognizing the prince's service on the Paraguayan battlefields, seems to have thought that such deeds did not justify the favour of the emperor: 'I really admire the Emperor's patience', he wrote in August 1883, 'because Sublieutenant Galvão is nothing more than a half-crazy man.'[2]

The life of a soldier did bring an extraordinary increase – both quantitatively and qualitatively – in contact between classes, races and regions in Brazilian society. In war, Cândido da Fonseca Galvão, the obscure son of an *Africano-forro* (a first-generation African who had obtained his liberty), whose horizons had reached no further

than the Comercial Vila dos Lençóis in the hinterland of Bahia,
would be exposed to the capitals of provinces, to his much-loved
capital of the empire, to foreign lands and to the frontier question.
We have seen how the campaign brought him into direct contact
with practically all levels of political power, from the old Conservative leader and Commander of the National Guard in his native
city to the most august political personalities and, at the very top, the
Emperor of Brazil himself, the first volunteer, 'father of the
Voluntários da Pátria'.

By the 1880s, Sublieutenant Galvão had established a link, albeit
a tenuous one, between that small underworld of Little Africa and
the wider world, where people of position debated the hegemonies
and the destiny of the new society in formation, heralded since the
abolition of the African traffic. The prince became a go-between
because of his leadership, his 'personal relations', his rank of
sublieutenant, his role in the press, his 'admirable majesty'.

Besides this specific post-war context, we can also place the prince
within the more general structures and common mentalities which
existed on a parallel plane to the ideologies of class. These were
capable of establishing a bridge, a common ground as Le Goff put
it, between 'Caesar and the humblest soldier in his legions'. Or, in
the case of Brazil, between the emperor and the least of his vassals:
the black prince.[3] Such ideological structures, present in the colonial
slave-owning format itself, have been characterized as the patriarchal 'spirit' or ethos. The patriarchal relationship is one of the
most central and controversial aspects of this sphere of study. I will
examine this point in more detail.

Paternalism and Slavery

I will turn first to Gilberto Freyre, since he makes this concept the
cornerstone of his interpretation of Brazilian society. In *Casa-
Grande & Senzala* (translated into English as *The Masters and the
Slaves*), Freyre rejects the supposition, implicit until then, that
colonization was a natural consequence, a creation, an imposition,
or whatever, of European civilization. It was a supposition that
assigned the blacks and indigenous Indian populations a very
marginal role in history. Freyre, in contrast, saw Brazilian colonization as the joint construction of whites, blacks, Indians and, above
all, of *mestiços*'.

'The patriarchal system of Portuguese colonization of Brazil ...', he writes as if explaining one of the precepts most dear to him, 'at the same time as expressing an imperialist imposition ..., an imposition of European forms ... on a tropical environment, also represented a compromise with the new conditions of life and the environment.' It was to become one of his constant explanatory themes, running through his entire work, and he used various terms for it: 'patriarchal spirit', 'slave-state patriarchy', 'Brazilian patriarchy', and so on. It was a new social system, characteristically Brazilian, not only encompassing its labour structure, but also its social relations, education, political style, religion, family life, sexuality, and so on.[4]

This first study of the 'formation of the Brazilian family under a patriarchal system', published in 1933, was continued in *Sobrados e Mocambos* (*The Mansions and the Shanties*), which focused on the decadence of the rural patriarchy and the development of the urban. Finally, in *Ordem e Progresso* (*Order and Progress*) Freyre studied the 'disintegration' of patriarchal or semi-patriarchal society under the free labour system in the twentieth century. Freyre intended that the three volumes should be read together. They would constitute 'an attempt at sociological and anthropological introduction to the history of patriarchal society in Brazil', from the time of its formation in the sixteenth century until the crisis of the First Republic in 1930.[5]

More recently, Genovese has made this same concept a fundamental axis for his analysis of another slave state. His interpretation of the slave structure in the 'Old South' of the United States differs from Freyre's Brazil in that he did not see it as a compromise that European slave-owners made 'with the new conditions of life and environment'. In Genovese's materialist approach to history, it was rather an ideological imposition by the masters, 'a way of mediating irreconcilable class and racial conflicts'. Nevertheless, for both Freyre and Genovese, resistance within such societies tended to be systemic rather than revolutionary. 'The slaves of the Old South', wrote Genovese, 'displayed impressive solidarity and collective resistance to their masters, but in a web of paternalistic relationships their action tended to become defensive and to aim at protecting the individuals against aggression and abuse.'[6]

This 'non-revolutionary' resistance, both in Freyre and in Genovese, should not be mistaken, I believe, for an idyllic vision of the slave state. On the contrary, both authors analyse a system of domination. In Brazil, according to Freyre, 'absolute winners in the military and technical sense over the indigenous population; absolute dominators

of the blacks imported from Africa ... the Europeans and their
descendants nevertheless had to transact with Indians and Africans
in the sphere of genetic and social relations.' Such relations, imposed
by the very business of colonizing the tropics, explain, in the course
of Freyre's work, not only the generalized miscegenation of which
Brazilians are the heirs but also many other social specifics. However
close they were, Freyre makes clear that such relations were still
fundamentally 'relations ... between "superiors" and "inferiors"';[7]
that the 'benignness of relations of masters with slaves ... cannot be
admitted ... except in relative terms' and that, in the final analysis,
'a master is always a master'.[8]

Negotiation and Conflict

The term paternalism might, all the same, seem inadequate if we
think of it only as a Machiavellian strategy of class domination
rather than a complex social phenomenon, built out of the mutual
and daily concessions and manipulations between masters and
slaves. Or, as Antônio Barros de Castro has suggested, negotiation
within conflict, where masters as well as slaves sought mutual
collaboration through socially available strategies and resources.
'These, trying to build a space for themselves; those, divided, partly
resisting, partly ceding', because both perceived the benefits of the
system.[9]

In Brazil, from colonial times onwards – not just for the new
arrivals but also for those who had been born there, the slaves,
freedmen and free men of colour – the need to create links with
society as a whole was a question of survival, the starting point of
a micro-policy of integration. If unsuccessful, the slave found himself
in the bitter condition of *boçal* (a word which originally described
an unacculturated slave and is today applied to any rude, unpolished
person), that is, a being of foreign tongue, religion and habits, and
thus someone with no place or patron in the new world. If
successful, he became *ladino* (again, a word originally used to
describe an acculturated slave and, today, extended to anyone who
is sharp and on the ball), the 'smart one' capable, in the phrase of
Antonil, 'of learning Christian doctrine, as well as seeking ways of
living life'.[10]

'Living life', as we know, presupposes a complex learning process,
not just of techniques and disciplines of work, but also, necessarily,
of other skills which lead to social integration. It is evident that the

destiny of every slave – and afterwards of every freedman and free man of colour, such as Cândido da Fonseca Galvão – could vary enormously according to the African or Brazilian background of each and to their personal or professional skills, their degree of domination of cultural symbols, and so on. It also varied, without doubt, according to whether they worked in the fields, wielding a scythe from dawn to dusk, whether they were foremen responsible for the work gang, or whether in domestic service, living in close contact with their masters in positions of trust such as cooks, wet nurses, dry nurses, nursemaids, ladies' maids, pages, messenger boys; or whether they had already escaped the eyes of the master and worked '*ao ganho*' (working for third parties and retaining a part of their earnings) as street sellers or handymen, and so on. All this would have depended on the slave's individual luck and the specific circumstances, disposition and needs of each individual master. It is therefore infeasible to suppose that such complex social processes – which evidently imply acts of personal will and initiative on the part of the slave – could have ever been entirely dependent on the arbitrariness of the master or the malign machinations of class domination. In truth, the slaves never gave their masters such a long leash.

Some died of *banzo*, that terrible depression caused by homesickness. But the majority would find the strength to win social alliances, to reinvent a family and a religion. Some set up religious brotherhoods and mutual assistance associations which, among other things, collected money to purchase freedom for their members.

These associations existed and prospered under the umbrella of the Catholic Church. Patricia Mulvey counted, without claiming to have made an exhaustive survey, no fewer than 165 black brotherhoods in Brazil.[11] In Salvador, for example, the *Sociedade Protetora dos Desvalidos* (Society for the Protection of the Needy), as it is known today, was founded by nineteen freed Africans, all men of courage. They included the author of the idea, Manoel Victor Serra, who worked for himself in the Canto da Preguiça; stonemasons and carpenters capable of book-keeping and running an association; a wagoner, Gregório do Nascimento, whose freight service was said to have made him rich; small entrepreneurs such as Theotônio de Souza 'who made vinegar', and a water seller, Roberto Tavares, who owned his own donkey. The founding meetings, at which the society was initially baptised, 'Irmandade de Nossa Senhora da Soledade Amparo dos Desvalidos' (Brotherhood of Support for the Needy of Our Lady of Soledade), took place on 10 and 16 September 1832,

[handwritten annotations in top margin: "In Prince of the Street he wanders from type to type with very little on Bolívar."]

respectively, in the chapel of *Quinze Mistérios* (Chapel of Fifteen Mysteries). The safe in which they saved their contributions was, for greater security, kept in the house of the parish verger, Father Joaquim José de Sant'Anna. In 1848 the Brotherhood was moved to the church of *Nossa Senhora do Rosário das Portas do Carmo*, where, three years later, its name was changed to that by which it is still known today.[12]

Among the many other societies it hosted, Salvador was the home of the *Venerável Ordem Terceira do Rosário* (The Venerable Tertiary Order of the Rosary) founded in the church of Nossa Senhora do Rosário dos Pretos in the Pelourinho in the eighteenth century by Angolans of 'unblemished reputation' who had 'honest means of subsistence', and who also obeyed the commandments of God and the Church. In the same fashion, Dahomey Jejes set up the *Irmandade do Senhor Bom Jesus das Necessidades e Redenção dos Homens Pretos* in the Igreja do Corpo Santo in the lower city in 1752 while Yoruba women from the Ketu nation organized their sisterhood of *Nossa Senhora da Boa Morte* in the church of Barroquinha.[13]

[handwritten annotation in right margin: "Slow Russell Wood's different emphasis"]

In contrast, resisting links with society at large meant a plunge into the difficult 'impersonal' relations of the slave-owning market, the ugly face of the system. Refusing to learn Portuguese (a long and difficult process, even in the second generation, as we can see from Dom Obá II d'Africa's writings) or becoming a Muslim represented a total rejection of the culture of the new world. This meant choosing political isolation, whether it was made by slaves, freedmen or free men of colour. Pierre Verger has shown how the refusal to integrate culturally sometimes translated into conversion to Islam, which had been brought from Africa by the Hausas, 'whose doctrine of disdain for the infidel contained the elements to attract the slave or humiliated freedman ... providing a religious basis for his resentment against those who kept him or who had kept him in a servile state.'[14]

Evidently, these micro-politics of negotiation, the so-called Brazilian '*jeitinho*', or 'way round', presupposed profound social differences of access to the sources of material and cultural riches, power and prestige. Brazil's colonial origins presupposed exactly those slave-owning relations which became established on the plantations. These were the primary base of the system – from there, they extended above and below, as society's organizational principle, to include the moral behaviour, political thought and relationships of its members: an ideological paradigm of a concrete society which involved slaves, masters, freed slaves and free men of colour. Everywhere – on the plantation, in the city, in the workshop, in the palace – Brazilian paternalism typically meant a relation of exchange, a negotiation within a potentially hostile environment of slavery. On one hand, service and loyalty; on the other, protection and recompense.

On that particular point, the prince and the emperor seem to have shared a common ethos. The emperor, as everyone knew, had been a real soldier, wearing a poncho and carrying a sword on the way to the recently reclaimed Vila de Uruguaiana. He was now the 'father of the Volunteers of the Fatherland'. It seems that the emperor considered it a specific duty, befitting his position; 'to be generous to those who have dedicated themselves to me and to the Nation,' as he expressly recommended to his daughter, in a private document written to prepare her to take over the delicate functions of the Regency while he was away on his first visit to Europe in 1871.[15]

Twelve years later, having arrived 'a little early' for the hand kissing audience, the immigrant Carl von Koseritz took advantage of the remaining daylight to walk round the Imperial palace at São Cristóvão. He noticed, astonished and admiring, that in the palace grounds the emperor maintained, at his own expense, 'a private school, run by three teachers and attended by more than 200 poor boys and girls'. Looking round, he observed that it was very well-equipped, with 'all modern teaching material and its own library'. It was also open at night for adult education. While he was passing time, Koseritz also noted that the emperor 'had, through his well-known generosity' settled many poor families, 'a true colony of families', giving them 'land and a roof' in the palace grounds.[16]

Although Dom Pedro II's philanthropic gestures have not yet warranted a systematic analysis, they would be of great interest in a history of collective ideas in Brazil. The emperor supported, from his personal budget, an unknown number of the disadvantaged, allocating fairly considerable sums to such charitable ends. Indeed, four days after the proclamation of the Republic, the new government recognized these to be in the public interest and transferred them to the National Treasury, to be met out of a charity budget.[17]

In fact, the distribution of alms was, like the hand kissing, one of the Saturday traditions at the Palácio Imperial da Quinta da Boa Vista. Dom Obá II d'Africa, the proud prince with no kingdom, seems to have attended these alms-giving sessions. In 1884, for example, 'on the occasion that he would receive the continuing charitable donation which His Majesty normally distributed to

Supports his paternalist them with references to Emperor's generosity.

however many of his subjects who chose to climb the steps to his palace, and, in particular, to the volunteers who had gone to defend the fatherland', the prince conducted himself meritoriously, according to one anonymous witness, when he prevented another sub-lieutenant, who was blind and overcome with emotion at having received a favourable despatch, from falling down the steps.[18] Some contemporaries from the elite seemed to understand, in fact, that this was the main motive for the prince's visits to the palace. 'On the days when he was broke', wrote Hermeto Lima, in a text which is clearly both imprecise and partial, 'Prince Obá would wait for the emperor at Quinta da Boa Vista and would pay him the usual obeisances. The emperor, with that generosity which everyone recognized, knew what that meant and ordered his butler to give Sublieutenant Galvão a few pennies.'[19]

'Courtesies and Affabilities'

Besides his weekly meetings with the emperor at the Saturday hand kissing, the prince also sought other points of support in the society of Rio de Janeiro, the highest strata of the empire. Mello Moraes, like many other contemporaries, would watch him walking through the city streets, gracious and exuding bonhomie, 'greeting without being greeted, distributing the courtesies and affabilities of a sovereign, crossing from one pavement to the other in order to exchange a few words ... with whatever distinguished person he came across.'[20]

While he was critical of the prince's 'audacity in appearing' at the palace and approaching the emperor as if he were an 'august colleague', Vicente Reis, a police official and man of letters, described him as a fundamentally 'calm man, with a cheerful expression, laughing and boastful', always pleasant and accessible, 'doffing his top hat to everyone of his own colour who paid him respects'.[21]

Not just in person, but also in his newspaper articles, the prince maintained that 'boastful' tone which so many of his contemporaries had commented on. 'In his articles', noted Lulu Senior, one of the journalists on *Gazeta de Notícias*, 'there are always words of praise and respect for the Brazilian and Portuguese monarchy, for the great men of Bahia and for the Senhor do Bonfim [Our Lord of Bonfim, the most popular Catholic church in Bahia]'.[22]

Even allowing for exaggeration on Lulu Senior's part, we can, nevertheless, say that the origin of the prince's patriotic sentiments was his fierce loyalty to Bahia. Not just Bahia as it really was, slave-owning and oligarchic, but the mythic land of All Saints, cradle to so many worthy men, scene of the first discovery of Brazil, of the first Catholic mass on dry land and the first 'Governador-Mor' sent by the Portuguese king. At the time of the Paraguayan War, Bahia once again earned itself a first by being the Brazilian province that supplied the most volunteers. A little like that young brave from Rio Grande do Sul whom we saw fighting side by side with our sublieutenant in the war and for whom the only place that existed was 'the Province' – his own beloved Rio Grande do Sul. The rest, he termed, generically, 'Bahia'. For the Baiano Galvão, his own province was the beginning and end of everything.[23] As a soldier and faithful subject, the prince felt himself to be an integral part of a territory that lay half-way between the historic and the mythic, 'that first-born Bahia that when the fatherland moans ... is the first to tremble'.[24]

After distant Africa, it was in the 'mother-homeland Bahia' that the prince's roots lay. The myth of his origin, and the moral strength that he drew from it, left roots on both sides of the Atlantic. On one side, the impossible Empire of Oyo, the inheritance of his grand-father Abiodun, which was distant both in historical time and in geographical space; on the other, his 'firstborn Bahia', his real birthplace in the New World, his sublieutenant's uniform, his campaign medals, his unshakable loyalty to Dom Pedro II. As was the case for so many other first-generation Brazilians, both sets of roots seemed to the prince to be noble and good, a source of confidence and self-esteem. In 1886, for example, he defended, in emotional terms, his 'Bahia – native province and motherland, fecund firstborn of Cabral – whose shining glories, laurels and noble rights sing out liberty for the whole world'.[25]

Such strong sentiments, did not, however, mask his critical sense when dealing with the reality of the province. 'That mother-homeland Bahia, everyone knows more or less that it has its faults,' he admitted in 1882, clarifying, nevertheless, that of all the prov-inces, Bahia was 'the first lover of monarchy and liberty'.[26]

Whether Bahia was or was not the first lover of monarchy and liberty, from the time of his first contacts during the war, Galvão was to remain, until the end of his life, faithful both to the old, Conservative leader of Lençóis, Colonel Antônio Gomes Calmon, to the Conservative party itself and to the great Conservative party leaders of the empire, above all, but not only, to those connected with his 'mother-homeland Bahia'.

Not only in the province of Paraíba studied by Linda Lewin, but throughout the Brazil of that time, politics and administration were still essentially bounded by 'bonds of kinship, political friendship and personal association'.[27] It was thus, in verses published in 1886, that the prince paid his homage to Senator Junqueira, 'Bahian friend', 'faithful and dedicated protector', a man whom he knew would carry out 'justice based on merit, not on colour'.[28] On other occasions, the prince claimed to be 'the friend of the sincere senators of the order of the late Rio Branco, Bom Retiro, Cotegipe, João Alfredo', all of whom were great conservative leaders of the Empire and all, with the exception of the Pernambucan João Alfredo, Bahians like himself.[29]

As a soldier and defender of the fatherland, the prince nurtured, throughout his life, a great admiration for his most illustrious commander, also a Conservative leader, 'the unconquered General Duque de Caxias' to whom he owed, as we have already seen, his incorporation into the Companhia dos Inválidos da Província da Bahia, in 1876.[30]

For the Conde d'Eu, grandson of the French king, Louis Philippe, husband of the presumptive heir to the throne and another of the commanders in the war against Paraguay, the prince reserved a very special form of address: that of 'most serene protector'.[31] The count, who was commander-in-chief during the last phase of the war, abolished slavery in Paraguay with a decree issued on 2 October 1869. In his memoirs (as we have already seen) the count made great account of the part played by men such as Sublieutenant Galvão. At one point he described the Bahian Zouaves as 'the most handsome troop in the Brazilian army', with their officers 'entirely *au fait* with all the smallest details of their service and proud of their battalion'.[32] When the war was over and many in the official world feared the return of the soldiers, particularly the Volunteers, who were mostly former slaves and free men of colour tempered by prolonged battle, the count was one of the few to raise his voice in their defence, threatening to resign his post and going so far as to call the Volunteers, in a private letter, 'companions in arms'.[33] This was no mean feat, considering the silence that his position imposed, both under the 1824 Constitution and at the request of his father-in-law, Dom Pedro II, who, before the marriage had warned the count not to touch on the delicate question of the Conservatives or the Liberals. His model was the non-interventionist stance of Prince Albert, consort of Queen Victoria. The emperor had also, on the eve of his first trip to Europe, insisted on this point with his daughter, Princess Dona Isabel.

> So that no ministry has the slightest jealousy of the interference of my daughter in public affairs it is indispensable that my son-in-law, the natural counsellor of my daughter, acts in such a manner as that no-one can be certain that his advice has really influenced my daughter's opinions.[34]

Be that as it may, contacts and social alliances such as these were important domestic conquests, subproducts of the war against Solano Lopes. One should not therefore be surprised that Dom Obá II d'Africa so often appealed to the 'Senhor Prince Conde d'Eu', or 'Empretérito e Ínclito Conde d'Eu' (Renowned and Illustrious Count of Eu), as he called the count. 'For a long time I have explained to the Most Serene Prince, the reasons why I sometimes burden him with requests,' Obá apologized, in 1886, only to ask in the next breath, 'but Senhor, am I the only one?' And then, as if anticipating the reply: 'It is certain that I am not.'[35]

'Requests', in truth, however inopportune they might be, were always necessary in 'Africa Pequena'. Owing to the slave-owning basis and the privileges of class inherited from the colony, the idea of civil rights, citizen's rights or the simple rights of a worker was practically non-existent. Masters disciplined slaves, as masters disciplined apprentices, as bosses were free 'to hire and fire, to set wages and to stamp out trouble among malcontents'. The action of the police, as well as the administration of the judicial system, did not fail to reflect these same oligarchic bases. Robert Levine summed it up thus:

> Unlike the English system, where law was debated in open court and therefore subject to public scrutiny, and unlike the two-tier system of England and France which permitted private individuals to file formal charges in court, Latin American judges sat behind closed doors, reviewed all evidence in writing, and passed sentence in kind. The judiciary functioned implicity as a tool for social control, not social justice.[36]

Such a system, while solid during the whole period and for some time later, could not, however, in a period of such profound transition, fail to generate conflict and apprehension, above all in the more complex and politicized social arena of Rio de Janeiro. In this sphere as well, starting from his personal relations and his African prerogatives (whether real or imaginary), the prince acted within the paternalistic web, rather as though he were a propitiating element, a link between state bureaucracy on the one hand and the urban masses with no social relationships on the other.

The prince did not merely 'stroll' through the streets in the centre of town, but, according to a critical article that appeared on the front page of the influential *Jornal do Commercio*, 'would burst boldly into public departments, principally those of the forum' where he would 'very often upset the work of our old and respectable judges, with foolish and impertinent questions'. On 23 April 1887, for example, we know that 'bold as only he can be', and, 'despite the protests of the doorman', Prince Dom Obá II d'Africa thrust his way into the austere headquarters of the *Tribunal da Relação*, in the city centre, 'in the name of his sovereignty and the power of his imaginary sceptre'.[37]

While considerably less well documented than his weekly visits to the Imperial palace, there is some evidence of the prince's action with agencies of the state. For example, two days before the Proclamation of the Republic, Lulu Senior recounted how the prince, among his many other activities, had arranged the release of a number of 'his subjects' from prison, and had, on several occasions, 'even given up his own liberty for them'. In order to obtain such desiderata, he explains, the prince 'climbs the steps to ministers, makes official requests, written in his own hand and stamped with the eloquence that God gave him'.[38]

But we do not know any more than this, at least at this stage. We do know, however, that a good relationship with such departments was a crucial point in the securing of those civil rights that were still so elusive in this long period of crisis in slave-owning society.

What did this prince, who was a regular visitor to the Imperial palace and who managed to get 'his subjects' out of jail, represent? More precisely, what were the social bases which he represented? I will tackle these questions in the following section, examining, not the emperor's faithful vassal, but his other persona, the street king in the empire of his reign.

Social Bases and Support

The identification of Dom Obá II d'Africa's social bases brings us once more to the Rio de Janeiro of the blacks and the brown-skinned, the Rio de Janeiro of Little Africa. Do the documents allow a more precise qualification, a more accurate characterization of the prince's followers?

The various witnesses on this point invariably provide only partial aspects, fragments of a larger reality, which were gleaned here and there by those who took their different individual routes through the city, while out shopping or while travelling to work. Thus, Mello Moraes refers in particular to the '*quitandeiras do Largo da Sé*' which, in the jargon of the age, meant the black women (either slaves, freed or free) who sold bananas, oranges, vegetables, sweet-meats, and so on in that public square, or who went from door to door with their wares on large trays carried on their heads, offering their products to householders.[39]

Another contemporary, Hermeto Lima, saw, besides these *quitandeiras*, the 'black herb-sellers of the Rua Larga de S. Joaquim' (today's Rua Marechal Floriano Peixoto). These herb-sellers were, doubtless, people linked to the worship of the *orixás* (the Afro-Brazilian deities). Some would have been freed Africans, others Brazilians like the prince, who knew the secrets of plants and the art of curing the evil eye or undoing sorcery. 'The *quitandeiras* of the Largo da Sé and the herb-selling blacks of the Rua Largo de S. Joaquim', wrote Hermeto Lima in his history of the Rio de Janeiro police, 'were convinced of his hierarchy and paid him real respects, kissing his hand, which was always gloved.'[40]

Besides these particular, localized experiences, other sources provide more general descriptions, not based on specific activities or places but on criteria of provenance or race. In this line, Mello Moraes included among Obá's subjects, in addition to the *quitandeiras* of the Largo da Sé, the 'Minas blacks', a term which, at the end of the nineteenth century, above all in Rio de Janeiro, was applied to Africans in general and not just to those who came from the Gold Coast, today's Ghana.[41] Similarly, in the early days of the Republic, the newspaper *O Paiz* identified them, generically, as 'sons of Africa'.[42]

One should bear in mind, however, that at that time, 'children of Africa' meant not just Africans, but blacks in general, not differentiating between those born in Africa and in Brazil. For the Conservative *Jornal do Commercio*, for example, the subjects of Dom Obá II were the 'crioulos and crioulas' (creoles, male and female) – that is, the blacks born in Brazil.[43] Putting together both sides of the equation, or both Africans and Brazilians, the Liberal *Diário de Notícias* identified them as people 'of his own race' (i.e. the prince's), while the police superintendent Vicente Reis, an observant man, noted that the prince was courted, universally, by 'all those of his own colour'.[44]

How did Obá himself define his flock? In his newspaper articles, the prince spoke mainly in the name of 'the African peoples' of the city of Rio de Janeiro, or, more globally, and always in capitals, of the 'Blacks and Browns'; or even, using a stronger expression that embodied a certain political exaggeration, of '*o povo em massa*' (the masses). According to the prince, it was precisely because of this widespread following that he was attacked harshly and unjustly from all quarters. 'For being Black', he wrote in 1886, 'and for enjoying the sacred confidence and favour of the masses'.[45] Once again, according to the prince, such campaigns of 'libels' and 'injustices' would never be able to undermine 'the credit that I have acquired in this heroic and great city of Rio de Janeiro'.[46]

Taking this evidence as a whole and taking into account the semantic customs of the time, we can circumscribe the kingdom of Dom Obá as one that included a portion of the African, creole and mixed race population, typically made up of slaves, freed slaves and free men of colour, among whom there were certainly many migrants and ex-combatants like the prince himself.

How can one explain his leadership? We have already seen how Alferes de Zuavo 'paraded his person' through the city and was, in all quarters, revered by these simple people who proudly hailed him and bowed on bent knees in the dust of the city streets to receive his blessing. Indeed, the documents are detailed on these aspects. Taking them together, it is possible to say, as the *Diário de Notícias* did after his death, that the prince lived 'acclaimed by those of his race', enjoyed 'immense popularity' and, finally, died 'in the majesty of a sovereignty which no-one dared to contest'.[47]

In 1887, while he was still alive, the *Jornal do Commercio* described the prince in his frock coat and cane, '*falando grosso* [literally, 'speaking strongly', with the voice of authority] to the creole men and women whom he calls his subjects'.[48] 'Speaking strongly', 'immense popularity' or 'sovereignty', the power of Dom Obá II d'Africa seems difficult to explain, or even to describe adequately. His contemporaries, who were, generally, reluctant to waste their time on the subject, seemed to believe that the person they were dealing with was what we, after Weber, today call traditional leadership or authority. Thus, according to how they were seen by their contemporaries among the elite, the 'subjects' or 'vassals' of Dom Obá merely re-enacted in Brazil the oldest rules, practices and customs brought from Africa.

In that Little Africa, so divided internally by questions of customs, survival and religion, at one and the same time, Sudanese, Bantu and Creole, what did a remote (although symbolically important) traditional Yoruba legitimacy mean? If we look more carefully at the title that he gave himself and displayed so proudly, the opinion of the prince himself seems to be decisive on this point. It means, effectively, a king (Obá in Yoruba), the second in a dynasty that was reborn with his father, Benvindo da Fonseca Galvão, Obá I of the diaspora. With the uprooting of his family to Brazil, however, Dom Obá's authority was no longer restricted to the old Empire of Oyo, but embraced all the ethnic groups of Little Africa: hence Dom Obá II d'Africa.

We are therefore talking about a tradition that was reinvented and expanded by charisma.[49] Dom Obá II d'Africa reigned, not simply by tradition, but through the extraordinary powers that his ample 'tribe of vassals' attributed to him. Such powers included, certainly, his real inheritance of Abiodun, his feats and war medals, his relationship with Dom Pedro II and perhaps, above all, his capacity for political action within the existing political circles, the *realpolitik* of the day.

Referred to, in places, as his 'admirable majesty', or 'his own particular body language', such charisma, in the sociological sense, was also perceived by his contemporaries among the elite. Several days after his death, the *Diário de Notícias* tried, in effect, a more coherent explanation:

> There was in him a prince of royal blood, African blood to be sure, but nevertheless the very good blood of a prince who was recognised and acclaimed by those of his own race, in front of whom he bore himself regally as their sovereign with a weighty aplomb in his manner and an air of domination that one could not fail to note.[50]

Finally, we will look at the finances of this prince of the diaspora. It is known that the support given to Obá was not limited to gestures of reverence, noisy exclamations and requests for blessings, but extended to real financial support. 'Due to his regal lineage, to his succession to the throne of Africa', wrote a contemporary, 'Prince Obá II receives a contribution, a tribute from his subjects.'[51] *O Paiz* also attributed the payment of this stipend – 'a type of tribute', according to the newspaper – 'to his lineage and his sovereign position'.[52] At the time of the prince's death, in the early days of the Republic, the journalist at *O Paiz* appeared to hesitate at using the word 'stipend'. He did concede that the prince lived 'at the cost of others' and finally died in misery, as was the wont of those 'who did not make work the principal support of life'. Here too he explained these contributions as being due to the 'supremacy which he wanted to have over the children of Africa'.[53]

It is certainly difficult to imagine today how much his 'stipend' could have been; the deeds, if they ever existed, have been lost. We can obtain some idea of the amount, however, from other evidence which is sufficiently well founded, First, these 'tributes from his subjects' constituted the principal source of the funds of one of the chronically unemployed in the Imperial capital. With such a 'stipend', the prince was able to support his modest representations of a sovereign, his family, his modest 'feijoada', his glass of paraty, his room in a rooming house in the Rua Barão de São Félix, his attire, which was always admired.

When Dom Obá II d'Africa strolled through the city streets he would never be described in the way that so many other veterans of Paraguay were: 'with his old uniform, his old-fashioned sword, his dirty collar, his worn-out boots and his penny cigar'.[54] On the contrary, contemporary witnesses – in both written documents and drawings – always, as we have already seen, remarked on his exaggeratedly regal bearing, his 'admirable majesty', his top hat, which he always sported at a fashionable angle, his white gloves, his gold pince-nez, the extravagant plumes of his sublieutenant's hat. For example, Carl von Koseritz attended the imperial hand kissing on four occasions and saw the prince at each. He described Obá as 'a tall, strong black', with a 'Henry IV beard', wearing 'fine black clothes and a gold pince-nez with a blue lens'.[55]

To go to the palace practically every Saturday, the prince hired a tilbury carriage. In the 'excess of emotion' described by Mello Moraes, he gave a note of 2 or 5 mil-réis to the sentries who had paid him military honours. Other contemporaries recounted a similar incident in Salvador, at the gates of the Governor's palace, when he handed over 'a silver coin', a substantial increase in the value of the donation.[56]

It was presumably through the same tributes that the prince was able to broadcast his ideas via the press, either by paying to have his articles published, or, more rarely, by paying to have the leaflets that he wrote published. According to the writer Lima Barreto, who barely knew him but who gathered information about him while it was still fresh in the oral memory of the city, such publications, in the prestigious Jornal do Commercio at least, cost about 10,000 réis. Obá 'wrote pages and pages'; he would then glue these together, forming one long scroll which he carried rolled up like an ancient manuscript. He also carried a pair of scissors, which he would use to cut off lengths of the roll in accordance with the rates charged by the newspapers' classified sections. Having obtained the quotation, the prince would then decide how much of his text could be published the following day. 'Thus, when his famous article reached the price of 10$000, or whatever, then the Prince Obá, II d'Africa, let it come out in the paid section.'[57]

A 2 or 5 mil-réis note, or a silver coin; the hire of the tilbury; 10 mil-réis for the article; food, rent and clothing: this was the size of the prince's 'stipend', the only way it can be estimated in a kingdom lacking bookkeeping or ledgers that was Little Africa. Such a quantity, collected penny by penny among slaves, former slaves and free men of colour, permits us, once again, to reflect on the extension of his domain: '*o povo em massa*', as the prince himself called it.

Brazilian Questions

... and from then on he has regaled the public, from time to time, with manifestations in the press, which are even less correct than they are interesting, in which he discusses Brazilian matters in the style of Obá II. He is naturally a monarchist and conservative, because he is a prince ...

Carl von Koseritz, 11 August 1883

Because of who he was, the political thinking of Dom Obá II d'Africa seemed to his contemporaries to be perfectly obvious and not at all interesting. Indeed, the majority of his contemporaries showed little inclination to waste their time on the subject. But a century later, it is clear that we see it very differently. After all, the prince, like the people of Little Africa, was dealing with questions which are keys to a much broader understanding of the transition from slavery and the forging of modern Brazil. Questions of political definition, questions of belonging and citizenship, questions of race. How did those at the bottom of society, who were emerging from the relationships of slavery, see these fundamental issues? The prince's thinking as a whole – and particularly in relation to these questions – is the object of both this and the following chapter.

The Fundamental Question

The prince, as we know, supported the emperor and was able to declare, without fear of contradiction, 'that my wrist will never reach out for the pen of weakness to write anything against the monarchies'.[1] He also said, with a certain exaggeration, that he would 'sacrifice' his own 'life and even ... [my] fortune' in defence of the institutions; this, he said, was well documented in 'long

107

articles which I have published in my political life over many long years'.[2]

Exactly what idea the prince had of this political institution is another question to be investigated. He was a constitutional monarchist and revered the 1824 Constitution, which he saw as a guarantee of internal order, the source that legitimized Dom Pedro II and, by extension, 'foreign princes' such as himself. In consequence, he frequently paid respect to 'the living reason of the Constitution', or the 'law of the State Constitution', or 'the law that guides us' in the title of his articles.

When he tried to explain the nature or the origin of monarchical power, however, it seems that the prince was in marked disagreement with the spirit of the 1824 Constitution. Brazil separated from Portugal during an age when monarchies could be better justified by 'the unanimous acclamation of peoples' than by the divine right of God, although both ideas were present to some extent. Brazilians are, in this sense, heirs to the 'new ideas' of the beginning of that century, and even more so to the ideas that spurred the Oporto Constitutionalist Revolution of 1820, the episode that, in a roundabout way, was to detonate Brazilian independence two years later. Brazil is simultaneously the heir to eighteenth-century French ideology and, in the realm of the practical organization of power, to English parliamentarianism. For Galvão, however, power seemed to come more from God than from any Rousseauesque social contract between men. And because it came from God, it was more an absolute power than a constitutional one.

> Because, at the beginning of the world men asked the Creator to guide them. The Creator felt sorry for them and appointed [kings] in several tribes, whose illumination was sent through providence. Thus men would obey whatever message was sent through the chosen one.[3]

Where did the prince's ideas come from? They were totally contrary to the 'doubly' liberal ideas which had guided both Independence in 1822 and the Carta granted by Pedro I in 1824. This 'origin of the Kings' reminds us of the historical books of the Old Testament which narrate the founding of the Hebrew monarchy in around 1050 BC. At that time, the Israelites, foreseeing poor government under the sons of Samuel, the last judge, and also fearing invasion from the Philistines and the Amorites, called upon God, through the voice of the elders from all the tribes, to send a king 'that may judge us, and go out before us, and fight our battles'.

Saul was chosen after the Lord had whispered his name in Samuel's ear:

> Tomorrow about this time I will send thee a man out of the land of Benjamin, and thou shalt anoint him to be captain over my people Israel, that he may save my people out of the hand of the Philistines: for I have looked upon my people, because their cry is come unto me.

The following day, after Samuel had met Saul, the Lord said: 'Behold the man whom I spake to thee of! this same shall reign over my people.'[4]

We have this and other evidence to show that Dom Obá II d'Africa used the Holy Scriptures both as regular reading and as inspiration. Nevertheless, the question of divine right, as well as the question of power, came from yet another source, an earlier source, received in the cradle – although it was also part of the cultural ambience of Little Africa. Once again, it was the idea of an absolute monarchy where, according to Rev. Samuel Johnson, 'The king is more dreaded than even the gods.'[5] It should be remembered that, unlike the Hebrew experience (and the explanation given by Dom Obá) the Yoruba institution originated, not in a request from men, but from the will and motivation of God. We can suppose that the prince knew this version which was an integral part of the Yoruba myth of origin and, because of this, one of the first principles of the worship of the *orixás*, in which, as we will see later, the prince was also involved. For the Yoruba, the monarchy was a creation of the supreme god, Oludumare, through his son and messenger Oduduwa, creator of earth and, on it, of men and the first city-state, Ile-Ife. Before dying, Oduduwa, the first king, gave each of his seven sons a beaded crown – the supreme symbol of monarchy – and sent them out across the world to found their own kingdoms; Ijebu, Ondo, Ilesha, Ketu, Save, Benin and the Oyo of Dom Obá II d'Africa. The number of Oduduwa's descendants, and, consequently, the number of cities originally founded, varies greatly in accordance with the different regional versions of the myth. In the course of time, other, similar kingdoms sprung up from these early kingdoms, out of the need for defence or because of internal dissension, forming an endless chain in which all were directly or indirectly linked to, and legitimized by, the Holy City of Ile-Ife, the seat of the first man, the first gods and the first king.

The Obá, or king, who was the focal point and symbol of political unity within each city, is conceived as a type of provisional reincarnation of the same divine Obá who had reigned since the time of Oduduwa. The beaded crown which covers his face and depersonalizes him is, according to recent interpretations, the symbol of this inner being that goes back to the supreme god. The divine character of these descendants of Oduduwa can be evaluated through the additional titles that were attributed to them. For example, the Alafin (Obá) of Oyo, the branch which the prince claimed to belong to, was known as 'Lord of the World and of Life', 'Owner of the Land' and 'Companion of the Gods'. In other cities they were known as *ekeji orisa*, that is, brother to the *orixá*. Thus the Yoruba also consecrated the principle of heredity, not precisely from father to son, but from ancestors to descendants through a complex process of election – more exactly, through a process of control and political consensus – within the royal houses. There were generally two or four in each city, which alternated in power.[6]

In synthesis then, Dom Obá II's concept of monarchy, as that of many of his subjects in Little Africa, was absolute, of divine right and hereditary. A blood right such as this, which goes back to Olodumare and Oduduwa, the Creator, could survive anything: the splintering of the Yoruba empire after the great Alafin Abiodun; the sack and destruction of the capital, Oyo, by the Fulani in *c.* 1837; the personal tragedies of the Atlantic traffic; the reality of American slavery. 'In consequence', Galvão believed, 'I have the right of God, entrusted to my Abiodun grandfathers.' Sometimes he wrote in a mixture of Yoruba and Portuguese, according to a formula which he probably learnt from his father: 'Omam obá min jó Obá' (omo-obaa mi je oba), 'which means, the son of the king is king'.[7]

The prince not only believed this, but acted on it, both in his own defence and in defence of the reigning political institutions. In 1887, for example, he was extremely irritated by the disrespectful treatment paid him by some of the city's scandal-sheets and reminded them of his hereditary rights. 'What I own I owe to the Creator and the sacred lineage of Abiodun,' he wrote. 'I have never begged for titles or positions of any sort.' He continued: 'Because I possess Divine Rights, I should not waste my precious time to reply, in any newspaper, to the articles written about me.'[8] At heart he believed that the press attacked him for the same reasons that it attacked Dom Pedro II – because it envied his 'royal rights' conferred by God, 'seeing that Princes are born and not made by monies or bread and butter.'[9]

Concepts like these were, no doubt, shared by many ordinary people, as we will see later. To those who tried to mock a king without kingdom and crown ('as almost happens in certain less civilized countries,' he said, in a veiled reference to Brazil) the prince would deliver a reminder of his many subjects in the city of Rio de Janeiro: 'the due respect which I have continually received from my African fellow citizens, as is their duty and as is confirmed by the law.' By 'duty', the prince meant the political and religious tradition of the Yoruba, and 'confirmed by the law' clearly referred to the Constitution of the Brazilian Empire.[10] For the prince, as for his subjects, the constitutional emperor, Dom Pedro II, was the 'God of the Brazilian Nation' and the empress and Princess Dona Isabel were 'goddesses'.[11]

For the prince there was no conflict of power or legitimacy between that ancestral Obá, which the prince reincarnated in the streets of Rio, and the royal emperor of the empire. 'Princes, even if they be foreigners', explained Dom Obá, 'cannot and should not be against the rights of the crown, just as this signatory is not, for living reasons.' He understood that in Brazil, it was not up to him 'to order, want, instruct and confirm'. That right could only be exercised in his own kingdom, the city-state of Oyo, not in Brazil, 'given that the royal house where the heirdom of Abiodun was born is over there,' he said.[12]

The Party Question

Given the divine origin of the kings, the question of monarchy was, for the prince, the fundamental political nexus, the non-negotiable nucleus of his thinking and action in history. We know that he was 'Conservative', or even 'naturally Conservative', as von Koseritz described it. But what exactly did this party option mean within the political culture of the time? What exactly did it mean to be a Conservative, a Liberal or a Republican during that period in which the slave state was being dismantled? The sense of nationhood, the 'people's opinion', as we have seen, was still only a speck on the horizon of history. And, for that reason, or rather, because of the absence of the effective expression of public opinion in the political sphere, 'consulting the nation', the very heart of the parliamentary system, was no more than a constitutional formality, subject to all sorts of pressures from the powerful. In fact, after the bitter regional conflicts which had lasted from the time of Independence until Dom Pedro II's coming of age (1822–41), ideas and programmes were no longer important components of the political game. This absence was most marked in the prince's time (the 1870s and 1880s), when the parties did not, in practice, appear to have any clearly different programme or opinion. Conservatives, the most fervent Liberals and even the Republicans almost invariably accepted the status quo on their plantations and in society as a whole. It had never been possible to set up 'an abolitionist party', as Joaquim Nabuco had wanted. 'What more must be said', asked Nabuco in 1883 in irritation at the lack of penetration of his abolitionist ideas, 'to assure us that the temerity with which our political parties assume the great names they use is gross political deception?' For the young Liberal, they were nothing more than 'seekers after sinecures and political honour, candidates for paid employment, clients of ministers and trainbearers to the government'.[13]

In his memoirs of the period, Dunshee de Abranches went as far as classifying Conservatives, Liberals and Republicans respectively as *'escravistas'*, *'escravocratas'* and *'escravagistas'* – all meaning exactly the same thing: supporters of slavery.[14] For the ordinary people, according to a popular saying of the time, 'there is nothing more like a Conservative than a Liberal in power', or, indeed, vice versa. On one occasion a Conservative declared in the Senate Chamber that 'the Conservative in Brazil is necessarily Liberal, because the Constitution of Brazil includes holy, liberal institutions; therefore he is Liberal.' To which the Liberal leader Zacharias de Góes e Vasconcelos promptly retorted that it was precisely the opposite, 'the Brazilian Constitution contains holy, liberal institutions; the Liberal party wants to maintain them; therefore only a Liberal can be Conservative.'[15]

It should not then be surprising that all the major liberalizing reforms of the empire were, after fierce battles, carried out by Conservative cabinets with the active support and prodding of the emperor. The reforms that come into this category range from the judicial reform of 1871 to every one of the laws of emancipation, starting with the law for the abolition of the African trade in 1850, the liberty of the newborn in 1871, the Sexagenarians Law in 1885 and final abolition in 1888.

Because there were no opinions or programmes, the question of party power reigned supreme. Given the centralizing nature of the regime – a legacy from colonial days and the basis of the independent state – all political and administrative life (in Rio as in Lençóis) depended largely on the so-called 'machine'. At the bottom rung of society, where slaves were already a minority, the concept of 'equal rights' continued incipient and fragile, given that the only education received by the workforce, whether they were slaves, freedmen or free men of colour, was for work, and usually meant learning on the job. Everything depended on the party in power, including the results of the elections. As soon as a new 'situation' was installed in power, it would unleash a purge of '*derrubadas*' (literally 'choppings' or 'feelings') in order to set up a new 'machine' of control.

In contrast to what the prince believed – that the crown, the symbol of the nation, was a higher power than the parties – it was the parties that were the privileged players in the political culture of the time. The fact that they functioned almost as extended clans explains the ruthlessness of the 'choppings' to remove 'political enemies' from all levels of public service. In the absence of appropriate social and institutional limits, the 'choppings' went down as far as the humblest cleaners and caretakers in public departments. The prince denounced this practice repeatedly, trumpeting his own case through the newspapers of Rio de Janeiro. As far as clientelism went, the prince benefited from being a Conservative. 'I would rather have the Conservatives', he said in 1882, during the Saraiva Liberal cabinet, 'because when they were in power they employed me.' In fact, after the war, in the last few years of the Conservative cabinet led by Visconde de Itaboray, the prince, or rather the honorary sublieutenant, was given a job in the Military Pharmaceutical Laboratory. Although no quantitative study exists on this specific point, it is reasonable to suspect that other Volunteers had been given similar jobs at this time. For example, in the early years of the Republic, Lima Barreto knew a certain Major Vital, an elderly boy Friday at the old War Arsenal, who 'always solemnly wore his uniform and an old-fashioned sword' from the war.[16] According to the prince, from 1868 to 1878 – during the war and immediately after, under the Conservatives – many ex-volunteers and many blacks and '*pardos*' were given public employment. 'When the Conservatives were in power they employed me', he wrote, going on to mention other examples of the black and brown-skinned elite of the time 'and Dr Santos Lima and so many others throughout the Empire, such as creole medical doctors and many *pardos*'.[17]

But in the case of the prince, the job did not last very long. When the Liberals came to power in 1878 with the Sinimbu cabinet, Dom Obá fell victim to a 'chopping' and returned to unemployment. When the Sinimbu cabinet fell there was a long period of crisis, with a new Liberal cabinet every year for seven years until the Conservatives returned to power in 1885. During these years, the prince was a radical Conservative and so partial that he was unaware that the 'choppings' were meted out by both sides. For him, the salary policy of the Liberals was 'just for an Englishman's eyes' ('*para inglês ver*', a Brazilian expression meaning simulation or falsity).

> And even so there are those who turn away from the Conservative party, without realising that at least when the Conservatives are in power, they eat well themselves but they also give to all the craftsmen and public and private employees who are able to eat without leaving their children hungry, not like the others who killed the poor honorary officers and the wounded of the fatherland.[18]

According to the dominant political culture of the time of Dom Obá II d'Africa, the party in power could not lose an election. Throughout the period, the chambers always ended up in unanimity, whether they were Conservative or Liberal. Under the Zacharias cabinet (1862–8), the Liberal party not only controlled an almost monolithically Liberal chamber of deputies, but virtually all the political and administrative positions from Rio de Janeiro to the smallest hinterland municipality, including Dom Obá's Lençóis. In 1868, under the Conservative Visconde de Itaboray, there was a complete reversion and the two chambers and all political posts emerged from the elections almost unanimously Conservative. Once again, with the Sinimbu cabinet, the two houses were almost completely Liberal. And so it continued, the only exception being the first direct election in 1882.

The alternation of the parties whenever there was a political crisis was only possible with the direct intervention of the emperor, who was always prompt at carrying out his constitutional duty. But exercising the 'moderating power', above parties, seemed something of an impossible mission. When they were out of power or out of step with the emancipation process (either because they thought it too fast or too slow), Liberals and Conservatives alike aimed critical darts at Dom Pedro II. They sniped at his 'Machiavellianism', his 'imperialism', his 'personal power' and 'centralizing absolutism'. They called him a 'caricature Caesar', the implacable witch of São Cristóvão with his 'blacklist' and 'fateful pencil'. When they were ousted from power, by a 'political inversion', their indignation could turn into anti-monarchism. For example, in 1868, when the Liberals were ousted by the Conservatives, they clamoured openly for 'Reform or Revolution'. During the next two years the more extreme Liberals founded, in quick succession, a Republican club, a Republican newspaper and a Republican party. Despite a formal split in 1870, the links between progressive Liberals and Republicans remained strong throughout Dom Obá II d'Africa's period. Indeed, many people believed that the Republicans were nothing more than a 'pronouncement' (the term used) of the Liberals. Then, in 1878, when the Conservatives fell and the Liberals returned to power, some of the most illustrious signatories of the Manifesto for the Republic eight years previously returned to the Liberal fold. They included Lafayette Rodrigues Pereira, who became a member of the Sinimbu cabinet; Saldanha Marinho, elected to the chamber of deputies, and Cristiano Benedito Ottoni, who became a senator.[19]

Like many in Little Africa, Dom Obá II d'Africa was unable to understand the attacks made by the opposition, whether Liberal or Conservative, on sacred institutions which were, for him, the symbol of the nation itself. With his profound dynastic conviction, Galvão was not, as he himself said, 'like many of those who are only interested in the public coffers, who are only friends of the Monarchy when they are attached to the coffers and when they are free from it want Reform or Revolution'. On the subject of progressive abolition – and not just finding a job – the prince held much more deeply rooted party convictions. He was, in his own words, 'a conservative to conserve what is good', and, on the other hand, 'a liberal to repress the murders that have taken place in the current time on the orders of certain potentates'. For him, it was better to improve Brazil little by little, enforcing the law, respecting 'the living reasons of the Constitution that governs us' than to overthrow everything and wreak a 'revolution' as some wanted.[20]

The Question of the Regime

From this one can understand the prince's acidity in relation to the Republicans, and above all to the so-called 'revolutionaries'. In his political and philosophical conception, the only motives that could set a man against sacred institutions were ugly sentiments such as greed and envy. From time immemorial, he reasoned, 'the Princes and Kings have been victims of traitors to the Crown, to the King, because of their great envy at not being Princes.' They were thus committing a grave sin, because 'all those who rise against these sacred rights ... will be rewarded with the chastisement of God and will die before their due day and hour.' The 'revolutionaries' should repent as soon as possible 'of their mistakes in ... being Republicans'. If they succeeded, they would be 'Traitor to the king, to the country and will be known as greedy for gold, with no love for God

Most of all, he was a monarchist, a believer in the devine right of kings and emperors

and human conscience'. He went on: 'After rising up against the king, wanting to be the king ... by force ..., even if they have a cardboard crown', they will have acted 'like the mother who becomes pimp to her own daughter, leading her to disgrace'.[21]

He allowed only one exception to these grave accusations: the liberal-democrat Quintino Bocaiúva, an 'evolutionary' Republican rather than a 'revolutionary' Republican like, for example, the young Silva Jardim. (The latter openly preached a *coup d'état* and saw the implantation of a positivist dictatorship as a modern solution, recommended by the great French masters, which would put Brazil in the forefront of the whole of humanity.) In making an exception for Quintino, the prince certainly took into account his extremely educated manners – also noted by the great writer Machado de Assis and the French journalist, Max Leclerc. Despite the fact that they supported opposite camps, the prince referred to Bocaiúva as 'my friend Quintino Bocaiúva'. And he put great store on the fact that the republican was known as 'the Prince of Letters' for the poetry and plays of his youth.[22]

It was in defence of the regime and his political and philosophical ideas that the prince went on the offensive on 15 May 1883, when the newspaper O Corsário published a fake letter, written in his style and bearing his signature, expressing criticism of the institutions and the emperor. His reply was published in O Carbonário, the rival scandal-sheet, under the general heading of 'The righteous word before God, his Majesty and all the people [*Universidades*]' (the truth before God, the Emperor and the world). The prince denounced the letter, not just as a joke in bad taste, but as a treasonable attempt to set the 'blacks and brown-skinned' of his reign against the monarchy. The prince thought it was the work of republicans seeking public support for a coup. 'Like those who say', he wrote, 'that we cannot carry out the revolution without the participation of the blacks and the brown-skinned' and for that reason 'would set them against His Majesty'. They attacked him 'to make me turn into a republican, like certain false monarchists who disgrace the poor'. He seemed to suspect that behind all of this there were those interested in delaying the course of emancipation. 'All this', he insisted, 'just because they do not want His Majesty to bestow value on the black colour, like he has frequently bestowed on me.' This was, he continued, 'while the false ones treat people like me who are friends of his majesty like a madman, while those who are false to the king, they say are wise'.[23]

Whether his fears were well founded or not, the fact is that from that moment on, the prince began to see perils on all sides while most of his contemporaries seemed confident in the stability of the regime until the very last moment. The best example of this was Silva Jardim, the spokesman of the 'revolution', who openly advocated a military coup and yet was taken by surprise when it happened. Jardim doubted that there was any possibility of a coup until the night of 14 November 1889, when the rumours were already circulating in Rio de Janeiro. That night he was dining with Alfredo Madureira at the fashionable Hotel Globo, in the equally fashionable Rua Direita. At the top of his voice, he peremptorily denied all the rumours. 'Revolution? But doesn't Madureira know that this Republican party run by Quintino, is a party which expects to arrive at the Republic by "evolution"?' Then, according to a witness, he sarcastically drew out the syllables: 'E-vo-lu-tion!'[24]

In contrast, during the last five years of the monarchy, the prince seemed to have been possessed by strange paranoias of coups, palace treachery, 'ambushes' and 'putsches by the false ... against the crown of the fatherland' despite the apparent institutional calm. It seemed to him that these dangers were imminent. In 1885 he made a point of renewing his pledge of loyalty to the crown, 'before everything that might happen in the future and the present'.[25] In March 1887, when the emperor was ill, he lectured the doctors whom the emperor had gone to consult abroad. 'Think well, you wise clinicians, maturely, with the weight of your consciences, of the best ways to save the sacred existence of the much-loved and generous God of the nation.' 'And as soon as the sacred Existence of the Wise Sovereign has been saved, these illustrious clinicians will be greater friends of the fatherland.' But if they did not proceed thus, there would not be 'waters to wash their souls; because God will not permit it to be otherwise'.[26] While the emperor was away undergoing treatment, the prince feared for the stability of the regime. His articles during this period were addressed directly to the State Council. 'These Councillors should, before the country, assume the responsibilities that they have to succeed in the exercise of legality in the absence of the august Emperors.' He feared, specifically,

> certain hypocrites whom I know very well, who in front of the Majesty, kiss the sacred hands, and in his absence want to be Kings even if they wear a Cardboard Crown ... as the country is not unaware, that, without being the God of the Nation, they want to drink the blood of humanity, the more that they become God of the State.'[27]

His articles shortly before the final Abolition harangued the 'enemies

of princes'. Eventually, he entrusted the fate of the monarchy to
Santa Bárbara, the 'virgin of Africa', always 'great in her miracles'.
Because of his unswerving faith in these powers, he also still believed
that, if the emperor 'would beware of those who surround him', he
would escape.[28]

This faithful vassal was a peacemaker, an advocate of reform
within law and order. In 1887, at the same time as the emperor's
health was worsening, weakened by diabetes, it was evident that
there was a secret correspondence between republicans, principally
the 'evolutionary' republicans, and the so-called 'military question'.[29] According to the prince, the emperor's failing health and
illness were caused by the anxiety generated by the 'military
question'. Obá was virtually the only one to point out that 'God
created the Kings to defend the people' and 'the armies to faithfully
defend their leader'. By now clearly in the reverse current of history,
Alferes de Zuavos called on the 'faithful soldiers' and former
Voluntários da Pátria, 'as soldiers who stem from the people,
defenders of the Brazilian monarchy'.[30]

Abolition and Citizenship

In terms of rights or the absence of rights, what did it mean to be a
slave, a freedman or a free man of colour in that society? What did
liberty mean, not just under the law, but in the daily life of men such
as Dom Obá II d'Africa? And not just the great abstract concept of
an abolitionist utopia, but liberty (or rather, *alforria*) in terms of the
effective rights of belonging and citizenship. And within this concrete
sphere, where did the prince stand? These are the questions which
will be tackled in the following section. We shall take the basic
elements of citizenship identified in Marshall's classic analysis as our
starting point. First, civilian citizenship, which comprises the rights
necessary for individual liberty, such as the right of free movement,
religious freedom, freedom of the press, the right to own property
and, fundamentally, as a guarantee of all the others, the right to
justice. Second, political citizenship, which means fundamentally the
right to participate in the exercise of power, whether as a member
of a body invested with political power or as an elector of such a
body. And finally, social citizenship, which refers to the minimum
levels of well-being and material security in accord with the
prevalent social standards.[31]

In the days of the Brazilian empire, before the Republic, the formal ruling structure consisted of a liberal, representative monarchy with a parliament based on the English system. The right to hold property, like the fundamental rights of free thought, free assembly, and so on were all guaranteed under the 1824 Constitution. Among the rights to property, under the law, the slave was included. Slaves were not citizens, did not hold power over themselves and, theoretically, were not part of the social pact. In the common parlance of the time, they were not *nacionais* ('nationals') as were the free men of colour; they were *de nação* ('of the nation', that is, the nation of Africa). Or they were *crioulos*, that is, born in Brazil.

The right to nationality and citizenship was not therefore the privilege of the whites in the empire; it was a right that belonged to the freeborn. Because he was a property, the slave, by definition, had no rights at all, whether the civil right to property, or the fruits of his labours, which belonged to his master (and there was no distinction between 'regular' or 'extra' work).

This was according to the 'theory' of the system. Yet, as the result of a long historical negotiation, things were slightly different in reality, as was noted, with a degree of astonishment, by the German artist Johann Moritz Rugendas on his second visit to Rio de Janeiro. Rugendas, an acute observer of the small cultural details of Brazilian life, was surprised by the fact that the Brazilians allowed slaves 'to buy their liberty with their own money' (meaning the masters' money) as, logically and according to the law, they could 'take the slave's savings, without giving him his freedom or any other benefit'. Despite Rugenda's surprise, a slave's right to keep his savings and buy his freedom was an unwritten, but well-established conquest of that society, although the lack of specific research means that it is not possible to establish when the custom began.

A social reality that existed outside the law, this custom represented a notable achievement. It was made possible by a sort of social consensus which united, in permanent form, overriding class differences and wide sectors of society – the slaves, former slaves and poor free men of all colours. In this case, the masters yielded to what had become the custom of the land, one which the poor population sustained in the moral sphere. This minor right to civilian citizenship, which is almost imperceptible in the macro-history of the system – was an important part of what one might call the social commitment to a harmonious life. Although the masters had the law on their side, they would pause before facing the indignation of a man who had saved up his pennies ('in his free time', as was the custom) to buy his freedom, especially in the 'Court' itself. If they tried, they would have to confront not only the personal revolt of the slave (who would flee or, even more frequently, simply refuse to work properly or collaborate efficiently), but also open social censure, the terrible 'big tongue' of the small people. This 'public opinion', irreverent and severe, which was typical of the 'lower rungs of society' as Rugendas put it, would always be demonstrated 'with great intensity', expressing disapproval of the master 'by every possible means'.[32]

It is significant that, by 1871, this 'small right' of property, which until then had been informal, was given the backing of the law. Because it was a widely accepted custom, recognition under the law did not need a specific legal vehicle. Instead, it came as a passenger, built into the so-called 'Law of the Free Womb'. Article 4 of this law consecrated, wholesale, various practices, which had become normal customs. It stated, 'The slave is permitted to build up savings that come to him by way of donations and inheritances and also, with the consent of his master, what he obtains from his work and budgeting.' In one fell swoop, it recognized a slave's right to leave an inheritance and to buy his own *alforria*, the right to 'contract his future services to third parties by instalments' and even the right to have a family and support children under the age of 12.[33]

Under the 1824 Constitution, the slave *de nação* (African-born) who had obtained his liberty, as Yoruba Benvindo, Galvão's father had done, automatically gained access to civilian citizenship via the clause on his certificate of *alforria*, which guaranteed him the same status 'as if he had been born from the free womb': freedom of movement, the right to hold property, to make contracts and, above all, as mentioned earlier, the right to justice. However, as he was still African, his freedom did not confer on him political citizenship, unless he went through the bureaucracy of applying for naturalization. If he did not naturalize – and judging by the rarity of such petitions in the Brazilian archives, very few did – he would remain, like Benvindo and the great majority of freedmen, *de nação*, and consequently a foreigner.

When the creole bought his freedom, he got better value for his money. Without the need for more procedures, his new status automatically included political citizenship. It was, though, still a preliminary political citizenship, restricted to the so-called primary, or local, elections. He was expressly forbidden from voting for deputies, senators or members of the provincial assemblies or, indeed, standing as candidate for any of the above positions by article 94, paragraph 2. Technically, being a freedman (a former slave) was not the same as being free, which was something one gained only at birth and was the necessary precondition for full Brazilian citizenship. Probably once again because of customs and public opinion, this distinction between freedmen and free men was also abolished, in one of the secondary articles of the electoral reform law of 9 January 1881. From 1881 onwards, therefore, the only legal barriers against the exercise of political citizenship by freedmen and free men were the established general requirements of personal independence:[34] a minimum age of 25, not being a private soldier or member of a religious order, being formally integrated into the labour market (for primary elections, for example, a relatively modest minimum net annual income of 100 mil-réis) and, finally, being literate which, in practice, meant being able to sign one's own name.[35]

However, for the prince, as for his subjects, the idea of 'rights' did not come from the Constitution, which the majority did not even know or, like the prince, knew only superficially. Slaves, freedmen and free men of colour had a very low educational level. In 1872 only 1 in 1,000 slaves knew how to read or write. For women, the situation was even worse, with only 0.6 in every 1,000. The generation that had been born in the mid-century and brought up in the aftermath of the abolition of the slave trade was going through an accelerated process of creolization and Brazilianization. Every year from 1850 onwards, as the links with mother Africa weakened, society began to make its first concrete commitments to this population. The starting point of this process, as the prince and others understood it, was the enlistment to fight against the foreign invader. And it was from the war that the idea of 'rights' and the proof of belonging and citizenship stemmed. 'As the patriotic soldier that I am', the prince frequently repeated, 'I understand that I have only being doing my duty ... in taking an active part in all the matters that I understand to be grave.'[36] The new-found dignity of a victorious soldier and citizen led to demands which until then were unimagined or had lain dormant. There was the demand for political participation. 'It is just that the fatherland', he advocated after the war, 'should listen to the voice of the defender of the fatherland as a soldier.' Or, when he asked, angrily, whether the blacks and the brown-skinned were only good for 'cornet players and soldiers?'[37] Once the war was over, not only slavery but Brazil's profound social inequalities seemed unacceptable. 'The government ... made a place for all of us to go to the theatre of war', argued the prince on a point which always inflamed him, 'today we are seeing our brothers dying of hunger, without having what is necessary for our subsistance.'[38]

For the prince, the acquisition of citizenship, in concrete terms, began with the enlistment for the war and continued, after the war, via the process of progressive abolition. Enlistment and citizenship, for him, seemed to be part of the same historical process. First of all, as he understood it, there was the decree of 7 January 1865 setting up the *Voluntários da Pátria*, which 'made a place for all of us to go to the theatre of war'.[39] In the following year, on 6 November, another decree enabled the slaves *da nação* (slaves belonging to the crown, not to be confused with *de nação*) to enlist as free men, extending this liberty to their wives, who, as we have seen, also went to the front to accompany their husbands.[40] Again, in 1868, while the war was still in progress, the Speech from the Throne presented emancipation, for the first time, as a political problem which demanded a legislative solution. Two years later, on 2 October 1869, with Asunción occupied, abolition was declared in the Republic of Paraguay on the initiative of a number of Brazilian officers, among them the Conde d'Eu.

This new feeling of belonging, or expecting to belong, was to grow with the process of emancipation proper. In 1871, the Rio Branco Law of 28 September declared the children of slaves born from that date onwards to be born free and, at the same time, set up a fund (financed by taxes and fines on slave-owning itself) for the gradual liberation, by compensation, of adults. Fourteen years later, in 1885, again on 28 September, the Saraiva-Cotegipe law (it took three successive governments to approve the law) granted a cosmetic liberation of slaves over 65 years old and also, in a bolder move, once again regulated 'the gradual extinction of the servile element'. Shortly afterwards, on 16 October 1885, still under Prime Minister Cotegipe, corporal punishment by whipping was removed from the legal statutes of the country.

As one would suspect, Dom Obá II d'Africa supported such measures unreservedly, not just in his published articles, but in his frequent visits to the corridors of power. Struggling against this 'horrible stain' of slavery, as he described it, 'we have known how to carry out our duty'. He was proposing total abolition in 1882, because 'it is not enough just to treat slaves well, as the experience of other governments has shown'.[41]

The prince was unsparing in his enthusiastic praise for the Conservative cabinets of the Viscount of Rio Branco (1871–5) and the Baron of Cotegipe (1885–8) who were responsible, respectively, for the Laws of the Free Womb and the Sexagenarians, which clipped the wings of the system and, at the same time, regulated its gradual extinction. 'All this was given during the wise cabinet which freed the wombs an idea which I, as a black soldier, have always militantly supported,' he wrote in 1886. 'Behold the cabinet of March 7, 1871 which has at its helm eminent statesmen of the ilk of the master, the immortal Rio Branco, and all its well-known members'. He continued in the same vein, 'as did the worthy Baron of Cotegipe in the honorable cabinet of August 20, 1885, both of which I have faithfully and militantly supported.'[42] Such a process of subversion of the traditional order, as the prince understood it, was carried out by the crown, in the name of the nation. The men responsible, in both cabinets, 'have already become eternal in life ... as the faithful servants and friends of the Crown of the God of the nation' and 'have served the honour and the glory of a nation'.[43] When Galvão felt that the process was in need of a helping hand, he appealed to his powerful Afro-Brazilian supernatural forces. We have already seen this in relation to the emperor, to the Conservative leaders Rio Branco and Cotegipe and to various members of their ministries, such as the minister of the empire in 1871, João Alfredo Correia de Oliveira (who was later head of the cabinet at the time of final abolition in 1888); and to Rio Branco's last minister of war, João José de Oliveira Junqueira. 'Because of this', confessed the prince on the occasion of the first anniversary of the abolition of whipping, 'I always ask for the well-being of councillors Franco and Junqueira who are ill ... in all my prayers ... to Saint Barbara and to all the other African saints.'[44]

In the more specific political sphere – although politics, religion and morals did not occupy separate areas in his thinking – it seems that the prince had clearly perceived the political vacuum that had befallen the empire when it lost its traditional pillars of support as a result of discontent at the emancipating process. Around the middle of 1886, a time when many plantation owners came out openly against the 'personal power' of Dom Pedro II and when others were already displaying republican leanings, the prince defended the hierarchy of royal power over the discontented coffee barons. 'The baronetcy does not make Princes,' he wrote. In the correct order of things, he pointed out, it was the other way round, that the latter 'make' the former.[45] Some years earlier, the prince had severely criticized those who defended the slave order. 'The only desire that certain ungrateful Brazilians have is to live in laziness, and not want the well-being of the country, nor to help the blind desire of the whole nation to wash itself once and for all of the great stain of slavery.' For these, he announced divine punishment. 'Because their fate will be to end up stark raving mad in order to pay for the consciences which they owe to God and the majesties as much as to the blacks and the brown-skinned'.[46] Such 'nobles ... for being the richest', according to the prince, want 'God for themselves and the devil for the rest ... in that they do not want to give freedom to slavery ...., as has been given in the most civilized places in Europe.'[47]

Although his criticism was harsh, the prince did not generalize to the point of considering all the land barons to be birds of the same feather. Just one year before final abolition, he attested to the existence of 'patriotic plantation owners who sincerely love the Brazilian monarchy', for these, guaranteed the prince, His Majesty 'was a sincere and faithful friend'.[48]

The question of corporal punishment is particularly crucial in the study of the ideas of this 'soldier-citizen'. Corporal punishment was part of the spirit of the age and this penalty existed in both the civil legislation for slaves and in the disciplinary rules of the armed forces. Article 179, paragraph 19 of the doubly liberal Constitution of 1824 expressly forbade 'whippings, torture, branding by hot iron and all cruel punishments'. Yet the Criminal Code of 16 December 1830, reinforced by a law of 10 June 1835 (both of which were passed during the Regency, a period of great political and social instability) brought back public whipping, determined according to the severity of the offence, for slaves who attempted to kill their masters, administrators and overseers or their respective families. The municipal ordinances of communities throughout Brazil also prescribed whipping as punishment for offences committed by slaves, who, as we know, were not citizens, but only *de nação* (Africans) or 'creoles'. One can imagine, therefore, the well-founded consternation among freedmen and free men of colour when they found that such punishment still existed in the armed forces in which they had enlisted. Such punishment, as the prince understood it, went against the dignity of the free man, a dignity which was the essential prerequisite for the good soldier and citizen. Because of this, he strove, possibly more than anything else, 'to free the army from beatings', because, as he argued, 'free men are not slaves to be castigated'.[49] For him, such punishments were 'the cancer which takes captive all the strong defenders of the fatherland'. Soldier-citizens were treated 'like thieves and assassins and horse thieves'. When the army abolished this form of punishment, soon after the end of the war, the prince believed it was as a result of his own tireless lobbying. As he interpreted it, the punishment had been abolished at his own request, through the initiative of the Baron of Rio Branco and the war minister, João José de Oliveira Junqueira, and with the support of the emperor. 'At the request of his intimate friend, and the consensus of the God of the nation,' the prince was to remind people repeatedly when the legislation for the abolition of whipping for slaves went before the senate and the chamber of deputies.[50]

'We have no lack of poets', he wrote, displaying a weariness of utopias, 'what we lack are statesmen of the nature of Councillors ... Cotegipe, João Alfredo e Junqueira, who knew how to free [the soldiers of] the Army from the whip, who up until then were in the same condition as slaves'. For this 'great benefit' the prince cease-lessly asked the protection of God for the minister of war responsi-ble. 'In paying for this noble deed', he said, 'all the soldiers and patriots who are friends of the freedom of the fatherland should pray to God for the continuing existence of councillor João José de Oliveira Junqueira and for all those who share the same senti-ments.'[51]

As late as the mid-1880s, punishments meted in the most severe cases could consist of up to 400 strokes of the lash – in effect a death sentence. In 1861 a ministerial statement reduced the maximum penalty to 200 lashes, but this was frequently ignored, especially in the municipalities of the hinterland. However, after the so-called Law of Sexagenarians of 1885, such abuses, which were carried out in the presence of judges, began to provoke reactions in the press and in political circles, leading Liberals and Conservatives alike to facilitate the exceptionally rapid voting of the law of 15 October, 1886, which removed whipping from the Brazilian Criminal Code. The prince hailed this political achievement, unsparing of adjectives or capital letters, lauding the Baron de Cotegipe: 'Congratulations to the Most Worthy Senhor Most Excellent President of the Council of Ministers of the Cabinet of August 20 1885,' he wrote, a few days after the law was approved.[52]

As the prince understood it, the process as a whole started with enlistment and continued into progressive abolition. Such an inter-pretation permitted the birth of new expectations, not just among the citizen-soldiers who returned with the laurels of victory, but among slaves, freedmen and free men of colour. From that time on, freedom in Brazil was no longer to mean only the traditional projects of buying manumission with hard work in their 'spare time', as so many had done; nor the rejection of society by 'fleeing away' and setting up *quilombos* or *mocambos* (hiding places or settlements) in places out of reach of the law and the slave-hunters (*capitães-do-mato*). After the war, freedom for men like Dom Obá II d'Africa had become an official project. It was not by chance that for the coloured population as a whole, the name of the emperor had, as a contemporary observed, become 'synonymous with social power and even with Providence', from that moment identified as being 'the defender of their cause'. For the slave in particular, 'these facts meant that the government ... would some day also attempt to grant citizenship to the brothers of these men who had gone to die for their country on the very day when they had become citizens'.[53]

A host of new ideas was thus beginning to stir the lower classes of the Brazilian empire. Ideas of nation, belonging, citizenship, as a prince of the people had shown, were absolutely central. From 1850 onwards, the idea of the African 'nation' of origin was fading faster and faster; since the war the idea of a fatherland understood only in paternalistic regional terms – 'that Father-Motherland Bahia' of the prince, or 'The Province' of the Gaúchos from Rio Grande do Sul, was fast becoming the fatherland-Brazil which they had defended as soldiers. Even the creole Galvão, who had much reason to nurture his African roots, was to define himself from then onwards by a type of dual nationality. He once said, 'I do not wish and cannot ever be false ... to the people of my fatherland [in the singular], both the first one and the second one, to which I have great pride in belonging.'[54]

In order to gain a more accurate vision of this process – and in order not to restrict it to the prince – we will look at some more general data. In 1798, while the African traffic was still in progress, slaves made up a narrow majority of the population (around 1,582,000 people). This was roughly balanced by the free sector, composed principally of whites (around 1,010,000) and, way down the scale, of an intermediate coloured population of freedmen and free men (not more than 406,000). By the time of the 1872 census, shortly after the war, we are looking at a different country: with a total population of 9,930,000, the majority of whom were free blacks and those of mixed race (around 4,245,000); followed by a large contingent of whites (around 3,787,000) and, finally, by a declining population of slaves (1,510,000) and non-acculturated Indians (387,000). The colour barrier had been broken, as many perceived after the 1880s. 'This means', concluded Joaquim Nabuco, 'that the black race gave us a people.'[55]

The Racial Question

The Paraguayan War, the 1872 census, progressive abolition: all these helped reveal the 'racial question' in the Brazilian Empire. The new reality – a country of *mestiços*, whites, blacks and Indians – posed challenges to the country's intelligentsia which were far from trivial. A veritable revolution in self-image and, in consequence, in self-esteem for that young community in formation. Profound existential doubts were raised about the possibilities of nationhood, above all after the 1880s. Finally, who were the Brazilians?

It was quickly perceived that they were neither *tupi* nor *tapuia* (Indians) as the first school of literature, the 1845–75 indigenist romantic movement, had led us to believe with the heroism of the Indians in Antônio Gonçalves Dias' poems *I-Juca-Pirana* and *Os Timbiras*; or in José de Alencar's novels *O Guarani*, *Iracema* and *Ubirajara*; or in Carlos Gomes' opera *O Guarani*, based on the Alencar novel, which had great success on opening at La Scala, Milan, in 1870. After the war, as if a spell had been broken, the indigenist movement was rapidly transformed into a literary fashion of the past.

The question now was much more serious. How could a country of *mestiços*, whites, blacks and Indians – an inventive melting pot of races who until then had bothered little with their own identity – reconcile itself with the ethnocentric scientific ideas dominating Europe? The growing prestige of biological evolutionism – principally following the publication of Charles Darwin's *The Origin of Species* in 1859 – was in the process of turning into social evolutionism. In the 1870s and 1880s, social and biological evolutionism not only guaranteed the whites a comfortable throne at the top of the evolutionary scale (at the very front of the long march of stages between the 'primitive barbarian' and the great civilization) but left little hope for Asia, Africa or Latin America. Did Brazil have a future?

In Dom Obá's time, the racial question became confused with the question of nationality. The so-called Recife School, a north-eastern intellectual movement of the period, was characterized by the common interest of staff and pupils at the Law School, one of two in the country, in European scientific philosophy and evolutionary theory. The key thinker of that movement was Tobias Barreto, a brilliant mulatto who seemed eternally dissatisfied. He was a veritable devourer of texts, turning, like many others, from the Positivism of Comte to the evolution of Spencer, the philosophy of

Kant and, finally, to the mechanical evolutionism of the German biologist Ernst Haeckel. His importance lay less in his originality than in propagating these concerns and readings among a new generation of intellectuals, such as Sílvio Romero, who recognized Barreto's influence.[56]

Joaquim Nabuco, on the other hand, like other abolitionists, was aware of ethnocentric evolutionism, but opted for a more pragmatic line. For him, it boiled down to the fact that 'we are not exclusively a white people and so should not tolerate this curse of colour. On the contrary, we should do everything possible to cast it off.'[57] Others, however, even against their own inclinations, adopted the theories out of an absolute, dramatic adherence to science and its principles. The best example of this was Raimundo Nina Rodrigues, another brilliant mulatto, professor at the Bahia School of Medicine and the first scientist to tackle seriously the question of the blacks, albeit, perhaps as was the custom of his profession, with a pathological approach. In his influential works, Rodrigues (1862–1902) took the 'scientific racism' of the period on board unreservedly. For him, the black was inferior and consequently Brazilian miscegenation meant degeneration. He is justly considered to be one of the founders of Brazilian anthropology, due both to the quality of his work and his choice of theme. Besides his two *obra primas*, *Animismo Fetichista dos Negros Baianos* (Fetishistic Animism of the Bahian Blacks) and *Os Africanos no Brasil* (The Africans in Brazil), he produced *Mestiçagem, Degenerência e Crime* (Miscegenation, Degeneration and Crime) (1898), *Paranóia entre os Negros* (Paranoia amongst Blacks) and *Antropologia Patológica: os Mestiços* (Pathological Anthropology: the *Mestiços*) (1890). For Nina Rodrigues, Science with a capital 'S' was lord and master. It did not recognize affinities, aversions or vested interests – only truths. Not even his own personal experience – of real merit and brilliance – went any way towards refuting or modifying the masters. Nor, indeed, did the example of any of his contemporaries, who included the great writer Machado de Assis, André Rebouças, Luiz Gama, José do Patrocínio and many other mulattos who made notable achievements in the Brazilian empire. 'If we know blacks or coloured men of undoubted merit, creditors of esteem and respect', wrote Nina Rodrigues, 'this fact cannot hinder the knowledge of this truth – that up until today the blacks have not been able to constitute themselves into civilized peoples.'[58]

In an impassioned attempt to reconcile Brazilian reality with the foreign 'scientific truth', other contemporaries reached different conclusions. One of these was Sílvio Romero, literary critic, essayist and a brilliant debater. Between 1870 and 1880, Romero was influenced by a succession of ideas, from Comtean Positivism (which he later rejected violently) to Darwinism, German materialism and the English positivists, above all Spencer. From this set of influences, Romero produced a theory that was, up to a certain point, original: while he accepted ethnocentric evolutionism (the very idea of white superiority), he was the first academic to criticize its unilinear character. One could say that Romero had found the theoretical way out for the 'problem' of Brazilian miscegenation. It was no longer an inheritance which doomed the present and future; it was a response to the challenge of a tropical environment, the enabling factor that made Brazilian colonization viable. 'Future victory in the struggle for life among us will belong to the white,' predicted Romero in 1888. 'But the latter, in order to achieve this victory in the face of the hardships of the climate, will have to capitalize on the aid the other two races can furnish, especially the black race with which it has mixed most.' And finally, 'after having rendered the necessary help, the white type will continue to predominate through natural selection until it emerges pure and beautiful as in the Old World. That will come when it has totally acclimatized on this continent.' With Romero, Brazil had found its own evolutionism (which was later to be classified, rather pejoratively, as the 'theory of whitening').[59]

In outline, that was the state of the question at the time of Dom Obá II d'Africa. Few in that last quarter-century could escape the influences of ethnocentric science. To do so would, we can imagine, have required a new paradigm, both in the sphere of biology and in social thinking; in other words, a scientific revolution. Or else it would have to have been situated on a different, cultural plane: one that was non-scientific, but contemporary and concurrent with that Victorian scientific discourse. Be that as it may, the documentation left by that black prince allows us to imagine, at least, how such questions were dealt with by the ordinary people, those who were, in their daily lives, carrying out Brazil's miscegenation. As we will see, for this population the 'theoretical justification' had little or nothing to do with the evolutionary ideas of *inevitability* (Nina Rodrigues and others) or the *desirability* (Sílvio Romero and others) of 'whitening', and, consequently, of white superiority. On the contrary, it had much to do with a strong sentiment: the idea of the fundamental equality of humankind. In a letter to the Conde D'Eu, who was French, the prince declared 'very respectfully' that he was

proud 'of being black', as well as of his African origin.[60] Because he
believed that no race was superior to another, the prince was 'the
friend of Whites [always referred to respectfully with a capital letter]
and of all the brave and sensible men who knew virtue and who were
able to evaluate, through observation, that personal worth does not
lie in colour'. It was precisely because of this that he almost
invariably ended his writings with phrases in Latin, Yoruba or
Portuguese, which he considered to be interchangeable. 'It is the
reason why', he explained, 'that I always conclude my articles with
"ego sum qui sum", which in Africa means: "Manamim Omam Obá
mim jó Obá". Or, "I am what I am" in Latin; "Don't beat me, the
son of a king is king", in Yoruba.'[61]

A letter written by someone from the same cultural milieu in
support of Dom Obá II d'Africa, remembers the absurdity of
prejudice and discrimination, 'seeing that the black man is similar to
all the other races'. Besides, such feelings and attitudes were not in
harmony, as the writer explains, with 'the sacred intentions of the
Constitution'.[62] Another letter, written in February 1887, in the
throes of the abolition crisis, goes as far as formulating 'a blackening
project' rather than the 'enwhitening' of the country. For the writer,
the black race was clearly not the problem, but the solution for the
empire. It was from this standpoint that he supported the nomina-
tion of Dom Obá II as plenipotentiary ambassador for the West
Coast of Africa, where he could serve usefully by

> ordering the transport of African colonists, so that Brazil need never
> again suffer decadence in its tobacco and coffee plantations ... and
> sugar and cotton need never cease to fertilize the soil where Prince Obá
> II d'Africa himself was born, the grandson of Abiodun.

Here too, in dealing with the racial question, discrimination was
held to be absurd, as, after all, 'every one was made as God wished
him'.[63]

The prince himself occasionally published abolitionist or anti-
discrimination poetry, although he did not always excel in the metre
of his lines:

> 'Não é defeito preta ser a cor
> E triste pela inveja roubar-se o valor.'
>
> 'It is not a defect to be the colour black
> It is sad that envy should rob it of its worth.'[64]

The prince believed that 'it is right that Brazil should give up the question of colour, because the real question is value and when a man has value one should not look at what colour he is'.[65] For him, it seemed not so much a 'racial question' but a question of culture, of maturity and social refinement. This idea is suggested to us in various places by his use of the concept of civilization. As we have already seen, the prince justified African (rather than European) immigration, not just in order to benefit Brazil's export plantations, but also 'for the good of the uncultured peoples of Africa'.[66] Thus, the 'question' was couched, not in terms of the inequalities between races, but in terms of the inequalities between human cultures. At the same time, as a citizen and a prince, he never wearied of reminding his contemporaries of the good example set by 'more civilized countries' such as Portugal and England where African princes, far from being despised, were received with due honour. On the same note, his adored native land occasionally drove him to despair:

> a country so new, where the true and desired civilization still does not reign completely because there are those who still believe in the foolishness ... of colour prejudice and where everywhere there are conquests and more conquests yet to be won and life is dust, mire, ... everything is nothing.'[67]

As we have already seen, the prince spoke in name of 'the Blacks and *Pardos*'. He also, on occasions, came out with apparently original formulations, arriving at an independent aesthetic perception not dissimilar to the 'Black is beautiful' of the United States in the 1960s. In another letter, written in support of the prince, black is held not only to be beautiful, but 'superior to the finest diamonds'.[68]

Sometimes it seems that, deep down, he espoused the idea of black superiority. Not apparently in a biological sense but in a moral one, as a result of the historical experience of the diaspora. For example, the prince once compared his experience of life, as that of his race, 'to being similar to the eye's pupil which, being black, for its virtue, is the first, better than the whites of the eyes'.[69] The same idea is again present when, in a fit of irritation, he considers himself 'far above those who, because I am Black, think ... themselves in high positions, higher than I.'[70] And as it is too when he compares his race, in its historical experience, with strong Catholic images. His 'humble black colour' was, thus, 'every one like God and Holy Mary, virgin, always pure without being a cost to the public coffers, without being an assassin of humanity ... because black is the envied colour.'[71]

Once again, this same idea is clearly expressed when he turns his attention, not just to refuting abstract ideas on the value of individual races, but to combating their practical corollary: an immigration policy concentrated on Europe, which applied the 'theory of whitening' to 'the question of labour for the plantations'. The prince's dream of an ambassadorship to the 'African coasts', which he nurtured for several years, was a practical counter-proposal to this official policy.[72]

As the prince understood it, Brazilian society did not harbour obdurate racist feelings. Such an immigration policy must therefore have been the work of a very powerful minority which always wanted 'God for itself and the devil for the rest'.[73] For the prince, the 'sensible men' of the country knew 'that the colours Black or *Parda* should not be looked down upon as they have been ... just because many believe in the colour White'.[74] Criticizing the fact that 'there are those who want weak immigration just because it is white', he recommended, 'it is more just that those who come are the blacks, who have never been false to coffee and tobacco ... and who took up arms as soldiers of courage, strong and brave, to defend His Majesty's Crown'.[75]

For the new Brazilians of Little Africa, immigration policy represented not just the 'substitution of slave labour' but, above all, the shrinking and near-collapse of the labour market which had enabled freedmen and free men of colour to survive. Herein lies the root of the increasing preoccupation over labour rights among this population in the transition from slavery. 'Creoles and *pardos* are recognized as the first Brazilians to go to the battlefield to defend the fatherland,' argued the prince. Thus, 'the fatherland should not allow that these be annihilated because they are coloured.'[76] The same idea emerges again in 1882 when he complains of 'this persecution which means we do not have the liberty and frankness of seeing blacks and pardos becoming scribes in any of the departments of the empire'. Because of this, as we have already seen in relation to the political question, 'better thus to have the Conservatives because when they were in power they employed me and Dr Santos Lima and so many others throughout the Empire, such as creole medical doctors and many *pardos*.' In the opinion of the prince, it was the right policy, based on the value of each person and not on the colour of his skin. 'Why is that now they bend what is right?' he protested.[77]

From the 1880s onwards, the great majority of the Brazilian population – freedmen and free men of colour (or, as the prince put it, 'all the middle classes') – fell victim to these policies as they were squeezed between the great traditional land barons on one hand and the slaves and immigrants on the other.[78] A career in the army continued to be the main channel of integration and ascension for coloured citizens, above all after the abolition of the whipping penalty. For Brazil's immense, recently freed proletariat, the army could thus be considered, as the prince put it, 'the home of the fatherland'.[79]

8

Sources, Presuppositions and Symbolic Power

The villagers may belong to a god, but the god also belongs to the villagers.

Ikwerre proverb

Character is a god: it supports you according to your behaviour.

Yoruba proverb

It should be made clear at the beginning that the prince himself did not conceive his ideas in terms of 'sources' or 'possible influences', as this chapter sets out to do, but as 'inspiration'. The writing process, the art of putting ideas on paper for him was more a God-given gift than the result of a scientific elaboration, conscious of provenance and theoretical dues. Ideas would come to him without his being able to explain why; it was a type of inspiration or poetical frenzy. And it was for this reason that he thought of himself first and foremost as a 'poet'. In his articles, he never refers to himself as a 'people's leader' or a 'man of ideas' or anything other than a 'poet', or occasionally, as we will see, as an 'oracle'. And this despite the fact that he very rarely produced verse. Poetic frenzy seems to have been something that was almost beyond his control. Sometimes it was painful, driving him to his glass of *paraty* and then to problems with the police. The prince himself would never admit that his imprisonments were caused, as others claimed, by the *paraty*. Rather, he was arrested because of his 'inspiration', his 'clear ideas'. 'Today ... when I drink in order to write', he explained in 1886, 'the police arrest me so that I do not clarify the ideas which have so purified poetry ... they arrest me arbitrarily, Bahia would attest to my clean record, as well as to whether I am a poet or not.' And after all, as

134

he used to say, 'as far as drinking goes, everyone drinks'.[1]

Because it was a gift, the inspiration did not need the consolation of any '*branquinha*' (wee white dram). 'A gift from heaven', explained a journalist of the time, 'which obliges him to get up from his bed in the middle of the night and disturb the sleep of the parrots, *araras* (macaws) and *sabiás* (thrushes) which share his dwelling, in order to put his inspiration down on paper.'[2] More modestly, the prince himself spoke of his 'weak language which blossoms', though often it was 'overshadowed by the veil of indifference'.[3]

An historian's instruments do not permit the examination of 'poetic inspiration'. But an examination of his writings does permit the elaboration of a set of influences which appear to be more concrete or, at least, suitable for historical investigation. What did he read and what sort of contact did he have with the 'world of letters'? What did he derive from his reading and what did he receive from the so-called dominant culture? What did he get from Africa, and from Brazilian working-class culture, the emerging culture of slaves, freedmen and free men of colour in the Brazilian Empire?

School, Books and Readings

Apart from learning how to read and write while in Lençóis, probably taught by his father, the prince's most visible encounters with the world of letters were only to occur after the war, when he moved to Rio de Janeiro. It was there that he demonstrated some type of proximity to elite culture and its symbols, above all to the best-known authors and books of the age. First, it was a physical approximation: in the early days in Rio he lived in an attic in Rua Uruguaiana, above the Externato Gama school and a bookshop, the Livraria Azevedo. Second, there was a more active exposure to the newspapers, which he not only read but visited, frequently turning up at their printshops, classified counters and even going into the newsrooms to deliver his contributions or to make comments.

There is evidence to suggest that he also maintained good personal relations with other bookshops. For example, in 1886, he managed to put his latest 'volume of poetry' up for sale, not just in the Casa Camões but in the printshop of *Gazeta do Povo*, where his work had probably been printed, and also in the Livraria Serafim in Rua 7 de Setembro.[4]

Traces of this contact with books and above all with poetry are to be found in his articles published in the mid-1880s. For example, the prince must have had at least some rudimentary knowledge of the life and work of 'the poet and martyr Castro Alves, envied Bahian, friend of blacks and *pardos*'. It is also probable that he had read at least some parts of the great Portuguese classic *Os Lusíadas*, by Luís de Camões. The prince remembered some verses of this sixteenth-century epic and adapted them to his own purposes. He once paraphrased a quotation from it to chide the coffee barons who were unhappy at progressive abolition (above all, after the Saraiva-Cotegipe Law of 1885) when he argued that it was monarchs who presided over the *'barões assinalados'* (the eminent barons) and not the contrary.[5]

On occasions the prince cited foreign 'authorities' from the most diverse fields. Here, though, his knowledge seems to have been more superficial, probably gleaned from the Rio press and especially from the prestigious *Jornal do Commercio*. 'Just as we see Glactone [Gladstone] imposing his ultraliberal ideas on Queen Victoria in the Irish question', expounded the prince, 'we also see a Gambeta … with his fluency imposing on the common people the great deeds, we also see Victor Hugo in French poetry singing the glory of his fatherland', and so on, with the evident intention of showing off his erudition and lending respectability to his own themes and arguments.[6] In the quest for a good argument, he seems to have, at least once, resorted to fraud, or to what students sitting exams call the 'inspired guess'. For example, as if to justify his own importance, he remembered a certain King Humberto I, who, according to him, 'was an exile who ended up ascending the throne' and promoted 'the greatest well-being to the country which he governed'.[7]

We can presume, by his impassioned references to, and defence of, the constitution (although he never went into the individual merit of its articles and paragraphs), that the prince was familiar with it. The same can be said – and here the evidence is abundant – in relation to the Scriptures. We have already seen the possible influence of the historical books of the Old Testament (in particular, Samuel 9, 15–18), when the prince attempted to explain the divine origin of kings. He often finished his articles with a phrase in Latin, taken from the second book of the Pentateuch, when the God of Abraham, Isaac and Jacob appeared to Moses, a humble goatherd, in a burning bush and entrusted him with the onerous mission of liberating his people who were suffering under the captivity of the Egyptian pharaoh. He would free them 'and bring them up out of that land unto a good land and a large, unto a land flowing with milk and honey'. The theme clearly attracted the attention of the prince, because he could identify with the question of captivity in a foreign land. When Moses asked his name, God said to him: *Ego Sum Qui Sum* ('I am what I am') 'and he said, Thus shalt thou say unto the children of Israel, I AM hath sent me unto you.' And God continues, 'this is my name for ever, and this is my memorial unto generations' (Exodus 3, 1–22). '*Ego sum qui sum*', therefore, that which is by the essence and necessity of nature. The prince understood the passage as the true stamp of authority. '*I am what I am*', by the right of God, an expression which he translated both into Yoruba and into Portuguese by 'the son of a king is king'.[8]

These examples seem sufficient for us to understand the importance of the Bible in the prince's written sources. It seems clear that no other book would have exercised a comparable influence on Dom Obá II d'Africa's thinking and overall vision of the world. We will return to this question later in this chapter. For the moment, as a general evaluation of his bibliographic sources, we might picture his likely library, carefully arranged in a corner of his attic. If such a 'library' did exist, the Holy Bible would have been its centrepiece. We can only speculate as to the other books in his collection: *O Navio Negreiro*, by his contemporary Castro Alves; *Os Lusíadas*, by the great Luís de Camões; perhaps a volume of Victor Hugo and a life of the black Saint, Saint Benedict.

Even if it had been more extensive, such a library, such reading, still seems little to explain the entire thinking and vision of Dom Obá II d'Africa. Although he left a relatively large written documentation, the prince lived in and witnessed a world which was basically oral, the pre-literary world of the slaves, freedmen and free men of colour of the capital of the Empire.

A Popular History of Brazil

Far more than any other written source the prince gained his inspiration from the font of traditions and experiences of the black and mixed race people of the New World. His writings reveal the existence of an historical memory of Brazil, rudimentary though it was, which was transmitted from generation to generation among slaves, freedmen and free men of colour. Although he may not have had any history books in his 'likely library', the prince had reasonably detailed information and even his own interpretation of, above all, the post-Independence period.

For example, he was particularly well informed on the *Sabinada*,

Also had popular knowledge of Brazilian history

the Bahian separatist (or federalist) movement of 1837 led by a mulatto, Medical Doctor Francisco Sabino da Rocha Vieira. The prince's source was probably his own father, Yoruba Benvindo, who, at the time of the *Sabinada*, would have been a slave or a freedman in the city of São Salvador. Yet whatever his source of information, the prince had received a version very different from the official version of the rebellion. For him, 1837 was a conflict between 'true Brazilians' on the one hand and the 'ingrates and false ones of the fatherland' on the other. On the side of right, according to the prince, were the black and miscegenated population of Salvador, 'blacks and *pardos* of the order of General Bigode, major Felisberto, Calado, Sabino who was president of the province of Bahia at the time, the black creole Neves and many others'. As a result of this struggle and the long period of regression that followed, the prince wrote, 'it is rare that you see a black or a *pardo* bearing a sword', not just in Bahia, but throughout Brazil.[9]

Further back in time there was the fight for the independence of Bahia, a battle that brought together, under the same banner, not just representatives of the local elite (plantation owners, prominent traders, clerics, military officers and intellectuals) but also free men of colour, freedmen and even some escaped slaves. The prince remembers, perhaps because of this great social confraternization, 'the patriotic days of that Bahia of July 2nd where I was born'.[10]

On the wider plane of national politics, the prince knew and admired the achievements of José Bonifácio de Andrada e Silva, Brazil's 'Patriarch of Independence' and the empire's first prime minister. In the General Constitutional and Legislative Assembly of 1823, while setting up the political organization of a new national state, Andrada e Silva also called for the urgent abolition of the African trade (within four or five years) and of slavery itself, 'in order', he explained, 'that we may be able, in a few generations, to form a homogeneous nation, without which we shall never be truly free, respectable and happy'. Although such thinking was in tune with the general ideas of freedom and equality which had guided and inspired the movement for separation from Portugal, it was to lead the patriarch to political ostracism.[11]

To ostracism, certainly, but not to being forgotten by the people, as Dom Obá II d'Africa and other isolated references show. In truth, in the 1880s, the better-informed slaves, freedmen and free men of colour held Andrada e Silva in great respect, not just for his role in Independence but also attributing to him the integrating conquests written into the Constitution of the Empire. It was this oral tradition that the prince echoed in 1886 when he praised Andrada e Silva for his nation-building achievements: 'our José Bonifácio, with his fluent tongue, leading the people on to great deeds'.[12] Another example of the potency of this oral tradition is supplied by another free man of colour or freedman, an anonymous contemporary of the prince, who, in 1883, was said to have knocked on Andradas' door and asked permission to come in and pay his last respects to Antônio Carlos Ribeiro de Andrada, the patriarch's brother, who was on his death bed. They asked why he had come. 'Don't you see my colour?' he replied. 'If it were not for the Andradas, what would we be in Brazil? It was they who gave us a country.'[13] Not just Nabuco, but the abolitionists in general knew this oral tradition and used it for their own propaganda. In this sense, it is worth quoting the powerful lines from Castro Alves anti-slavery poem, O Navio Negreiro, which the prince admired so much:

> Andrada! tira esse pendão dos ares!
> Colombo! fecha a porta dos teus mares![14]
>
> (Andrada! Lower this flag from the skies
> Columbus! close the portals of your seas!)

It seems, however, that the prince was less well-informed on earlier history, before the arrival of his father. He knew, in effect, something about that great Portuguese voyage in 1500 when Captain Pedro Alvares Cabral discovered and took possession of the 'Isle of Vera Cruz'. The central stage of Brazil's inaugural event was, once again, the prince's adored native province, 'the first land of Cabral'.[15] But from then onwards, over the next three long centuries of colonial history that followed the discovery, it seems that the prince knew little. For example, the question of the origin of slavery was very nebulous for the prince of the people. His father Benvindo doubtless knew the institution in Africa. If we can trust in Benvindo's royal origin, then he knew slavery first as an African master, second as a Brazilian slave, and finally, as a freedman. We can suppose that for Benvindo, slavery was part of that 'natural order of things', that wider panorama found within every society which did not require an explanation. The prince, however, needed to know the 'origin', because he wanted it to have an 'end'. Although he did not have any information (either oral or written) on the subject, the prince believed that soon after discovery all the ordinary people in Brazil, blacks and whites alike, were slaves. 'Nobody is unaware', he wrote, that both the Portuguese and Africans came to Brazil 'all as foreigners subject to the slavery fabricated by Spain and Portugal'. In consequence, the transition to freedom was not just a contemporary question, but the very backbone of the history of Brazil, the land of liberty. First of all the whites had, 'as the more civilized, freed themselves by their own efforts.' Now it was the turn of the blacks and browns to free themselves as his father Benvindo had done, 'by his hard labour, his only protection that of Providence'. This explanation seemed, for the prince, to fill the gap between the oral tradition and the nationalist rhetoric disseminated at the time (above all in Bahia) that explained independence as the 'liberation of Brazilians' who, until then, had been subject to 'exploitation' and 'slavery' from the old metropolis. If the Brazilians had freed themselves from the 'slavery' of Portugal and Spain, who could, fifty years later, deny the same right to the black and miscegenated population? For the prince, it was more a moral dilemma than a political one. 'How could they want these sons to deny their forebears, as we are seeing?' he wrote in 1882. How could they not continue to free the slaves completely, down to the 'few old Africans who remain?' It was at this point that the prince's indignation, for the first and only time, overruled his sense of being Brazilian when he considers not only 'old Africans', but blacks in general as 'foreigners'. Why did not all enjoy equal civil rights? 'Can it be because white Brazilians only want to cheat the foreigners of their true rights because they know they are the strongest and bravest workers?' 'Can it be', he continued, 'that Brazilians will always be doctors, priests and engineers, seeing that they never undertake manual labour, and ... that ... the blacks and browns ... are only good for hanging their heads low as cornet players and private soldiers?'[16] 'Can it be?' asked the prince.

The Search for Truth

Besides that relatively restricted popular history of Brazil to which the prince had access, he was steeped in the rich Portuguese–African–Brazilian oral tradition, which by that time had become the common cultural heritage among slaves, freedmen and free men of colour, who expressed themselves in verse, in fables and, above all, in proverbs. These were not mere figures of rhetoric, but the basic, underlying precepts, the theoretical-methodological parameters through which the prince made his analysis of reality. 'When the truth is missing', goes a Yoruba proverb, 'we ride towards discovery on proverbs'; or, as another proverb was to describe it, 'The proverb is the driving force in a discussion.' We are, thus, dealing with something that in Yoruba culture – a very relevant heritage for the prince – is clearly perceived as a theoretical tool for understanding reality, 'the driving force' of argument and discovery. The Reverend Samuel Johnson, doyen of Yoruba historiography, made extensive use of proverbs in his *History*, above all in the chapter on the traditional manners and customs of the people. As he states in his preface, Johnson, who was also a Yoruba from Oyo, stopped writing in 1897.[17] Nearly half a century later, in 1939, Dr Nathaniel Akinremi Fadipe presented a PhD thesis in the University of London in which he explicitly defended the role of proverbs in Yoruba culture, especially in his chapter on social psychology. 'Most frequently', he wrote, 'the proverb is used in bringing out clearly the meaning of obscure points in arguments. Thus, to the Yoruba, "the proverb is the driving force in a discussion". If an argument becomes entangled, the proverb is used to restore clarity.' He continues,

knowledge of proverbs is evenly distributed throughout the population, and it is not the possession of only a few wise men. The average Yoruba punctuates his remarks at intervals with proverbs and he would make use of, at least, half-a-dozen proverbs in the course of a day.

Proverbs were thus an inextricable part of the education and socialization of the Yoruba youngster, of his introduction to the codes, customs and beliefs of society.[18]

In Brazil, too, proverbs had a decisive role in the process of socializing slaves, freedmen and free men of colour, whether they were Yoruba, Sudanese or Bantu. For many, abandoned to their fates in a slave society, this was virtually all the education they had. In this school of life, as another Yoruba saying has it, the acquisition of knowledge seems to have depended not just on the opportunities that were available but also on the effect of each one in seizing them. 'If you never offer palm-wine to your uncle', goes the saying, demonstrating the customary respect for the elders, 'you will not learn many proverbs.'

In his writings, the prince helped fix this age-old wisdom, which embodied the ethical parameters, world-view and hopes of the slaves, freedmen and free men of colour, giving them an historical date and a precise social substratum. Examining the proverbs which the prince used in accordance with the needs of his arguments, one is immediately struck by the positive philosophy that they embody, a basically optimistic and confident way of seeing the world. This philosophy of life was noted by Charles Darwin when he visited Rio de Janeiro in 1832 during his famous study tour on board the *Beagle*. 'It is impossible to see a negro and not to feel kindly towards him ... such cheerful, open, honest expression and such fine muscular bodies,' he wrote. Indeed, he was so impressed that when he returned to England, where the debate on the abolition of colonial slavery was in progress, he was a more convinced abolitionist than ever before. After getting to know the people of Rio, he wrote, 'I have seen enough of slavery and the dispositions of the negroes, to be thoroughly disgusted with the lies and nonsense one hears on the subject in England.'[19]

Half a century later, returning to the Yoruba proverbs, one can gain a deeper understanding of the qualities that struck Darwin during his brief stay. That population knew that 'there is no victory without a great battle'. On this point, the prince even went so far as to invert the meaning of another traditional saying, probably of Portuguese origin, by removing the 'no'. 'Against force, there *is* resistance,' insisted the ever-optimistic prince, certain that 'the devil is not as strong as God' and 'when God wills, even plain water is medicine.'[20] In respect of the hardships of life, the prince expressed a deep-rooted practical sense, the certainty, as he put it, 'that nobody is immune to the falsities of life'.[21] What has recently been termed 'the virtue of contentment' or 'the negative capability' is present in innumerable Yoruba proverbs and held to be essential to social and political stability. 'Having been made a king you begin to prepare a lucky charm,' goes one of them. 'Do you want to be made a god?' Or, in the same vein: 'The fowl eats corn, drinks water and swallows pebbles, yet she complains she has no teeth; does a goat which has teeth eat iron?'[22] The prince shared this philosophy. For example, when he addressed those who were plotting against the reigning institutions, he issued a plea for calm, saying that 'if things are bad with God, they will be worse with the devil who is the enemy of the spirit ...'[23]

In the political sphere, he seems to have been well-prepared to deal with empty promises. The prince endorsed the saying that 'great men with good hearts are known by their acts' and not by their fine words.[24] It was with this in mind that, in 1882, he classified the wages policy the Liberals had drawn up for 'public and private' workers as being *para inglês ver* (for an Englishman's eyes).[25] For the prince, as for the average worker in the period of the transition, a wages policy was needed because 'those who work deserve just payment'.[26] Once again, in relation to the treasonous political scenario of the last quarter-century, the prince was very well aware 'that not all truths can be spoken'[27]; that 'the dead do not speak' (implying: be careful what you say otherwise you might meet an untimely end); and that 'every betrayal only becomes known after it has been committed'. Because of this, tact was essential. 'What saves us, the creoles of Bahia', he explained 'is that we are wise old monkeys who do not fall into traps.' These ever-prudent Bahians knew that in the Brazilian empire, 'when a monkey scratches itself, it is asking to be shot at' (in other words, if you are defenceless, keep still and be quiet).[28]

This was an ancient piece of advice. The social virtue of patience, the wisdom of the weak, seems to have occupied a place of honour in Yoruba culture. Both Rev. Johnson, who researched and wrote between 1877 and 1897 and Dr N.A. Fadipe, writing in 1939, recognized patience as being one of the basic behavioural traits in traditional culture. As a virtue, patience should evidently not be mistaken for cowardice. For Johnson, the proverb which best embodies this 'trait of character' is, 'One who has not grasped the handle of his sword should not attempt to avenge the death of his father.' Fadipe offers an alternative saying: 'Keep the blood down in the system and spit out white saliva.' According to Johnson,

> no nation is more remarkable for cautiousness and for putting themselves generally on the safe side. When powerless they would submit to oppression and wrong to any extent so long as they find resistance useless; but when an opportunity offers for asserting their rights and overthrowing their oppressors, they are never slow to embrace it.[29]

The ideal of justice seems to have been equally important. The prince held that in a free society it should be the value of each which distinguishes individuals and not considerations of race or material riches. For him, knowledge was more precious than money. 'The gift of science ... is the greatest jewel of mankind', and 'science is the greatest asset' and, to underline his point, 'gold is worth nothing'. Against discrimination in general, not just of colour, he drew on that vast store of Brazilian popular knowledge built up over the preceding centuries. Within this moral philosophy of the poor, the colour of a man's skin was no yardstick of value. Thus, as the prince argued, in a single paragraph, 'when a man has value, you don't notice his colour'; 'you will be recognized for your value alone'; 'only the deserving will be rewarded'; 'you will receive according to what you deserve'.[30]

Such a train of thought – fruit of a multi-racial society – was current long before the prince's time, pre-dating the 'theory of whitening' which, as we have seen, was becoming established during his lifetime under the influence of the new ethnocentric ideas. In 1821, a year before Independence, an obscure leaflet, written in a popular style, argued for exactly those same ideas of equality among men who should be valued and distinguished by their moral and intellectual qualities. The author identified himself as coming from the São Francisco river valley, possibly, like the prince himself, from the hinterland of Bahia. Unlike the prince, however, he was white, in the original Brazilian conception of what that meant. 'It is necessary to observe ... that I am white', he begins candidly, 'despite the fact that one of my nicknames is "Moreno" [a Brazilian racial description meaning a coffee-skinned person with straight dark hair].' He explained, 'it does not hurt to put a comb through my hair.' Once again, it is the voice of the Brazilian racial experience speaking. He takes examples from history and the common-sense precepts of his own time to defend, in synthesis, that 'the Blacks ... are susceptible to all the good and bad sentiments, to dignified and great deeds as well as to low and dreadful deeds, in just the same way as we, the whites, are.'[31]

At the end of the nineteenth century, the same idea can be found in the most varied popular manifestations throughout Brazil. The following lines of north-eastern challenge, collected at the beginning of the twentieth century by Leonardo Mota, are notable for their similarity to the prince's:

Isso de cor e bobagem,
A cor branca é vaidade
O homem só se conhece
Por sua capacidade
Pela *pronunça* correta
E pela moralidade

(This colour business is nonsense
The colour white is vanity
A man is only known
For his capacity
To pronounce words correctly
And for his morality)

And

Você falou em Caim?
Já me subiu um calor!
Nesta nossa raça preta
Nunca teve um traidor:
Judas sendo um homen branco,
Foi quem traiu Nosso Senhor ...

(You spoke of Cain?
I'm already heating up!
This black race of ours
Has never bred a traitor:
It was Judas, a white man,
Who betrayed Our Lord ...)[32]

To the common citizen-soldier, slavery was nothing more than a discrimination among Brazilians, the work of heartless men, the eternal supporters of 'God for me and the devil for the rest.' The prince and his people, on the contrary, were God-fearing and knew that 'he who lives by the sword dies by it' and that 'pursuing and killing is for God alone'. To those who insulted them, they were even able to say, 'Pity them for they know not what they do'.[33]

The pacifist prince – a *Filho de Ghandi avant la lettre* – believed in the force of ideas. 'The element of war is the sword', he liked to explain, 'the element of my triumph has to be my pen'.[34] A profound spirit, he rued superficial men who lived their lives 'like the butterfly, which flutters from flower to flower without appreciating the perfume of any of them'.[35] When confronted with men like this, above all those who dealt in intrigue, he would exclaim, like he did wearily in 1883, 'Ah! God of pity and goodness, what a world!'[36]

A Choice of Faith

For that prince of the black diaspora, the voice of God and religion made itself heard through diverse cultural traditions. Galvão, the Brazilian, however, does not seem to have had any doubt as to his fundamental choice of faith. As he himself saw it, he was a Catholic prince. Not just because Catholicism was the official state religion, but because of its concrete and fundamental influence on his thinking and way of seeing the world. In August 1874, for example, when he thought he deserved a decoration for his bravery in battle, his dream was to receive the *Ordem de Cristo* decoration, because, as he explained it, 'I am Catholic'.[37] As a good Catholic, he saw that his children were baptized. In 1882, he solemnly announced to the emperor the birth and forthcoming baptism of his heir, Vincente Abiodun da Fonseca Galvão.[38] When he was widowed, like a good Catholic, he paid for a mass to be celebrated in memory of his 'virtuous wife', Raiza-me de Abiodun, a name both Bantu and Yoruba.[39]

A God-fearing man, the prince believed in eternal life for the just and the good. On the death of Conselheiro Ernesto Ferreira Franca to whom the prince attributed a decisive role in the abolition of whipping, he wrote, 'he did not die . . . his soul has flown to the feet of God.' For him, life was both 'a suffering' and 'a dream'. Death, on the other hand, besides being 'inevitable', was the true 'rest'.[40] In 1883, the prince drew on both Catholic and Yoruba tradition when he spoke out vehemently against 'the bad invention of cremation', which some were at that time considering introducing to the empire in order to modernize the burial procedure. Human beings, he said, were not 'pigs' to be 'roasted'.[41]

It seems clear that the image that most struck the prince was the resignation and humility of Christ, persecuted and crucified by men 'because of their envy that he was a king of the world and a wise man'.[42] Like Our Lord Jesus Christ, the prince also carried, year after year, 'his heavy Cross', as he put it.[43] He was probably inspired by the dramatic statue of *Nosso Senhor Bom Jesus dos Passos*, the patron saint of diamond prospectors, in his hometown Lençóis: a Christ doubled under the weight of the cross with a crown of thorns crushed down on real human hair and open wounds. The prince must have been familiar with the statue and probably also saw its festive arrival from Portugal on 2 February 1852, when it was carried to the church on the left bank of the River Lençóis, almost facing the Praça das Nagôs, where it has remained until this day. The date is still celebrated with fireworks and a procession, attracting rural pilgrims from miles around who arrive in the town crammed into overcrowded trucks.[44]

Another important influence was that of Saint Benedict the Black. Born in 1526 on an estate near Messina in Sicily, Saint Benedict was the son of a slave, probably a Nubian. Like so many in the kingdom of Dom Obá, he was illiterate and worked modestly in the kitchen of the Franciscan friary at Palermo. Despite his humble position, he distinguished himself for his virtue and saintliness and went on to become the superior and, in 1578, novice-master of his congregation. Saint Benedict was canonized in 1807, his story and example passed on orally among slaves, freedmen and free men of colour throughout the empire. By the end of the nineteenth century and the beginning of the twentieth, many free men made an affirmation of faith and negritude by baptizing their sons after São Benedito, thus establishing a strong link throughout Brazil between the name and the race. Saint Benedict, a saint of the Catholic Church, seems to have been a strong argument in the affirmation of fundamental equality between the blacks, whites and browns of the Brazilian empire. 'Miraculous black saint', argued the prince. Because of his own merit and in the absence of discrimination, Saint Benedict 'had the right of being God's cook'.[45]

While an ardent Catholic, the prince did not abandon his ethnic religion. Everything that he wrote (and, as we will see later, the visual symbols that he adopted) seems to indicate that there was no serious conflict between that 'God of pity and goodness', the saints, including Saint Benedict, who surrounded Him in paradise and the prince's belief in *Olorun*, 'the owner of Heaven' and his emissaries to the world of men, the *orixás*. On the contrary, the prince understood that the word 'saint' was synonymous with *orixá*, both in expressions such as *pai do santo* and *mão do santo* ('saint father' and 'mother', a direct translation of the Yoruba '*babalorixá*' and '*ialorixá*) and in everything else that he wrote about the '*povo do santo*', that is, the 'saint people' or devotees of the '*orixás*. For example, in 1886, when he felt his honour as a 'black soldier' had been slighted, the prince thanked Saint Barbara, 'virgin of Africa', who had never denied him, 'strength enough to know calmly how to react'. He was also protected 'by the weapons of Ogun', who, as he explained it, 'is Saint George in Brazil'.[46]

From an historical point of view, it is interesting to note the identification between Saint Barbara and the powerful Alafin Xangô, warrior chief of a still legendary Oyo, justice-maker and avenger, the vain master of the two-edged sword and the 'lightning stones'. In this case, in contrast to the present-day practice, identification transcended gender. The rays of lightning were the fundamental feature. 'As sure as the rays of Saint Barbara, Virgin of Africa exist', the prince was fond of saying when he wanted to emphasize the truth of his words.[47]

Besides this identification, which in the prince's time was the one most commonly made in Rio de Janeiro, there existed variations from region to region and even from '*terreiro*' to '*terreiro*' – from one religious centre to another. Research by Nina Rodrigues, Manuel Querino, Artur Ramos and Edson Carneiro shows that in Bahia, Xangô was identified not just with Saint Barbara but also

with Saint Geronimus, Saint Michael and Saint John.[48] Today, both
in Rio and in Bahia, the identification with Saint Geronimus seems
to predominate. In present-day Cuba, however, the 'syncretism' with
Saint Barbara is still the dominant one, just as it was in Rio at the
time of the Prince.[49]

Saint George, a warrior wearing armour and bearing a shield and
an iron spear, is still, to this day, identified in Rio de Janeiro, Recife
and Porto Alegre, with *Ogum*, a civilizing god, *orixá* of technology
and iron, protector of smiths and soldiers. But in Bahia the prevailing
identification is not with *Ogum* but with *Oxossi*, *orixá* of hunting
and master of the forests.

Among the prince's ethnic beliefs were the divining methods of the
traditional Yoruba oracle, which consisted of casting cola nuts or
cowrie shells. For example, in 1887, during the period of fierce
political discontent and unrest on both left and right caused by the
progressive abolition of slavery, the prince perceived the danger in
the air, both to the institutions and to the monarch himself. From
then onwards, he openly confirmed the influence of the saints and
'the Oracle that Defends the Fatherland and the Divine Majesty' in
his political activities and writings. Judging by the content of these
articles, it seems that the shells had not forecast a propitious future
for the monarchy. First and foremost, Obá reminded his readers that
betraying the king was a sin. He opened each article by declaring, in
good creole, 'The gods have ordered that we do not betray the king.'
Addressing 'faithful subjects everywhere', he recommended many
prayers to God for the emperor's life and continued reign, just as he
himself was doing in his 'fervent African Prayers'.[50]

The meeting and interlacing of cultures was becoming increasingly
visible in the years following the war and progressive abolition. It
was at the end of this process that the prince, happy with the
abolition of slavery and the recovery of the emperor, decorated his
sublieutenant's uniform with 'African feathers' and set off for the
city palace. As we have seen, his exuberant symbolic gesture landed
him in prison. Despite the impropriety of the act of putting feathers,
or any other symbol, on a military uniform, it is interesting to note
that from the time of Dom Obá onwards cultural syntheses were to
end up imposing themselves as the very mark of Brazilian culture.
For example, the traditional *Ranchos de Reis*, the origin of the
escolas-de-samba, which I have mentioned earlier, became more
distanced from their old religious origin as every year went by.

FIGURE 2   The prince's official portrait, 1882

The Symbols

Another set of western and Yoruba symbols, deeply entwined, can be seen in the prince's 'official portrait', a type of family crest or stamp of authority, which he occasionally had published in the press or reproduced on his most solemn manuscripts such as the letter he wrote to the emperor in 1882 to communicate, officially, the birth of his son, Abiodun da Fonseca Galvão (see Figure 2). In the centre was the prince in his military uniform; around him, symmetrically arranged in pairs, western insignia (the dove of the Holy Spirit, the royal crown) and Yoruba ones (the fetishes of *Ogum* and *Oxossi*). In terms of the mental concepts built into these objects – that which is signified by the signifier – it is not easy to distinguish isolated cultural traits. As we have already seen in the prince's writings, the surviving African symbols and those with a western influence are not separate. Rather they form part of their own cultural complex, the fruit of the Brazilian historical process. The Holy Spirit, as the prince points out, is *Ossun* (*Oxum*); *Ogum*, as we have already mentioned, 'is Saint George'; 'Ochoce'

(*Oxossi*) was, throughout Rio's Court and up to the present day, Saint Sebastian, the patron saint of Rio de Janeiro.

We will look at the signs themselves, with their historical association of objects and meanings. The analysis of the 'African group' does not seem to present any difficulty in that both the symbols are well known to specialists today, not only in Brazil but also in Nigeria and Benin. On the right of the portrait, a horizontal line with the ends curved round and seven small vertical dashes emerging from it at regular intervals. This is clearly an abstract representation of the fetish known as *ferramenta de Ogum* ('Ogum's staff'). Ogum, one of the most worshipped and feared *orixás* of Yoruba culture, is the god of iron technology, protector of ironsmiths and, by extension, of the activities where iron implements are essential such as farming, hunting and, above all, war. Ogum can be represented by an iron sword or (if emphasizing the civilizing aspect of technology, as was the prince's case) by an iron staff or bow on which miniature arms and work implements were hung – a sword, spear, hammer, sickle, arrow head, and so on. There were nearly always 7 (Ogum's number according to many traditions), 14 or 21.

It is interesting to note that it is this *orixá* rather than any other that is placed at the right hand of the prince. According to tradition, as collected by Rev. Johnson, Ogum was established by the great King Abiodun as the specific *Orilé* (totem) of the Alafins of Oyo, the symbol of their long lineage.[51] The same symbol took on additional meaning in Brazil where *Ogum*, the iron warrior, became identified with Saint George, Christ's knight in shining armour who, with his spear and sword, conquered the dragon of evil. In the time of the prince, Saint George was the patron saint of Brazil, one of the country's national symbols, with a national day celebrated with solemn masses, processions and popular festivities.

The next symbol in the prince's 'crest' is the bow and arrow (also know as the *Ofá* or *Damatá*) of *Oxossi*, or *Odé*, the Yoruba god of the hunt. *Oxossi*, the 'King of the Forests' of Rio de Janeiro *macumba*, was identified with another important patron saint, Saint Sebastian , protector of the 'Most Loyal and Heroic City of Saint Sebastian of Rio de Janeiro', the Corte of the empire.

In the following group (the dove of the Holy Spirit and the royal crown), the Catholic dove is identified, as the prince pointed out, with *Oxum*. According to Yoruba tradition, *Oxum* was one of the queens of Oyo, the youngest, and probably the best loved, despite being the least faithful, wife of Xangô, the fourth *Alafin* of Oyo. After her death she became an *orixá* of good deeds, the goddess of the river Oxum and, by extension, of the fresh waters so essential to life, of fertility and a certain jovial feminine grace. Judging by the specialist literature, her historical identification with the Holy Spirit seems to have been entirely superseded and the identification prevailing today, whether in the *macumbas* of Rio, the *candomblés* of Bahia, the *Xangôs* of Recife or even in Cuba, is with one of the manifestations of the Virgin Mary, most frequently Nossa Senhora das Candeias, Nossa Senhora da Conceição, Nossa Senhora dos Prazeres and, in Cuba, Nossa Senhora de la Caridad del Cobre.[52]

It is also necessary to look at the question of models, the specific images which the prince used. We can suppose that particular *dove*, that particular *crown* could be read and understood immediately not just in Rio, but throughout the Empire. The way that the prince drew the dove could be understood from north to south of the country because of the highly popular *Bandeiras do Divino Espírito Santo* (flags of the Divine Holy Spirit) carried by the small processions, known as *Folias do Divino*. In the days preceding the 'Festa do Divino Espirito Santo' (Festival of the Divine Holy Spirit), the 'follas' went knocking from door to door, singing and beating drums as they went, asking for contributions for the festival. Both the festival and the *folias* had been extremely popular in the metropolis since the Middle Ages. They originated in fourteenth-century Portugal, started by Isabel, the sixth queen of Portugal (1271–1336), who later became Saint Isabel, during the building of the Espírito Santo church in Alenquer. The day of the Divine was ten days after the Thursday of the Ascension. The festivities were (and still are, in the few places where the tradition has not died out) presided over by an *Imperador do Divino* (Emperor of the Divine), a child or an adult chosen by the community who enjoyed regal powers for the day: in some parts of Brazil and Portugal he was even permitted to free prisoners. These festivities enjoyed such prestige and social importance throughout the colony that, according to the folklore expert Câmara Cascudo, they were the reason that Dom Pedro I chose the title of Emperor rather than King of Brazil after independence.[53]

In the same book as he writes about the prince, Melo Morais Filho describes the *folias* in the Rio de Janeiro of his time, with obvious dislike, as 'festive gangs of white, creole and *mestiço* youths'.[54]

The *folias* were also famous in Lençóis. In his novel *Bugrinha*, Afrânio Peixoto records some of the social aspects of the *Império do Divino* and also describes the dove on the flag, which was identical to the dove in Dom Obá's 'official portrait'. 'The contrite multitude draws near, kisses the red cloth of the sacred flag in whose middle

FIGURE 3   'O Príncipe Obá', drawing undated

there is a dove with open wings, gliding and irradiating the glory of the Holy Trinity in all directions.'[55]

Lastly, on the question of the *crown*, we can be briefer. There is no doubt that it is the same Christian crown as the one that appears on the early Brazilian flag, in the position today occupied by a blue globe containing the constellations and the motto Order and Progress. Exactly the same symbol, as I have shown in a recent work, was used as a tattoo in Rio de Janeiro at the beginning of this century which was popular among priests of *candomblé* and *macumba* as well as with many others of similar background to the prince.[56]

The importance of this 'official portrait' of the prince in his military uniform, surrounded by such powerful Brazilian symbols, cannot have escaped his contemporaries. Melo Morais Filho, for one, pondering the 'origin of the absolute, spontaneous submission' of slaves, freedmen and free men of colour to the authority of the prince, cited, among other reasons, the 'proclamations and manifestos (with portrait) published in the daily newspapers and read by one or the other in the shops or at home'.[57]

To end, we will return to the figure of the prince as he was described by his contemporaries, sporting his top hat, frock coat, trousers, black shoes, pince-nez, gloves, cane and umbrella; with his 'gigantesque' height, 'thick moustache' and 'pointed goatee' (Figure 3). All these fashionable accessories bring to mind Gilberto Freyre's (1959) definition of the canes used at the end of the nineteenth century and beginning of the twentieth as 'insignia' of belonging to the Brazilian elite. Beards and, above all, large moustaches twisted into points were equally potent badges of status.[58]

Besides this symbolism of the imperial elite that the prince adopted, item by item, there is the more specific question of the umbrella. Not that such an object was not part of upper-class elegance (the emperor himself was often seen walking in Petrópolis with his top hat, overcoat and black umbrella) but in the case of the prince, it is clearly a parallel symbolic code, not to the elegance of Rio, but to the privileges of the Obás. Contemporaries frequently refer to his 'exaggeration' in carrying both a cane and an umbrella, and to the 'gallantry' with which he wielded the latter. This can be seen in several caricatures of the time (Figure 4) and in an oil portrait painted by Belmiro de Almeida (1858–1935), dated 1886 and today in the collection of Ambassador João Hermes Pereira de Araújo in Rio de Janeiro (Figure 5). It was apparently this 'exaggeration' and 'gallantry', plus some other minor details, which identified the prince as something of an eccentric, 'with a physiognomy that is absolutely *sui-generis*', or 'an eminently characteristic personality'.[59]

The Rev. Samuel Johnson tackled the question of umbrellas, not in his chapter on 'manners and customs' but in the chapter on 'government', which deals with the nature of power. 'Umbrellas in this country are part and parcel of state paraphernalia,' he wrote in Oyo in 1897. In the time of the great Alafin Abiodun in the Old-Oyo and for many years subsequently, 'private individuals dared not use

FIGURE 4   'Aventura de Sua Alteza o Principe Ubá 2 da Africa', 1886

FIGURE 5   'Principe Oba', oil painting, 1886

an umbrella', which was the regalia of the Alafin. Johnson explains that this privilege only began to be contested during the long period of invasions and social instability, which followed the break-up of the Oyo empire. For the first time in the city of Ibadan, 'The war boys were allowed to enjoy themselves in any way they liked, and use any materials of clothing and ornament they could afford, as it might be for only a few days before they laid down their lives on a battlefield.' Even in the New-Oyo of Johnson's time, a period when cheap umbrellas were imported from Europe, 'those of a chief are easily distinguished now by their size and quality'. Many were decorated with 'certain emblems indicative of rank'.[60]

N. A. Fadipe also broached the subject in his 1939 doctoral thesis, including it in a chapter on the social psychology of the Yoruba, in the section on rivalry, imitation, leadership and inventiveness. Even at that time, the political symbolism was so strong and well defined that 'for many years even after the establishment of British rule, it was forbidden to any other person but the king to wear shoes made of beads or use an umbrella'. And, 'In some communities, after this prohibition was relaxed, it was still forbidden to anyone to go past the royal palace wearing shoes of this kind, or using an open umbrella.'[61] As recently as the 1940s, the symbolic question was to surface as the epicentre of a political crisis caused by the Mahadiyyat movement, an apparently rare case of pacifist Islamic millennialism studied by Peter Clarke. The 'large, wide, brightly coloured umbrella' used by the leader of the movement, the Mahadi-Messiah, was interpreted by the established powers and by the *Awujale* (king) of Ijebu-Ode to be a sign of 'disrespect' and 'insulting behaviour'.[62]

It is therefore not surprising that this, like other persistent symbols, should have been transplanted to the Brazilian empire and in particular to the regions where the Yoruba concentration was greater, such as Salvador and the small town of Lençóis. Half-way through the century, James Wetherell, the British Vice-Consul, was struck by 'the almost universal habit of carrying umbrellas'. Being a practical man, Wetherell soon copied the habit, adopting for himself the 'small protection of one of these despised sunshades'. It was an efficient way of avoiding 'a scorched nose or parched and cracked lips'. Wetherell does not seem to have realized the symbolic value of the object which he himself had started to carry, with true British dignity. But he did think it curious that 'even the blacks' who were accustomed to the tropical sun, 'readily avail themselves of an umbrella, as a luxurious article of their toilet'. At this time, umbrellas 'were imported in large quantities from Europe' and made 'of many different coloured silks', above all, in Salvador, of 'blue, crimson, and green with these tints intermixed'. In the interior of the province, where Lençóis was located, 'crimson' seems to have been the predominant colour.[63]

A relative abundance of photographs of freedmen and free men of colour dating from the end of the nineteenth century can be found in both public and private collections. They are almost invariably portrayed with their dignified umbrellas which, like Dom Obá's, seem to have been black. In Lençóis, we find this symbolism embodied in the very geography of the region in 'a legend from the time of slavery' (or, 'from the time of the *nagôs*'). It concerns an imposing inland cliff of great beauty, the *Morro do Pai-Inácio*. Composed of quartzite from the Paraguaçu series, the Pai-Inácio rises 500 metres above the surrounding countryside. From the peak, with its crest of thick vegetation, it plunges in steep precipices on all sides. The only way up is by one hidden trail. From its flat top, there is a splendid view of the surrounding region, with its beautiful range of spurs rising from the plain, stretching as far as the eye can see. The origin of the toponymy is the 'legend of Pai-Inácio', the story of a very special *nagô* slave, as is indicated by the title 'Pai', or Father, which was awarded only to the oldest slaves, those best versed in the traditions. But Pai-Inácio was young and owned an umbrella. More than this, he was involved in a secret affair with the plantation mistress, the '*sinhá-dona*' herself. When the affair was discovered, Inácio fled to the fields and hills with the enraged master in hot pursuit, leading a small army of '*valentões*' (hired assassins), '*jagunços*' (thugs) and '*capitães-do-mato*' (slave-hunters) all keen to prove themselves and be the one to pull the trigger in this backlands vendetta of honour. Pai Inácio seems to have defied not just his master, but the whole system. Finally, they tracked him down to his hiding place, the escarpment which was to bear his name. Unable to escape down the single trail, Pai-Inácio was faced with the abyss. At the last moment he saved himself, leaping into space, his umbrella opened aloft like a parachute.[64]

Conclusion

In the preceding chapters we have studied the life and thinking of one nineteenth-century Brazilian and, through him, attempted to glimpse the society and culture in which he lived, a world that was still inhabited by masters, slaves, freedmen and free men of colour.

This Brazil was swept away by the abolition of slavery on 13 May 1888. In the perception of many, even the stones in the province and city of Rio de Janeiro trembled that day. In the Largo do Paço a crowd estimated at 10,000, larger than had ever been seen before, waited for the signing of the law, shouting '*Vivas*' to the Princess Regent, or 'Queen' as the simpler folk called her. 'The music played, the people embraced each other ... and everyone everywhere bustled with joy,' wrote one journalist. A 'man of colour' carried a placard declaring 'Long Live Abolition'. The majority could not write out placards; instead, they decorated their hats and clothes with sprigs of Independence, a green and yellow tropical tree, which had gained its name in 1822. Some brandished branches of Independence, stripping the gardens of the city bare.

It was a memorable occasion and few managed to sleep that night. When dawn broke the next day, several districts had been festooned with decorations; it was 'a rare house' which had not been strung with bunting. The Chamber of Deputies, realizing that the city had been taken over by the people and wanting to 'associate itself with the movement of celebration', suspended its sessions until the 16th. On the morning of the 17th an open air mass was celebrated in the rain in the Campo de São Cristóvão for a crowd calculated at 20,000 people. The days went by but the enthusiasm did not abate. Besides the banquets held by the abolitionist elite, for which it was necessary to have a written invitation, there were free performances in the theatres, free races at the Derby Club, an open air ball on Largo do Paço, school parades, and other events. The celebrations continued to Sunday, 20 May, when there was a 'big civic march', 6 km long, with representatives of 'all the classes' of Rio de Janeiro. 'It was as if an enemy in occupation had suddenly evacuated, leaving us free and independent, in possession of our fatherland!' Joaquim Nabuco is reported to have said. 'It was like breaking out of total darkness into a spring day,' said a contemporary.[1]

History cannot ignore the impact of such changes. The law had decreed that masters were no longer masters; slaves no longer slaves. The distinction between 'freedmen' and 'free men of colour' no longer existed. Brazil had finally been redeemed from inequality. 'Capitães-do-mato' were no longer needed, slave quarters were now dormitório dos camaradas ('dormitories of comrades'). It was the old world turned upside down.

Further inland, on the hillside coffee plantations, former slaves sung a simple chorus, over and over again, for three days and nights:

> Eu pisei na pedra, pedra balanceou
> Mundo tava torto, Rainha endireitou!
>
> (I stepped on the stone, the stone tottered
> The world was twisted, the Queen straightened it!)[2]

Things were happening so fast that it was difficult to keep pace. Four months later, in the city of Rio de Janeiro itself, a small advertisement appeared in the newspaper O Paiz offering, 'For rent: a free person to cook' which elicited the criticism of another newspaper: 'What the hell! Do we still have slaves in Brazil?'[3]

No. Neither slaves nor masters existed. Both had to find their proper place within a new society whose rules were as yet untested. It is not by chance that two telling phrases emerged during this period: the senhorial: 'Você Sabe com quem está falando?' ('Do you realize whom you are speaking to?') used by the former masters to impose their authority;[4] and, equally important, the reply: 'Tão bom como tão bom' ('Equal to the best', implying 'I'm as good as you').

'"Equal to the best" is the phrase on the tip of the tongue of low-class individuals, because everyone considers themselves equal ... and no one wants to obey,' observed the Viscount of São Boaventura, particularly impressed with the city of Rio de Janeiro, where he considered there was no longer any 'respect' or 'order'.[5]

Indeed, after 13 May, it seemed that there was no longer any place for former political fidelities in the Brazilian empire. 'To the extent that joy reigns in the Empire, in some rural districts, the farmers conspire against the State and declare themselves Republicans', denounced a cartoon by Angelo Agostini, published just two weeks after the signing of the law, showing coffee planters quickly swapping their Panama hats for red Republican caps.[6]

In the city of Rio de Janeiro, the chief topic of conversation, from the top to the bottom of the social scale, in the streets, the trams, the coffee houses and even in the kitchens among the domestic staff, was 'the art of governing peoples'. 'Sometimes, when we are reading a newspaper, relaxing in our dining room', wrote a contemporary 'we hear ingenuous voices from the region of the cooker saying that the Republicans are against the Princess because she signed the abolition.' In the kitchens, as in the living rooms, 'imaginations' were 'full to the brim with governmental crises ... bloody elections ... impossible dissolutions'.[7]

In Little Africa too, the new situation brought challenges. Here as well, there was no space for the old political loyalties, nor even for princes of the people. Dom Obá II d'Africa's kingdom began to disintegrate. The decline of his authority was evident, particularly in his diminished capacity for levying revenue from his subjects. He practically disappeared from the paid columns of the newspapers, publishing only one article in 1888 and another in 1889 compared to the 35 between 1886 and 1887. The letters of support, which had totalled six between 1886 and 1887, vanished, as if by magic.

As one newspaper put it, 'The anarchy of free ideas ... began to bring everyone to the same level and rebellion began to appear amongst those who had so greatly ... listened and contributed' to Dom Obá II d'Africa. On 12 November 1889, a mere 18 months after abolition, the prince found himself in an ugly brawl with two men and two women in a desperate attempt to assert his waning authority. It took place in a modest house on Rua da Prainha and the only information available comes from the crime pages of the newspapers. Challenged by the 'African people', the prince fiercely defended his prerogatives, hammering the traitors with 'his umbrella and cane wielded as a single weapon'. When the police arrived, it was the prince, and not his challengers, who was arrested.[8]

Three days later, on 15 November, the emperor himself was to fall. Seventeen days after that, the prince donned his full dress uniform, sword and plumed hat to lead 'the shrill' protest march that was to be his last public act in the streets of Rio de Janeiro.

A few months later the newspapers were to report, 'alone in the world, abandoned by all those who had once, reverent and humble, bowed themselves to him, Dom Obá has succumbed to Death's scythe'.

'Let the earth not weigh heavy on him', requested the anonymous author of his obituary, 'because his glories will remain in this world to be recounted to the peoples of Africa, of whom this eccentric prince was a most rare example.'[9]

Appendices

Appendix A

Letter in which Alferes Cândido da Fonseca Galvão claims that he finds himself unable to find means of subsistence as a consequence of wounds suffered in combat in the Paraguayan campaign and asks for a pension and a decoration (1874), ASE, Cândido da Fonseca Galvão file.

Imperial Senhor
Saldando a Vossa Magestade Imperial vem com profundo respeito um dos súditos do excelso trono de Vossa Magestade com a presente carta, cujo seu conteudo é primeiro felicitar a Vossa Majestade e Sua Augusta Família Imperial, pela qual invoco ao Altíssimo Deus onipotente amplas prosperidades e vigorosa saúde para amparo de seus súditos, vassalos e sustentáculo da Nação brasileira. Senhor em 1865 tendo sido agredida e vilipendiada a honra e integridade Nacional, pelo déspota ex-governo do Paraguai, inspirado pelo Sacrossanto amor do Patriotismo alistei-me como verdadeiro soldado nas fileiras das valentes falanges dos briosos Voluntários da Pátria que marcharam depois que me achava na referida Companhia feito em diversos combates, tive de lamentar a perca de minha extremosa mãe que sucumbiu cheia de dores e aflições em consequência eu ter marchado para guerra em defesa da Pátria, além desta perda sensível exauri os pequenos pecúnios pecuniários que podia dispor para minha subsistência. Sendo ferido em combate fiquei inutilizado da mão direita, que priva-me grangear o pão para subsistir-me e minha família como provo com os atestados do distinto Dr. em medicina e outros [illegible] e diretor da faculdade de Medicina da Bahia [illegible] que sirvo de arrimo a um pai com idade 87 anos, que há nove anos se acha em um leito de dor sofrendo de moléstia incurável; que desde a idade de 15 anos que tem prestado serviços ao país não tendo tido compensação alguma. Vossa Magestade, atendendo os meus serviços na Campanha concedeu-me as honras de Alferes do Exército, porém me achando inválido também sou

digno de uma pensão e sem esta, não posso viver com dignidade como exige a minha pequena posição na sociedade por isso imploro a Vossa Magestade Imperial a graça de conceder-me uma posição correspondente ao meu posto, assim como uma honra honorífica preferindo o oficialato da Ordem de Cristo por ser a legião da minha Pátria Católica Romana a qual professo. Confio no magnânimo Espírito de Vossa Magestade Imperial espero as graças empetradas. O humilde súdito de Vossa Majestade Imperial.

Rio de Janeiro 16 de maio de 1874.

Cândido da Fonseca Galvão
Alferes Honorário

Imperial Senhor

Hailing Your Imperial Majesty, one who is a subject of the excelsius throne of Your Majesty approaches you with profound respect to present this letter, in which the contents are first to wish happiness upon Your Majesty and Your August Imperial Family, for which I invoke omnipotent God on High to bestow ample prosperities and vigorous health upon you, for the support of your subjects, vassals and the sustenance of the Brazilian nation. Senhor, in 1865, when National honour and integrity was assaulted and vilely sullied by the despotic former government of Paraguay, inspired by the Sacrosanct love of Patriotism, I enlisted as a true soldier in the ranks of the valiant phalanges of the brave *Voluntários da Pátria* who marched to war. After I found myself in the above-mentioned Company and proved myself in various battles, I had to lament the loss of my most loving mother who succumbed, full of pains and afflictions as a result of my having marched to war in defence of the Fatherland, besides this considerable loss, I exhausted the modest, pecuniary savings that I had for my subsistence. Having been wounded in combat, I was unable to use my right hand, which deprived me of earning the daily bread for the subsistence of myself and my family as I offer proof with the testaments of the distinguished Dr. in medicine and others [illegible] and director of the Bahia faculty of Medicine [illegible] that I support an 87-year-old father who for the past nine years has been on a bed of pain suffering from an incurable disease; that from the age of 15 I have served the country without receiving any compensation. Your Majesty, to attend my service in the Campaign you conceded me the honours of an Army Sublieutenant, however, finding myself an invalid I am also worthy of a pension and without such, I cannot live with the dignity that my modest position in society requires and for this I implore Your Imperial Majesty the grace of conceding me a position befitting my rank, as well as an honorary honour, in preference membership of the Order of Christ for being the legion of my Roman Catholic Fatherland that I profess to. I trust in the magnanimous Spirit of Your Imperial Majesty, I await the asked for graces. The humble subject of Your Imperial Majesty.

Rio de Janeiro 16 May 1874

Cândido da Fonseca Galvão
Honorary Sublieutenant

Appendix B

Letter to Dom Pedro II, 1882, MIP, Manuscript Archives, Bundle 187, document 8473.

Senhor
Como subdito obediente e devotado servidor de Vossa Magestade Imperial, venho communicar a Vossa Magestade Imperial que foi Deus servido abençoar o meu consórcio, concedendo-me um filho, que viu a luz no dia 22 do corrente, e que troce o nome de Vicente Abiodum da Fonseca Galvão, e se eu for feliz em chegar crial-lo e chegar a ser homem, como espero da Divina Providência, terá Vossa Magestade Imperial n'elle um tão devotado servidor e tão obediente subdito, quanto eu me honro e préso de ser. Communico também a Vossa Magestade Imperial que o dicto meu filho vai receber o sacramento do baptismo no dia 4 do proximo mez de fevereiro, sendo seu Padrinho meu primo o Príncipe de Oyó, que aqui chegou no vapor em que vieram suas Altezas os Senhores Conde d'Eu e a Sereníssima Virtuosa Princeza Imperial. Por esta occasião, peço reverentemente permissão a Vossa Magestade Imperial, para fazer publicar pela imprensa o Manifesto que meus subditos africanos dirigem a todas as nações da terra, e especialmente aos povos de oyó e Eubá,[1] na África, reconhecendo meu filho como Príncipe do referido Estado e meu herdeiro com o nome Africano da realeza a que pertence de Obá 3°.

Peço finalmente perdão a Vossa Magestade Imperial por servir-me d'este meio para fazer a communicação e o pedido supra, em razão de achar-se Vossa Magestade Imperial ausente d'esta cidade.

Deus conserve a precioza saúde e a vida de Vossa Magestade, de Sua Magestade a Imperatriz e de toda a Família Imperial como todos os Brasileiros havemos mister. Sou, Senhor, com o mais profundo respeito De Vossa Magestade Imperial reverente e submisso subdito.

Rio de Janeiro 31 de Janeiro de 1882.

Cândido da Fonseca Galvão Alferes Honorário do Exército Brasileiro, Príncipe Obá 2° d'Africa.

---

1. 'Povos de Oyó e Eubá' [Egba]   Related sub-groups of the Yoruba-speaking people. According to Rev. S. Johnson, 'all the principal families of the Egbas trace their origin from Oyo, hence the common saying "Egbas who have no their root in Oyo are slaves"'. Cf. *The History of the Yorubas*, pp. 15–18.

Senhor

As an obedient subject and devoted servant of Your Imperial Majesty, I come to communicate to Your Imperial Majesty that God has seen fit to bless my union, granting me a son, who was born on the 22nd of this month and who goes by the name of Vicente Abiodum da Fonseca Galvão, and if I should be fortunate enough to be able to bring him up and see him become a man, as I hope that Divine Providence will allow, Your Imperial Majesty will have in him as devoted a servant and as obedient a subject as I honour and pride myself to be. I also communicate to Your Imperial Majesty that my aforementioned son will receive the sacrament of baptism on the 4th of the upcoming month of February, his Godfather being my cousin the Prince of Oyó who arrived on the steamship in which the Highnesses the Senhor Conde d'Eu and the Most Serene and Virtuous Imperial Princess travelled. On this occasion, I reverently request Your Imperial Majesty's permission to publish in the press the Manifesto that my African subjects address to all the nations of the earth, and especially to the peoples of Oyó and Eubá, in Africa, recognizing my son as prince of that State and my heir to the African name and the royality to which he pertains as Obá 3.

Finally, I ask that Your Imperial Majesty pardon me for using this means of communicating the fact and the above request, in view of the fact that Your Imperial Majesty is absent from the city.

God protect the previous health and life of Your Majesty, of Her Majesty the Empress and all the Imperial Family as all Brazilians must desire.

I am, Senhor, with the most profound respect for Your Imperial Majesty, your reverent and submissive subject.

Rio de Janeiro 31 January 1882

Cândido da Fonseca Galvão Honorary Sublieutenant
of the Brazilian Army, Prince Obá 2 d'Africa.

Appendix C

'A Justa Palavra Perante Deos, a Magestade e Universidades' (I),[2] *O Carbonário*, 4 June 1883, p. 4.

---

2. 'Universidades'   All the people, everybody.

Publicando o Corsário[3] de 15 do mez passado uma carta adrede preparada com o fin de comprometer-me atribuindo-se-me a sua paternidade, declaro ser inverídica essa atribuição, pois que, eu não sou o finado que obrigadamente fizeram todas as falsidades e fizeram eles acreditarem, como iludiram o pobre Sabino, Pedro Ivo, Bento Gonçalves e tantos outros. O certo é que o paiz me conhece mais do que [os que] são titulares e falsos a monarchia, e fiéis ganhadores, sacrificando o direito do povo, e usurpando vexatoriamente o sangue da pobreza com impostos e mais impostos, e a pobreza morrendo à fome, sem emprego, e alguns que estão empregados deitam para fora afim de ficarem desesperados pela fome e continuar o desmantelo da Nação, como estamos vendo todos os dias assassinatos, roubos de toda a ordem, intrigas de todas as espécies, tudo pela ganância de dinheiro, pois os que são pobres querem a força ser ricos, e quem é rico, os invejosos querem ver ficarem pobres até da proteção de Deos e da Magestade, motivo este que venho obrigado como sempre é costume meu onde tenho gasto somas de contos de réis desde 1847, sem ser preciso, como muitos, que quando escrevem é porque ganham do Tesouro Nacional

Principe Obá II d'Africa
(continua)

'A Justa Palavra Perante Deos, a Magestade e Universidades' (II), *O Carbonário*, 8 June 1883, p. 4.

Quem no Brasil não conhece que eu não sou falso, como muitos que, fingem-se amigos da monarchia para saberem o segredo dela, para poder darem-lhe a queda de morte, e como eu não sou como muitos, que julgam-se inteligentes, e precisam ter um mentor para fazerem figura no parlamento, consistindo seus feitos nos – apoiados e na má invenção da cremaçáo, como porcos que matam e afinal é tostado o cabelo; o certo é que tanto hão de fazer, que estes das invenções, que atrevemse a querer saber adivinhar o segredo de Deos, e continuam com as intrigas, cometendo todos os atos de falsidade, pois o fim deles é acabarem doidos varridos para pagarem as consciências que devem a Deos e as Magestades; tanto quanto aos pretos e pardos, que só o único desejo que certos ingratos brasileiros tem é serem acompanhados da preguiça, e não desejarem o bemestar do paiz, nem coadjuvar o cego desejo da nação inteira em ser de uma só vez lavada a grande mancha da escravidão, pois eles desejam acabar a existência de quem deseja a extinção

---

3. *O Corsário* (*The Corsair*)   Tabloid newspaper issued on Wednesdays and Saturdays in Rio de Janeiro city from 1881, containing crude criticism of the Emperor, whom it referred to by demeaning sobriquets. Declared circulation of 20,000–25,000.

dessa grande mancha que o chorado Visconde do Rio Branco tanto fez com a sua imorredora idéia.[4]

Príncipe Obá II d'Africa
(continua)

'A Justa Palavra Perante Deos, a Magestades e Universidades' (III), O *Carbonário*, 11 June 1883, p. 3.

Por isso eu disse no *Cruzeiro* de 15 de Abril hodie mi crastib,[5] que ninguem estaria isento das falsidades da vida tão certo que fazem comigo este vil enrêdo com a monarchia para depois eu virar republicano, como certos monarchistas fingidos que fazem a desgraça da pobreza como quem diz: – nós não podemos fazer a revolução sem os braços dos pretos e dos pardos; e assim vamos enredal-os à magestade, como certos bem conhecidos pelo paiz, que do monarcha na Bahia diziam cobras e lagartos, até pela imprensa, que não podem mais na face do paiz negar estas verdades, e hoje são inimigos de quem as patenteiam, porque pensarão talvez que o paiz já esqueceu-se do passado; como sou amigo dedicado e sincero da monarchia que tenho sempre defendido, jamais passou-me pela memória o ligeiro vestígio de ofensa a mesma, com quanto os falsos tratem de doido quem como eu é amigo da magestade, e quem é falso a ela dizem que tem juízo, porque alguns destes já foram ministros como o ximango,[6] tudo isto só porque não querem que S.M. dê valor a cor preta, como eu tenho frequentemente tido, ao ponto de ser tecido esta carta pelos baianos bem conhecidos como falsos, por eu ser considerado pela magestade só o que desejam é verem-me morto. Ah! Deos de misericórdia e de bondade, que mundo!
O certo é que com o dom que Deos confiou-me não podem.

Principe Obá II d'Africa.

---

4. 'Imorredora idéia' Rio Branco Law (no. 2.040) of 28 September 1871, also known as the 'Law of the Free Womb'. From the signing of the law up to 1883, when the prince was writing, an average of 11,000 slaves were set free every year under this law (cf. *Jornal do Commercio*, 28 September 1882, editorial). In contrast to Dom Obá II d'Africa, the abolitionist movement criticized such results as far too slow, proposing immediate abolition without compensation. Cf. Joaquim Nabuco, *Abolitionism . . .*, p. 144.
5. 'Hodie mi crastib' [hodie mihi, cras tibi] Latin phrase which means 'today me, tomorrow you', often employed in old epitaphs to remind viewers, as the prince explains, 'that nobody would be exempt from the misfortunes of life'.
6. 'Ximango' Falcon-like bird (*Milvago chimango*) common in the extreme south of Brazil; deprecatory name given to the Liberals by the Conservatives who were themselves called 'cascudos' ('hardshells', *teleósteos fish*, from the family of the *loricarideos*). It refers here, specifically, to the Liberal cabinet then in power, headed by José Antônio Saraiva (1823–95).

'The Rightful Word Before God, the Majesties and the Universities (I)', O Carbonario, 4 June 1883, p. 4.

The Corsário, having published on the 15th of last month a letter maliciously written for the purpose of compromising me, attributing its authorship to myself, I declare that this attribution is untruthful, because I am not the deceased person to whom people always attribute all the falsities and make others believe them, as was done to poor Sabino, Pedro Ivo, Bento Gonçalves and so many others.

The truth is that the country knows me better than those who have titles and are false to the monarchy, yet earn regularly at the cost of the people, sacrificing the right of the people and vexfully usurping the blood of poverty with taxes and more taxes, and the poor are dying of hunger, without a job, and some that are employed are thrown out only to become desperate with hunger and the Nation continues to decay as every day we see murders, robberies of all sorts, intrigues of all species, all for the love of money because those who are poor want to be rich at any cost and those who are rich, the envious ones wish to see poor and even to lose the protection of God and your Majesty, which is the reason that I am obliged as always and as is my habit, to spend money (NB: to pay to have this text published), as I have done since 1847, unlike so many others who when they write it is because they are receive money from the National Treasury.

Prince Obá II d'Africa
(to be continued)

'The Truthful Word Before God, His Majesty and the Universities' (II), O Carbonário, 8 June, 1883, p. 4.

Who in Brazil does not know that I am not false, as so many are who feign to be friends of the monarchy in order to know its secrets, in order to deal the moral blow, and as I am not like so many others, who think themselves intelligent, yet need to have a mentor in order to appear in parliament, their acts consisting of chorusing 'Hear, hear' to others and in the evil invention of cremation, like pigs who are slaughtered and their hairs singed off; in truth, those people want to go so far with their inventions that they will soon want to go even further and try to divine the secret of God, and continue with their intrigues, committing all the acts of falsity, their fate will be to end up out of their minds in order to pay the consciences that they owe to God and Your Majesties; and to the blacks and the brown-skinned, because the one desire that certain ungrateful Brazilians have is to live in idleness, and they do not desire the good of the country, nor to help the blind desire of the entire nation to be for once and for all cleansed of this great stain of slavery, instead they want to put an end to those who desire the extinction of this great stain, that the much-lamented Visconde do Rio Branco did so much to remove with his immortal idea.

Prince Obá II d'Africa
(to be continued)

'The Rightful Word Before God, the Majesties and the Universities' (III), *O Carbonário*, 11 June 1883, p. 3.

For this I say in the *Cruzeiro* on April 15 hodie mi crastib, that no one will escape from the falsities of life just as they did with me this vile ploy with the monarchy so that later I should turn republican, just as certain feigned monarchists who make the disgrace of the poor, just as those who say: we cannot have the revolution without the sweat of the blacks and the brown-skinned; and thus let us indispose him with the majesty, just as certain men well known in the country, that in Bahia say all the dreadful things they please about the monarchy, even in the press, and who cannot anywhere in the face of the country deny this what they have done, and are today enemies of those who say the truth about them, because they perhaps think that the country has forgotten the past; as I am a dedicated and sincere friend of the monarchy whom I have always defended and against whom it has never entered my mind to make the slightest vestige of an offence, despite all this the false ones treat as crazy one such as I who is the friend of his majesty, and those who are false to the king claim to be wise, because some of them have been ministers like the *ximango*, all this just because they do not want Your Majesty to give value to the colour black, as I have frequently held, to the point of having this letter written by Bahians well known for being false, just because I am well-considered by Your Majesty, all they want is to see me dead.
Ah! God of mercy and goodness, what a world!
In truth, do what they will, they can do nothing against one such as I, with the gift entrusted to me by God.

Prince Obá II d'Africa.

Notes

Abbreviations

APEBA	Arquivo Público do Estado da Bahia (Salvador)
ASE	Arquivo Seletivo do Exército (Rio de Janeiro)
CNPq	Conselho Nacional de Desenvolvimento Científico e Tecnológico (Brasília)
FCRB	Fundação Casa de Rui Barbosa (Rio de Janeiro)
IHGB	Instituto Histórico e Geográfico Brasileiro (Rio de Janeiro)
INL	Instituto Nacional do Livro (Brasília)
MEC	Ministério da Educação e Cultura (Brasília)
MHN	Museu Histórico Nacional (Rio de Janeiro)
MIP	Museu Imperial de Petrópolis (Petrópolis, RJ)
PP	Parliamentary Papers

Introduction

1. Cf. Raul Pompéia, *Obras* (VI), organization and notes by Afrânio Coutinho, Rio de Janeiro, Civilização Brasileira, 1982, pp. 118–19.

2. *O Paiz*, 3 December 1889, p. 1.

3. 'Honras mandadas cassar'. Session room of the provisional government of the Republic of the United States of Brazil, 6 December 1889. Section of the Ajudante General, *Coleção das Ordens do Dia*, Rio de Janeiro, Typ. de G. Leuzinger & Filhos, 1889, p. 984.

4. *Diário de Notícias*, 9 and 14 July, 1890, p. 1; *O Paiz*, 9 July 1890, p. 1; *Gazeta de Notícias*, 9 July 1890, p. 1.

5. Lima Barreto, 'A Matemática Não Falha'. In *Bagatelas*, São Paulo, Brasiliense, 1956, p. 183 (original article, 1918).

6. Quoted in Eloy Pontes, *A vida exuberante do Olavo Bilac*, Rio de Janeiro, José Olympio, 1944, 1. v., p. 226.

7. Quoted in Raimundo de Menezes, *Emílio de Menezes, o último boêmio*, 2nd edition, São Paulo, Saraiva, 1949, p. 148.

8. Carlo Ginzburg, *O queijo e os vermes; the daily life and ideas of a miller persecuted by the inquisition*, translation from the original Italian by Betania Amoroso, São Paulo, Companhia das Letras, 1987, p. 30 (1st edition, 1976); Robert Darnton, *O grande massacre de gatos*, Rio de Janeiro, Graal, 1986,

pp. 106–7 (originally published in English, 1984). For the theoretical discussions that arose after the publication of Darnton's work, see Roger Chartier, *Cultural History; between Practices and Representations*, trans. Lydia G. Cochrane, Cambridge, Polity Press, 1988, pp. 95–111 (original article, 1985); Pierre Bourdieu, Robert Darnton and Roger Chartier, 'Dialogue à propos de l'histoire culturelle', *Actes de la Recherche en Sciences Sociales*, no. 59, September 1985, pp. 86–93.

9. Carl von Koseritz, *Imagens do Brasil*, trans. Afonso Arinos de Melo Franco, São Paulo, Martins, 1943, pp. 159–60 (1st German edition, 1885).

10. Rodolpho Galvão, *Das concepções delirantes; seu valor diagnóstico*, Rio de Janeiro, Typ. de G. Leuzinger & Filhos, 1886, pp. 49–50.

11. Mello Moraes Filho, *Quadros e Crônicas*, Rio de Janeiro, Garnier, s.d., pp. 251–7. The same text (around 1,200 words) was republished in another collection by the same author published for the first time in 1895. See *Festas e tradições populares do Brasil*, 3rd edition, Rio de Janeiro, Briguiet, 1946, pp. 543–8.

12. Hermeto Lima, 'O Príncipe Obá', *Revista da Semana*, Rio de Janeiro, 21 February 1925, p. 30. The same article was republished, years later, in a co-authored work. See Mello Barreto Filho and Hermeto Lima, *História da polícia do Rio de Janeiro: aspéctos da cidade e da vida carioca, 1870–1889*, Rio de Janeiro, A Noite, 1944, pp. 149–51. Hermeto Lima was an author who specialized in police matters, and published, among other technical works, *A identidade do homen pela impressão digital* (Identity of Man through Fingerprints), Rio de Janeiro, Imprensa Nacional, 1913; *O alcoolismo no Rio de Janeiro* (Alcoholism in Rio de Janeiro), Rio de Janeiro, Imprensa Nacional, 1914; *A infâmia alcoolatra* (Alcoholic Notoriety), Rio de Janeiro, Imprensa Nacional, 1916; and *Os crimes célebres do Rio de Janeiro* (Famous Crimes of Rio de Janeiro), Emprensa de Romances Populares, 1921.

13. Vicente Reis, 'O Rio de Janeiro no Crepúsculo da Monarquia; Aspéctos de Sua Vida Social e Comercial', *Revista do IHGB*, no. 345, Oct./Dec. 1984, p. 70.

14. Arthur Ramos, *O folclore negro do Brasil; demopsicologia e psicanálise*, 2nd edition, revised and illustrated, Rio de Janeiro, Casa do Estudante do Brasil, 1954, p. 232 (1st edition 1935).

15. Luís da Câmara Cascudo, *Dicionário do folclore brasileiro*, 4th edition, revised and expanded, São Paulo: Melhoramentos; Brasília: INL, 1976, pp. 635–6; R. Magalhães Júnior, *O Império em chinelos*, Rio de Janeiro, Civilização Brasileira, 1957, pp. 260–3.

16. Reis, op. cit., pp. 70–1; Moraes Filho, op. cit., s.d., pp. 253–4.

17. Claude Lévi-Strauss, *O pensamento selvagem*, 2nd edition, São Paulo, Companhia Editora Nacional, 1976, p. 285 (original in French, 1961).

18. Darnton, op. cit., pp. xv, 106 and 335.

Chapter 1: The Illusion of the Mines

1. Johann von Spix and Karl von Martius, *Viagem pelo Brasil, 1817–1822*, São Paulo, Melhoramentos, 1976, 2 vols., p. 118.

2. Ibid., pp. 115–18.

3. Ibid., p. 119.

4. In the time of Spix and Martius, Rio de Contas, for example, which was founded in 1724, had around 900 inhabitants. Spix and Martius also referred to gold prospecting in river beds, especially in the Rio Brumado, and to the mining of lesser minerals such as alabaster in the Rio Santo Antônio region and the 'beautiful amethysts, famed for their deep colour' mined at places along the route between Caetité and Rio Pardo. Op. cit., pp. 111–16.

5. Ibid., pp. 113 and 116.

6. Ibid., p. 119 and passim.

7. Ibid., p. 113. The importance of this inlet of individual economy within the slave system has aroused increasing academic interest. For a preliminary evaluation, see Stuart B. Schwartz, 'Resistance and Accommodation in Eighteenth-century Brazil: The Slaves' View of Slavery', *Hispanic American Historical Review*, 57 (1), 69–81, 1977; Ciro F. S. Cardoso, *Escravo ou camponês?* São Paulo, Brasiliense, 1987; Eduardo Silva, 'A Função Ideológica da Brecha Camponesa'. In E. Silva and J. J. Reis, *Negociação e Conflito; a resistência negra no Brasil escravista*, São Paulo, Companhia das Letras, 1989, pp. 22–31.

8. Spix and Martius, op. cit., pp. 117, 120–1.

9. Ibid., p. 112.

10. Sílvio Fróes Abreu, *A riqueza mineral do Brasil*, 2nd edition, São Paulo, Companhia Editora Nacional, 1975, pp. 104ff. The region is described in a small number of late nineteenth-century works, such as Charles Frederick Hartt, *Geology and Physical Geography of Brazil*. London, Trübner, 1870, pp. 306–7. Systematic geological research was not undertaken until the twentieth century, after the pioneering studies of Orville A. Derby, published in 1904 and 1906. For a brief history of subsequent studies, see Centro Integrando de Estudos Geológicos, *Morro do Chapéu, Bahia*, Brasília, Departmento Nacional da Produção Mineral, 1987; John C. Branner, 'The Tombador Escarpment in the State of Bahia, Brazil', *American Journal of Science*, New Haven, 30 (179), 335–43, 1910.

11. Abreu, op. cit., pp. 104–5.

12. Chemist João de Miranda Neves, *Manuscripts*, 'Livro I', pp. 284–92. Document belonging to the *Private Collection of Mestre Oswaldo*, Lençóis (BA). This documentation consists of three large volumes of miscellaneous manuscripts and cuttings, unnumbered, collected from the beginning of the present century by João Miranda Neves, chemist in the Vila de Estiva (now renamed Afrânio Peixoto) district of Lençóis. It includes notes on the treatment of backlands diseases, curiosities and even reconstructions of regional history via interviews which the chemist conducted with his older clients. His account of the diamond rush was punctuated with expressions such as 'this was the story that I was able to find out', and 'Sr Antônio Barbosa said that', and 'as you can see in the account of old Pedro Antônio da Cruz, who died recently', and so on. Based on the examination of each volume (some of the cuttings and poems are dated) I used, for practical ends, the following classification: 'Book I' (c. 1908 until at least 1912); 'Book II' (c. 1916–17); and 'Book III', which the author himself opens with '3rd Book of Miscellaneous Encyclopaedia, 1917'.

13. Afrânio Peixoto, *Bugrinha*, 10th edition, Rio de Janeiro, Conquista, Brasília, INL, 1972, p. 45 (1st edition 1922).

14. Instituto Brasileiro de Geografia e Estatística, *Enciclopédia dos Municípios*, Rio de Janeiro, 1958, vol. 20, p. 389.

15. Nadir Ganem, *Lençóis de outras eras*, Brasília, Thesaurus, 1984, p. 16; field research, 1986–7.

16. Letter from the president of the province, Barão de Caçapava, to the minister of justice of the Empire. Salvador, 31 July 1845. APEBA, Seção Histórica, Correspondência, livro 689, doc. 101.

17. Letter from the president of the province, Barão de Caçapava, to the finance minister of the empire, Salvador, 31 July 1845. APEBA, Seção Histórica, Correspondência, livro 689, doc. 113.

18. James Wetherell, *Brazil: Stray Notes from Bahia: being Extracts from Letters, etc. during a Residence of Fifteen Years*, ed. William Hadfield, Liverpool, Webb and Hunt, 1860, p. 29.

19. Abreu, op. cit., p. 112.

20. Chemist João de Miranda Neves, *Manuscripts*, 'Livro I', pp. 287–9; Afrânio Peixoto, op. cit., p. 132; Fernando Sales, *Lençóis, coração diamantino da Bahia*, Salvador, s. ed, 1973, pp. 6–7.

21. Salvador, 31 July 1845. APEBA, Seção Histórica, Correspondência, Livro 689, doc. 113.

22. On the difficulties of communication, the need for roads and so on, see letter from the president of the province to the minister of the Empire, Salvador, 13 August 1845. APEBA, Seção Histórica, Correspondência, livro 689, doc. 61.

23. See Provincial Law nos 428 and 946 (20 May 1864). Also 'Auto da Instalação da Câmara Municipal da Nova Vila dos Lençóis, contendo a Lei Provincial que criou a dita Vila e Freguesia, e Juramento e Posse dos Vereadores' (12 April 1858). APEBA, Presidência da Província, Governo Câmara de Lençóis (1858–81), doc. 1.340, 167 pp.

24. Peixoto, op. cit., pp. 134–5.

25. Such registers were found in both local memory and in local historiography. Field research, 1986.

26. Peixoto, op. cit., pp. 38 and 41.

27. Circular of 12 April 1858. APEBA, Presidência da Província, Governo Câmara de Lençóis (1858–81), doc. 1,340, 167pp. There is also mention of another cholera epidemic in January 1889. See Governo Câmara de Lençóis (1859–89), doc. 1,341, 195pp.

28. The system of *meias-praças* (tied labourers) became the norm after 1888. The term was used in both Bahia and Minas Gerais, where the system doubtless originated, arriving in Bahia together with the prospectors and traders from Rio das Velhas and the Distrito Diamantino who flooded in during the 1845 rush.

29. The bridge, one of the architectural attractions of the city, was built in 1860 from local stone, whale oil and egg yolks. See Sales, op. cit., p. 17.

30. Eduardo Silva, *Barões e escravidão; três gerações de fazendeiros e a crise da estrutura escravista*, Rio de Janeiro, Nova Fronteira, 1984, p. 80.

31. Pedro Calmon, *História social do Brasil*, 2 tomo, Espírito da Sociedade Imperial, 3rd edn., São Paulo, Companhia Editora Nacional, 1937, pp. 152–3; Peixoto, op. cit., p. 43; Abreu, op. cit., pp. 108–9.

32. Carbonate, which until then had been ignored, was worth $500 a gram in 1880. Four years later it was worth 8$000 and, shortly after, 65$000. Calmon, op. cit., p. 153.

33. Peixoto, op cit., p. 46. Most of the main and secondary characters in his novel are historical, such as João Sobral (the first republican in the city), the priest, and so on. The principal character, Jorge de Castro, bears many similarities to the author, who was also one of the 'favoured sons' of the city. Afrânio Peixoto was born in 1876, graduated in Medicine from Salvador and died in Rio de Janeiro in 1947.

34. The practice of adopting the surname of a former master, although not rare, does not seem to have been the most usual among freedmen. In Bahia, at least, recent studies show a preference for Portuguese surnames relating to saints, symbols, ceremonies or festivities of the Catholic Church. It is interesting to note that the immense majority of freedmen in Benvindo's time, simply did not choose any surname at all when they gained their freedom. During the nineteenth century, only 10 per cent of the freedmen and free men of colour in Bahia had surnames. Of these, around 69 per cent seemed to have opted for Portuguese surnames with a religious connotation. Cf. J. Tavares-Neto, and E. S. Azevedo, 'Racial Origin and Historical Aspects of Family Names in Bahia, Brazil', *Human Biology*, 49 (1977), 287–99; Eliane S. Azevedo, *Análise antropológica e cultural dos nomes de família na Bahia*, Centro de Estudos Afro-Orientais, Universidade Federal da Bahia, 1981. On the social importance of the surname adopted by Benvindo, it is worth remembering that many prominent men belonged to the various branches of this large patriarchal family: the Viscount of Maracaju, minister of war in the last cabinet of the monarchy, and General Deodoro da Fonseca, who was to depose him in 1889 with the proclamation of the Republic. See Walter Fonseca, *Fonseca, uma família e uma história*, São Paulo, Obelisco, 1982. Although there is no specific study on the subject, either historical or genealogical, the prestige of the Fonseca Galvão in Bahia can be attested beyond a shadow of a doubt by the palace in Salvador known as 'Solar dos 7 Candeeiros', which today houses the Bahian section of the *Pró-Memória* heritage foundation and is one of Brazil's most important examples of eighteenth-century colonial architecture. Over the main entrance hangs the coat of arms of Captain Antônio Elias da Fonseca Galvão, patriarch of the Bahian branch of the family, originally from the Capitania of Pernambuco. The arms were granted to Fonseca Galvão in a letter from the king of Portugal dated 26 April 1768. For further reading on the patriarch and the 'Solar dos 7 Candeeiros', see Egon Prates Pinto, *Armorial Brasileiro*; illuminations by Luís Gomes Loureiro, Rio de Janeiro, Revista da Semana, 1936; Tom Maia and Teresa Regina de Camargo Maia, *Velha Bahia de hoje*, Rio de Janeiro, Expressão e Cultura, 1985, p. 104. In the first half of the nineteenth century, when Benvindo was in Salvador, members of the family were active and prominent in local affairs, whether among the editors of the local *Jornal da Sociedade de Agricultura*, the house organ of the farmers' association; or among the citizens who, on 1 January 1836, delivered a petition to the provincial legislative assembly protesting against the substitution of a 60 per cent tax on sugar cane rum by one of 2$000 for each slave owned. No less than three members of the family signed this petition, the first of whom, coincidentally or not, was called Cândido A. da Fonseca Galvão. See APEBA, Assembléia Legislativa, Petitions, 1835–6. See also Wanderley Pinho, 'A Bahia, 1808–1856'. In Sérgio Buarque de Holanda (org.), *História geral da civilização Brasileira*, São Paulo, Difusão Européia do Livro, tomo II, 2 vols., p. 305.

35. J. B. Magalhães, *A evolução militar do Brasil; anotações para a História*, Rio de Janeiro, Biblioteca do Exército, 1958. Quoted in Claudio Moreira Bento, 'O Exército e a Abolição'. In Arno Wehling (org.), *A abolição do cativeiro*. Rio de Janeiro, IHGB, 1988, p. 84.

36. *O movimento da Independência: o Império Brasileiro (1821–1889)*, 2nd edition, São Paulo, Melhoramentos, s. d., p. 429.

37. Dionísio Cerqueira, *Reminiscências da campanha do Paraguai, 1865–1870*, Rio de Janeiro, Biblioteca do Exército, 1980, pp. 62–3 (1st edition, Paris, 1910).

38. As early as 1865, the central government suspended the embarkation of

volunteers, causing much disappointment in the province. See Notice of 22 June 1865. APEBA, Avisos Recebidos, Ministro da Guerra, maço 828. For a detailed analysis from the military point of view, see Paulo de Queiroz Duarte, *Os Voluntários da Pátria na querra do Paraguai*, Rio de Janeiro, Biblioteca do Exercito, vol. I, 1981, pp. 231–5. Quotation from p. 233.

39. Letter from Câmara Municipal de Lençóis to the president of the province, Luís Antônio Barbosa de Almeida. Lençóis, 3 February 1865. APEBA, Presidência da Província. Governo Câmara de Lençóis, 1859–89, Doc. 1341.

40. In the Republic, from the end of 1919 until 1930, Lençóis became the headquarters of Horácio de Matos, one of the archetypal figures of backlands 'Coronelism' prior to the 1930 revolution. For an overall account of the question, see Vitor Nunes Leal, *Coronelismo, enxada e voto*, 2nd edition São Paulo, Alfa-Omega, 1975 (original edition, 1949); Raimundo Faoro, *Os donos do poder*, Porto Alegre, Globo, 1958; Marcos Vinicius Vilaça and Roberto de Albuquerque, *Coronel, coronéis*, Rio de Janeiro, Tempo Brasileiro, 1965; Maria Isaura Pereira de Queiroz, *O mandonismo local na vida política brasileira*, São Paulo, I.E.B., 1969. For a specific analysis of the phenomenon in Bahia, see Zahidé Machado Neto *et al.*, *O coronelismo na Bahia*, Salvador, Universidade Federal da Bahia, 1972; Eul-soo Pang, *Bahia in the First Brazilian Republic; Coronelism and Oligarchies, 1889–1933*, Gainesville, University Press of Florida, 1979. For a recent revision of the earlier studies, see José Murilo de Carvalho and Eduardo Silva, 'Entre a Enxada e o Voto', *Acervo; Revista do Arguivo Nacional*, Rio de Janeiro, vol. 2, no. 1, January–June 1987, pp. 23–8. On local power, hierarchy and enlistment in the National Guard, see Antônio E. Martins Rodrigues, Francisco José Calazans Falcon and Margarida de Souza Neves, *A Guarda Nacional no Rio de Janeiro, 1831–1918*. Rio de Janeiro, Pontificia Universidade Católica, 1981, pp. 71–96.

41. Aristarchus, pseud., 'Bahia; Negócios dos Lençóis; Especulação de Patriotagem', *Jornal do Commercio*, 22 July 1865, p. 4.

42. Justiça, pseud., 'Bahia; Termo de Lençóis', *Jornal do Commercio*, 23 July 1865, p. 1; idem, 'Bahia; Negócios dos Lençóis', *Jornal do Commercio*, 24 July 1865, p. 2; idem, 'Bahia; Negócios dos Lençóis; Ao Público de Todo o Império: Muita Atenção', *Jornal do Commercio*, 9 August 1865, p. 1; idem, 'Bahia; Negócios dos Lençóis; Um Herói Proclamado Por Si Mesmo', *Jornal do Commercio*, 28 August 1865, p. 1.

43. Medeiros e Albuquerque, *Quando eu era vivo, 1867–1934*, 2nd edition, Rio de Janeiro, Livraria Globo, 1945, p. 112.

44. Dom Obá II d'Africa, 'A S.M. Imperador', *Jornal do Commercio*, 28 February 1885, p. 5.

45. ASE, Pasta Cândido da Fonseca Galvão, 'Memorial', Bahia, 21 March 1872.

46. Ibid., 'Memorial', Rio de Janeiro, 16 May 1874.

47. Cerqueira, op. cit., p. 147.

48. ASE, Pasta Cândido da Fonseca Galvão, 'Memorial', Bahia, 21 March 1872. The prince also refers to this fact, with much emphasis, in a later article. See *Jornal do Commercio*, 28 February 1885, p. 5.

49. Cerqueira, op. cit., p. 212.

50. Ibid., p. 207; Lima, op. cit., p. 468; Richard Graham, 'Os fundamentos da ruptura de relações diplomáticos entre o Brasil e a Grã-Bretanha em 1863: "A quest ão Christie"', *Revista de História*, 24:49 and 50 (1962), 117–38, 379–402.

51. Cerqueira, op. cit., pp. 46–8 and 58.
52. Ibid., p. 56, 76, 97, 113 and 216.

Chapter 2: The Battlefields

1. *Jornal do Commercio*, 5 July 1865, p. 2.
2. ASE, 'Oficiais dos Corpos de Voluntários da Pátria em Sua Organização', manuscript, 1865, p. 61.
3. Dionísio Cerqueira, *Reminiscências da campanha do Paraguai, 1865–1870*, Rio de Janeiro, Biblioteca do Exército, 1980, p. 111.
4. Conde d'Eu, *Viagem Militar ao Rio Grande do Sul*, São Paulo, Companhia Editora Nacional, 1936, p. 135.
5. Paulo de Queiroz Duarte, *Os Voluntários da Pátria na Guerra do Paraguai*, Rio de Janeiro, Biblioteca do Exército, vol. 2, Tomo III, 1984, p. 181.
6. Cerqueira, op. cit., p. 56.
7. Duarte, op. cit., p. 182.
8. *Jornal do Commercio*, 23 June 1865 (2o. clichê), p. 1.
9. Letter from Joaquim Antônio da Silva Carvalho, Coronel Comandante Superior, to the president of the province, Baltazar Araújo de Aragão Bulcão. Quartel da Casa da Moeda, 1 June 1865. APEBA, Guerra do Paraguai, Maço 3668.
10. Decree of 5 June 1865. APEBA, Atos do Governo, Maço 976, folha 274. Also ASE, Companhia de Zuavos, Pasta 9, 'Voluntários de Diversos Estados que Marcharam para a Guerra do Paraguai'.
11. Quoted in Duarte, op. cit., pp. 182–3.
12. *Jornal do Commercio*, 13 July 1865, p. 2.
13. *Jornal do Commercio*, 23 June 1865, p. 1.
14. Virtually with the same words: Mello Moraes Filho, *Quadros e crônicas*, Rio de Janeiro, Garnier, s.d., p. 251; Mello Barreto Filho and Hermeto Lima, *História da Polícia do Rio de Janeiro; aspéctos da cidade e da vida carioca, 1870–1889*, Rio de Janeiro, A Noite, 1944, p. 149.
15. *Jornal do Commercio*, 3 July 1865, p. 1.
16. *Jornal do Commercio*, 4 July 1865, p. 1.
17. Conde d'Eu, op. cit., p. 135.
18. Duarte, op. cit., p. 188; Abid Murad, *A batalha de Tuiuti e uma lição de civismo*, Rio de Janeiro, Biblioteca do Exército, 1957, 'esboço 2'.
19. See especially, Umberto Peregrino, 'Estudo Biocrítico de Dionísio Cerqueira'. In Cerqueira, op. cit., pp. 17–44.
20. Cerqueira, op. cit., pp. 153–5.
21. For a comprehensive evaluation from the military point of view, see Murab, op. cit., pp. 13–49.
22. Cerqueira, op. cit., p. 162.
23. George Thompson. Quoted in Duarte, op. cit., pp. 193–4.
24. Ibid., pp. 181–99.
25. Cerqueira, op. cit., pp. 104 and 326.
26. Moraes Filho, op. cit., p. 251. The author, however, was mistaken, as he thought the battle was that of Curupaity.

27. Dom Obá II d'Africa, 'A Justiça e a Consciência', *O Carbonário*, 29 April 1887, p. 4.

28. Francisco Fernandes de Souza, alias Chico Diabo, was then 27 years old. He was reported to have died old and in poverty but 'surrounded by his companions of arms also old themselves' in 18 October 1917, at Fonte Nova do Desterro, in Salvador. See *A Tarde*, Salvador, 19 October 1917, p. 1.

29. Cerqueira, op. cit., p. 72. The same was noticed by Conde d'Eu, op. cit., p. 103.

30. Ibid., p. 50. In the same vein, p. 147.

31. Ibid., pp. 96 and 148.

32. Ibid., p. 72. In the same vein, pp. 84, 90, 106 and 137.

33. Ibid., pp. 98–9.

34. Ibid., p. 132.

35. Ibid., p. 192.

36. Ibid., p. 233.

37. *O Paiz*, 26 October 1887, p. 1.

38. Cf. Gilberto Freyre, *Ordem e progresso*, Rio de Janeiro, José Olympio, 1959, tomo I, pp. 67–88.

Chapter 3: The Homecoming

1. ASE, Pasta Cândido da Fonseca Galvão, 'Memorial', Bahia, 21 March 1872.

2. Oliveira Lima, *O movimento da Independência; o Império Brasileiro, 1821–1889*, 2nd edition, São Paulo, Melhoramentos, n.d., pp. 424–5.

3. ASE, Pasta Cândido da Fonseca Galvão, doc. 2.724–49, Bahia, 31 March 1871.

4. Letter from Manoel da Cunha Wanderley Luís, Brigadeiro Comandante das Armas, to Dr Francisco José da Rocha, vice-president of the province, Quartel General do Comando das Armas da Bahia, 31 May 1871, ASE, doc. 246.

5. ASE, doc. 1.602. 2a. Secção, *Repartição do Ajudante General*, 31 October 1871.

6. *Coleção das Ordens do Dia da Repartição de Ajudância General Publicadas no Ano de 1872*, Rio de Janeiro, Typ. do Diário do Rio de Janeiro, 1874, p. 576. See also 'Papéis que Serviram de Base ao Decreto de 25 set. 1872, Concedendo Honras do Posto de Alferes a Cândido da Fonseca Galvão', ASE, manuscripts file.

7. ASE, Pasta Cândido da Fonseca Galvão, 'Requerimento a Vossa Majestade Imperial', 29 November 1873.

8. Cf. Lima, op. cit., p. 424.

9. ASE, Requerimento do Alferes Cândido da Fonseca Galvão ao Ilmo. Exmo. Duque de Caxias, Ministro e Secretário de Estado dos Negócios da Guerra, Rio de Janeiro, 6 June 1876. The favourable dispatch, with the same date, is in the document itself.

10. ASE, Pasta Cândido da Fonseca Galvão, Requerimento ao Ilmo, Sr Duque de Caxias, Ministro e Secretário da Guerra, Rio de Janeiro, 6 June 1876.

11. ASE, Maço 539. Letter from José Pedro Dias de Carvalho to Tenente-General Visconde de Pelotas, Ministro da Guerra, Rio de Janeiro, Paço do Senado, 16 September 1880.

12. ASE, Ministério da Guerra, 1a. Secção. Repartição Fiscal, doc. 1.184, 13 November 1880. In the same vein, see letter of the director of the *Repartição Fiscal da Guerra*, Francisco Augusto de Lima e Silva, 10 September 1885.

13. Lima Barreto, 'A Matemática não Falha'. In *Bagatelas*, São Paulo, Brasiliense, 1956, pp. 177–84. Quotations on pp. 181 and 184. The article was originally published in December 1918.

14. ASE, Ofício no. 411. Parte from Comandante of the *Asilo de Inválidos da Pátria*, to Conselheiro Tenente-General and Barão da Gávea, Ajudante-General do Exército, Salvador, 9 May 1876. On the same episode, see Partes from Capitão Antônio da Cunha Frota and Alferes Francisco Lucas against Alferes Galvão, *Asilo de Inválidos da Pátria*, Quartel na Ilha de Bom Jesus, 9 May 1876; finally, letter no. 4596, from Barão da Gávea to Conselheiro de Guerra, Marechal do Exército, Duque de Caxias, Presidente do conselho de Ministros, Ministro e Secretário dos Negócios da Guerra. Quartel General da Corte, 12 May 1876.

15. ASE, Letter from João do Rego Barros Falcão to Conselheiro Marechal de Exército Duque de Caxias, Ministro e Secretário de Estado dos Negócios da Guerra, Quartel General do Comando das Armas da Bahia, 9 January 1877.

16. Robert Edgar Conrad, *Tumbeiros*, São Paulo, Brasiliense, 1985, p. 194.

17. Louis Couty, *Le Brésil em 1884*, Rio de Janeiro, Faro e Lino, 1884, p. 388.

18. Stanley J. Stein, *Vassouras, a Brazilian Coffee County, 1850–1900*, Princeton, Princeton University Press, 1985 (original edition, Harvard, 1958). For a case study, see Eduardo Silva, *Barões e escravidão; três gerações de fazendeiros e a crise da estrutura escravista*, Rio de Janeiro, Nova Fronteira; Brasilia, INL, 1984.

19. Leslie Bethell, *The Abolition of the Brazilian Slave Trade; Britain, Brazil and the Slave Trade Question, 1807–1869*, Cambridge, Cambridge University Press, 1970, pp. 375; Robert E. Conrad, *Os últimos anos da escravatura no Brasil, 1850–1888*, Rio de Janeiro, Civilização Brasileira; Brasília, INL, 1975, p. 67 (original edition, California, 1972).

20. Cf. Robert Slenes, *The Demography and Economics of Brazilian Slavery, 1850–1888*, PhD Thesis, Stanford University, 1976, p. 138; Jacob Gorender, *O escravismo colonial*, São Paulo, Ática, 1978, pp. 325ff, Robert E. Conrad, *Tumbeiros*, São Paulo, Brasiliense, pp. 196–7.

21. Sebastião Ferreira Soares, *Notas estatísticas sobre a produção agrícola e carestia dos gêneros alimentícios no Império do Brasil*, Rio de Janeiro, Typ. Imp. e Const. de J. Villeneuve, 1860, pp. 135–9 and 216.

22. Conrad, *Tumbeiros*, op. cit., pp. 198–9 and 216.

23. Câmara dos Deputados, *Anais do Parlamento Brasileiro*, Rio de Janeiro, 1854, vol. IV, p. 349.

24. Roberto Simonsen, 'Aspéctos da História Econômica do Café, *Anais do 3 Congresso de História Nacional*, Rio de Janeiro, IHGB, 1941, vol. IV, pp. 211–99. See especially p. 269.

25. Afonso d'Escragnolle Taunay, *Pequena história do café no Brasil*, Rio de Janeiro, Departamento Nacional do Café, 1945, p. 548.

26. Cf. Stein, op. cit., p. 228.

27. Silva, op. cit., pp. 141.

28. Kátia M. de Queiros Mattoso, Herbert S. Klein and Stanley L. Engerman, 'Notas Sobre as Tendências e Padrões dos Preços de Alforrias na Bahia, 1819–1888'. In J. J. Reis (org.), *Escravidão e invenção da liberdade; estudos sobre o negro no Brasil*, São Paulo: Brasiliense; Brasília: CNPq, 1988, pp. 60–72.

29. Cf. Stein, op. cit., pp. 229ff.

30. *Gazeta da Tarde*, Rio de Janeiro, 5 January 1881, p. 1.

31. Kátia M. de Queirós Mattoso, 'A Propósito de Cartas de Alforria; Bahia, 1779–1850', *Anais de História*, Assis (SP), no. 4, 1972, pp. 23–52. For the previous period, see Stuart B. Schwartz, 'The Manumission of Slaves in Colonial Brazil; Bahia, 1684–1745', *Hispanic American Historical Review*, 54 (4), 603–35, 1974.

32. Queirós Mattoso, Klein and Engerman, op. cit., p. 61.

33. Pierre Verger, *Fluxo e refluxo do tráfico de escravos entre o golfo do Benin e a Bahia de Todos os Santos*, São Paulo, Corrupio, 1987, p. 534.

34. Gilberto Freyre, *Ordem e progresso*, Rio de Janeiro, José Olympio, 1959, Tomo I, pp. 328–9.

35. Queirós Mattoso, Klein and Engerman. op. cit., p. 62.

36. See Maria Inês Côrtes de Oliveira, *O liberto: o seu mundo e os outros; Salvador, 1790–1890*, São Paulo: Corrupio; Brasília, CNPq, 1988, pp. 26–7, 42 and 94.

37. On the formation of communities of 'Brazilian' returned in Africa, see Verger, op. cit., pp. 599–636; Manuela Carneiro da Cunha, *Negros, estrangeiros; os escravos libertos e sua volta à Africa*, São Paulo, Brasiliense, 1985.

38. On the origins of the *samba* and the 'schools of samba', see Edison Carneiro. *A sabedoria popular*, Rio de Janeiro, MEC/INL, 1957, pp. 113–22; Eneida, *História do carnaval carioca*, Rio de Janeiro, Civilização Brasileira, 1958; Vasco Mariz, *A canção brasileira*, Rio de Janeiro, MEC, 1959, pp. 180–8; Ary Vasconcelos, *Panorama da música popular brasileira*, São Paulo, Martins, 1964, vol. I, p. 17; Sérgio Cabral, *As escolas de samba*, Rio de Janeiro, Fontana, 1974; Jota Efegê, *Ameno Resedá, o rancho que foi escola*, Rio de Janeiro, Letras e Artes, 1975; Roberto Moura, *Tia Ciata e a pequena África no Rio de Janeiro*, Rio de Janeiro, FUNARTE, 1983.

Chapter 4: Life in Rio de Janeiro

1. On the support of the *fazendeiros*, see Eduardo Silva, *Barões e escravidão; três gerações de fazendeiros e a crise da estrutura escravista*, Rio de Janeiro, Nova Fronteira/INL, 1984, pp. 69ff.

2. Dom Obá II d'Africa, 'As Vivas Razões da Constituição ...', *Jornal do Commercio*, 25 February 1885, p. 5.

3. Rebecca Baird Bergstresser, *The Movement for the Abolition of Slavery in Rio de Janeiro; Brazil, 1880–1889*, PhD Thesis, Stanford University, 1973, pp. 49ff.

4. Campos Sales, *Da propaganda à presidência*, São Paulo, s. edn, 1908, p. 252; Artur Bernardes, 'Mensagem Presidencial', quoted by Delgado de Carvalho, *História da cidade do Rio de Janeiro*, Rio de Janeiro, Secretaria Municipal de Cultura, 1988, p. 109.

5. Stanley J. Stein, *Vassouras, a Brazilian Coffee County, 1850–1900*, Princeton, Princeton University Press, 1985, p. 29 and passim; Silva, op. cit., p. 188 and passim.

6. Oliveira Lima, *O movimento da Independência; o Império brasileiro (1821–1889)*, 2nd edition, São Paulo, Melhoramentos, n.d., p. 467.

7. Afonso Arinos de Melo Franco, *História do Banco do Brasil*, quoted by

Francisco de Assis Barbosa, *Jk: uma revisão na política brasileira*, Rio de Janeiro, José Olympio, 1960, p. 96.

8. For a comprehensive vision, see Francisco Agenor de Noronha Santos, *As frequesias do Rio antigo*, Rio de Janeiro, Cruzeiro, 1965; Francisco de Assis Barbosa (org.), 'Cadernos do IV Centenário', *Jornal do Brasil*, January–December 1965.

9. Silva, op. cit., pp. 80–3, 138ff.

10. Max Leclerc, *Cartas do Brasil*, trad., prefácio e notas de Sérgio Milliet, São Paulo, Companhia Editora Nacional, 1942, p. 46.

11. Brasil, *Recenseamento do Rio de Janeiro (Distrito Federal) realizado em 20 de setembro de 1906*, Rio de Janeiro, Oficina de Estatística, 1907, pp. 13–14.

12. On slavery in the city, see Mary C. Karash, *Slave Life in Rio de Janeiro, 1808–1850*, Princeton, Princeton University Press, 1987; Leila Mezan Algranti, *O feitor ausente; estudo sobre a escravidão urbana no Rio de Janeiro*, Petrópolis, Vozes, 1988; Sam C. Adamo, *The Broken Promise; Race, Health, and Justice in Rio de Janeiro, 1890–1940*, PhD Thesis, University of New Mexico, 1983; Luís Carlos Soares, *Urban Slavery in Nineteenth-Century Rio de Janeiro*, PhD Thesis, University of London, 1988; Sidney Chalhoub, *Visões da liberdade; uma história das últimas décadas da escravidão na Corte*, São Paulo, Companhia das Letras, 1990.

13. Brasil, *Recenseamento do Distrito Federal de 1890*, Rio de Janeiro, Oficina de Estatística, 1901, p. 78; idem, *Recenseamento de 1906*, op. cit., pp. 100ff.

14. Dom Obá II d'Africa, 'Ao Exmo. Sr. Conselheiro Ernesto Ferreira França', *O Carbonário*, 13 March 1889, p. 4.

15. Recenseamento de 1890, op. cit., p. 78. For a specific study, see Sandra L. Graham, *House and Streets: the Domestic World of Servants and Masters in Nineteenth-century Rio de Janeiro*, Cambridge, Cambridge University Press, 1988.

16. Recenseamento de 1890, op. cit., 'Introdução', p. XXXI.

17. On Brazilian racial ideology and whitening theory, see Thomas E. Skidmore, *O preto no branco; raça e nacionalidade no pensamento brasileiro*, Rio de Janeiro, Paz e Terra, 1976.

18. Recenseamento de 1906, op. cit., p. 108.

19. Ibid., pp. 116–20.

20. Nícia Vilela Luz, *A luta pela industrialização do Brasil*, São Paulo, Difusão Européia do Livro, 1961, p. 58.

21. See June Hahner, 'Jacobinos Versus Galegos: Urban Radicals Versus Portuguese Immigrants in Rio de Janeiro in the 1890's', *Journal of Interamerican Studies and World Affairs*, 18(2) 125–54, May 1976; Wilma Peres Costa, 'Notas Sobre o Jacobinismo Brasileiro', presented at the Seminar Rio Republicano, FCRB, 1984; Gladys Sabina Ribeiro, *'Cabras' e 'pés-de-chumbo': os rolos do tempo. O antilusitanismo na cidade do Rio de Janeiro, 1890–1930*, Tese de Mestrado, Niterói, UFF, 1987.

22. Quoted by Bergstresser, op. cit., p. 28.

23. Dom Obá II d'Africa, Untitled (IV), *O Carbonário*, 1 November 1886, p. 4.

24. Mello Barreto Filho e Hermeto Lima, *História da Polícia do Rio de Janeiro; aspéctos da cidade e da vida carioca, 1870–1889*, Rio de Janeiro, A Noite, 1944, p. 151.

25. *O Carbonário*, 24 May 1886, p. 2.

26. *O Carbonário*, 28 November 1887, p. 3.

27. *O Carbonário*, 3 February 1888, p. 2.

28. *Gazeta de Notícias*, 9 July 1890, p. 1.

29. Figures for 1861–73. See Eduardo Silva (org.), *Idéias políticas de Quintino Bocaiúva*, Brasília, Senado Federal; Rio de Janeiro, FCRB, 1986, 1 vol., 'Introdução', p. 94. For the following period, see *As Queixas do Povo*, Rio de Janeiro, Paz e Terra, 1988, pp. 87ff.

30. João do Rio, *As religiões no Rio*, Rio de Janeiro, H. Garnier, s.d., p. 8. The articles were originally published in 1904. On the author, see Antônio Arnoni Prado, 'Mutilados da Belle-Epoque; Notas Sobre as Reportagens de João do Rio'. In Roberto Schwarz (org.), *Os pobres na literatura brasileira*, São Paulo, Brasiliense, 1983, pp. 68–72.

31. Lulu Senior, 'Principe Obá', *Gazeta de Notícias*, 13 November 1889, p. 1.

32. Roberto Moura, *Tia Ciata e a pequena África no Rio de Janeiro*. Rio de Janeiro, FUNARTE, 1983, p. 62; José Murilo de Carvalho, *Os bestializados; o Rio de Janeiro e a República que não foi*, São Paulo, Companhia das Letras, 1987, p. 41; Silva, *As Queixas do Povo*, op. cit., pp. 79–80.

33. Ary Vasconcelos, *Panorama da música popular brasileira*, São Paulo, Martins, 1964, vol. I, pp. 18–19; Moura, op. cit., pp 46 and 66–7.

34. Heloisa Tolipan, 'Sambista Centenária', *Jornal do Brasil*, 28 February 1987, Caderno Cidade, p. 5.

35. Vasco Mariz, *A canção brasileira*, Rio de Janeiro, Serviço de Documentação do MEC, 1959, pp. 180–8; Vasconcelos, op. cit., p. 63; Moura. op. cit., pp. 46 and 63–4.

36. Moura, op. cit., p. 64.

37. Ibid., pp. 62, 64 and 66.

38. João do Rio, op. cit., pp. 2–7.

39. Ibid., p. 17.

40. Cf. Pierre F. Verger, *Orixás; Deuses Iorubás na África e no Novo Mundo*, São Paulo, Corrupio, 1981, pp. 174–85.

41. *Jornal do Brasil*, 28 February 1987, Cad. Cidade, p. 5.

42. Aluísio de Azevedo, *O Cortiço*, São Paulo, Martins, 1965 (1st edition, 1890).

43. Lilian Fessler Vaz, 'Notas Sobre o Cabeça de Porco', *Revista do Rio de Janeiro*, 1(2), January–April 1986, pp. 29–35.

44. *O Paiz*, 3 December 1889, p. 1.

45. *Gazeta de Notícias*, 9 July 1890, p. 1; *Diário de Notícias*, 14 July 1890, p. 1.

46. Francisco Peixoto de Lacerda Werneck, Barão de Pati do Alferes, *Memória sobre a fundação de uma fazenda na província do Rio de Janeiro*; edição original de 1847 e edição modificada e acrescida de 1878, edited by Eduardo Silva, Brasília, Senado Federal; Rio de Janeiro, FCRB, 1985, pp. 38, 59 and 95.

47. Luís Peixoto de Lacerda Werneck, *Idéias sobre colonização precedidas de uma sucinta exposição dos princípios gerais que regem a população*, Rio de Janeiro, E. and H. Laemmert, 1855, pp. 36ff; Caetano Furquim de Almeida, 'Carestia dos Gêneros Alimentícios'. In *Relatório do Presidente da Província do Rio de Janeiro*, Rio de Janeiro, 1858, Anexo K; Sebastião Ferreira Soares, *Notas estatísticas sobre a produção e carestia dos gêneros alimentícios no Império do Brasil*, Rio de Janeiro, Typ. Imp. e Const. de J. Villeneuve, 1860, pp. 17–21 et passim.

48. Soares, op. cit., p. 288.

49. Ibid., p. 289. For a longer period, see Aureliano Restier Gonçalves, 'Carnes

Verdes em São Sebastião do Rio de Janeiro, 1500–1900', *Revista de Documentos Para a História do Rio de Janeiro*, vol. III, Rio de Janeiro, Arquivo do Distrito Federal, 1952, pp. 307–8.

50. The British Library, PP, 1886, vol. 65, p. 329; idem, 1882, vol. 70, p. 175.

51. The British Library, PP, 1878, vol. 75, pp. 24–6; idem, 1881, vol. 89, p. 539; idem, 1882, vol. 70, pp. 181–203; idem, 1886, vol. 65, pp. 329–53.

52. *O Paiz*, 3 December 1889, p. 1.

53. Stein, op. cit., p. 245.

54. Américo Jacobina Lacombe, Eduardo Silva e Francisco de Assis Barbosa, *Rui Barbosa e a queima dos arquivos*, Brasília, Ministério da Justiça, Rio de Janeiro, FCRB, 1988.

55. Lima, op. cit., pp. 461–4.

56. See Sandra Lauderdale Graham, 'The Vintém Riot and Political Culture; Rio de Janeiro, 1880', *Hispanic American Historical Review*, 60(3), 432–49, August 1980; Bergstresser, op. cit., pp. 18–22.

57. Quoted by Nelson Werneck Sodré, *História da Imprensa no Brasil*, Rio de Janeiro, Civilização Brasileira, 1966, p. 266.

58. Bergstresser, op. cit., pp. 18ff.

59. Dom Obá II d'Africa, 'A Cruel Inveja Contra o Príncipe Dom Obá II d'Africa, Apesar que Contra a Força há Resistência, o Certo é que o Diabo não Pode mais que Deus' (III), *O Carbonário*, 22 November 1886, p. 4. Ver ainda: *O Carbonário*, 23 February 1887, p. 4.

60. Bergstresser, op. cit., p. 30.

61. Dom Obá II d'Africa, 'Ao País e ao Respeitável Público', *O Carbonário*, 8 September 1882, p. 4.

62. Idem, 'A Justa Palavra Perante Deus . . .', *O Carbonário*, 4 June 1883, p. 4.

Chapter 5: The Faithful Vassal

1. R. Magalhães Júnior, *O Império em chinelos*, Rio de Janeiro, Civilização Brasileira, 1957, pp. 261–2.

2. Mello Moraes Filho, *Quadros e crônicas*, Rio de Janeiro, Garnier, n.d. (1890s), p. 255.

3. Ibid., p. 254.

4. Ibid., pp. 255–6.

5. MHN. Visitors' book of the Quinta da Boa Vista Palace, 1882–5, Arquivo, IMr2.

6. Ibid.

7. Ibid., pp. 66–7.

8. Ibid.

9. Carl von Koseritz, *Imagens do Brasil*, Tradução de Afonso Arinos de Mello Franco, São Paulo, Martins, 1943, pp. 160 and 219 (1st edition in German, 1885).

10. Leslie Bethell, *The Abolition of the Brazilian Slave Trade: Britain, Brazil and the Slave Trade Question, 1807–1869*, Cambridge, Cambridge University Press, 1970, p. 377.

11. von Koseritz, op. cit., p. 221.

12. MHN, Visitors' book, op. cit., pp. 41–2, 45–6, 55–6 and 66–7.

13. von Koseritz, op. cit., p. 217.

14. Ibid., p. 158 and 218.

15. Ibid., p. 219.

16. Ibid., pp. 219–20.

17. On the Senador Vergueiro's sharecrop system, see Thomas Davatz, *Memórias de um colono no Brasil*, Tradução, introdução e notas de Sérgio Buarque de Holanda, 2nd edition, São Paulo, Martins, 1951; Sérgio Buarque de Holanda, 'As Colônias de Parceria'. In S. B. de Holanda, (org.), *História geral da civilização brasileira*, Tomo V, São Paulo, Difel, 1960, pp. 245–60; José Sebastião Witter, *Ibicaba, uma experiência pioneira*, 2nd edition, São Paulo, Arquivo do Estado de São Paulo, 1982. On the transition to free labour in other coffee areas, see Emília Viotti da Costa, *Da senzala à colônia*, São Paulo, Difel, 1966; idem, *Da Monarquia à Republica: momentos decisivos*, São Paulo, Grijalbo, 1977, pp. 149–77; Warren Dean, *Rio Claro: um sistema brasileiro de grande lavoura, 1820–1920*, São Paulo, Paz e Terra, 1977; Ademir Gebara, *O mercado de trabalho livre no Brasil*, São Paulo, Brasiliense, 1986; Ana Lúcia Duarte Lanna, *A transformação do trabalho: a passagem para o trabalho livre na Zona da Mata mineira, 1870–1920*, 2nd edition, Campinas, Editora da UNICAMP, 1989. On the legislation related to work contracts, especially the 1871 law, see Maria Lúcia Lamounier, *Da escravidão ao trabalho livre*, Campinas, Papirus, 1988.

18. von Koseritz, op. cit., p. 221.

19. Ibid., pp. 222–3.

20. Ibid., p. 219.

21. Luís Peixoto de Lacerda Werneck, *Idéias sobre colonização precedidas de uma sucinta exposição dos princípios gerais que regem a população*, Rio de Janeiro, Eduardo & Henrique Laemmert, 1855, p. 21.

22. Louis Couty, *L'Esclavage au Brésil*, Paris, Librairie de Guillaumin, 1881, p. 87. It is interesting to note that the *Revista do IHGB*, the most important Brazilian history periodical, had published only three articles on the participation of blacks in the history of Brazil, since its inauguration in 1838, up to the final abolition in 1888. See João José Planella, *Índice por assuntos gerais da Revista do IHGB, 1838–1983*, Porto Alegre, mimeo, 1983, p. 55. See also Américo Jacobina Lacombe, 'A Cultura Africana no Brasil', *Jornal do Brasil*, 27 November 1988, p. 7 (Caderno B/Especial).

23. von Koseritz, op. cit., p. 160.

24. Stanley J. Stein, *Vassouras, a Brazilian Coffee County, 1850–1900*, Princeton, Princeton University Press, 1985, pp. 59–62.

25. Eduardo Silva, *Barões e escravidão; três gerações de fazendeiros e a crise da estrutura escravista*, Rio de Janeiro, Nova Fronteira, 1984, pp. 195–6.

26. von Koseritz, op. cit., p. 217.

27. See Barão de Pati do Alferes, *Memória sobre a fundação de uma fazenda na província do Rio de Janeiro*, edição original de 1847 e edição modificada e acrescida de 1878, ed. Eduardo Silva, Rio de Janeiro, FCRB; Brasília, Senado Federal, 1985, pp. 63 and 101.

28. Cf. Silva, op. cit., pp. 195–6.

29. Werneck, *Idéias sobre colonização ...* op. cit., pp. 63–4.

30. Idem, 'Breves Considerações Sobre a Posição Atual da Lavoura do Café', *Almanak Administrativo Mercantil e Industrial da Corte e Província do Rio de Janeiro*. Rio de Janeiro, 12, 2a. série (7), 93–109, 1885, p. 106.

31. Ibid., p. 107.

32. Idem, *Idéias sobre colonização* ... op. cit., pp. 75–9.

33. Quintino Bocaiúva, *Idéias políticas de Quintino Bocaiúva*, ed. Eduardo Silva, Brasília, Senado federal, Rio de Janeiro, FCRB, 1986, vol. I, p. 243.

34. Ibid., pp. 24–5 and 244.

35. Ibid., pp. 250–1.

36. Ibid., p. 241.

37. For further details on the wages of the Asian workers, see Bocaiúva, op. cit., pp. 260–1.

38. Ibid., pp. 261–2.

39. Ibid., p. 264.

40. Nicolau Joaquim Moreira, open letter to Quintino Bocaiúva, 6 September 1870. Quoted in Bocaiúva, op. cit., pp. 266–7. On the *Sociedade Auxiliadora da Indústria Nacional*, see José Luís F. Werneck da Silva, *Isto é o que me parece: a Sociedade Auxiliadora da Indústria Nacional na formação social brasileira, 1827–1904*, Tese de Mestrado, Niterói, Universidade Federal Fluminense, 1979, 2 vols.

41. Nicolau Joaquim Moreira, open letter to Quintino Bocaiúva, 13 September 1870. For a complete discussion, see Bocaiúva, op. cit., pp. 263–75.

42. Joaquim Nabuco, *Cartas aos abolicionistas ingleses*, ed. José Thomaz Nabuco, Recife, Fundação Joaquim Nabuco/Massangana, 1985, p. 44, letter of 8 April 1880. On the intellectual origins of anti-slavery thought and the inter-connections between British and continental abolitionist movements, see David Brion Davis, *The Problem of Slavery in Western Culture*, New York, Oxford University Press, 1988 (1st edition 1966); idem, *Slavery and Human Progress*, New York, Oxford University Press, 1984, pp. 168ff. Seymour Drescher, *Capitalism and Antislavery; British Mobilization in Comparative Perspective*, London, Macmillan, 1986; David Richardson (ed.), *Abolition and its Aftermath*, London, Frank Cass, 1985.

43. Dom Obá II d'Africa, 'Untitled', *O Carbonário*, 25 March 1887, p. 4.

44. Idem, 'As Vivas Razões da Constituição da Lei que nos Rege e nos faz Respeitá-la', *Jornal do Commercio*, 25 February 1885, p. 5.

45. Idem, 'Untitled', op. cit.; idem, 'A Justiça e a Consciência' (V), *O Carbonário*, 2 May 1887, p. 4.

46. Idem, 'A Paixão de N. S. Jesus Cristo', *O Carbonário*, 26 April 1886, p. 4; 'Plano Maldito dos Adversários; a Inveja e a Razão Convence os Espertalhões dos Direitos de Deus e dos Reis' (II), *O Carbonário*, 21 June 1886, p. 4.

47. Idem, 'Cruel Intriga', *O Carbonário*, 29 November 1886, p. 4.

48. Idem, 'Untitled', op. cit.

49. Bethell, op. cit., pp. 376–7.

Chapter 6: Prince of the Streets

1. Mello Moraes Filho, *Quadros e crônicas*, Rio de Janeiro, Garnier, n.d., p. 254.

2. Carl von Koseritz, *Imagens do Brasil*, Tradução Afonso Arinos de Melo Franco, São Paulo, Martins, 1943, p. 160.

3. J. Le Goff, 'As Mentalidades, uma História Ambigua'. In Le Goff e Pierre

Nora (orgs), *História: novos objetos*, Rio de Janeiro, Francisco Alves, 1976, p. 68.

4. Gilberto Freyre, *Casa-Grande & Senzala*, 25th edition, Rio de Janeiro, José Olympio, 1987, 'Prefácio à la. Edição' (1933), pp. lv–lxxxviii, especially pp. lx–lxii. Strongly influenced by Freyre, would emerge, in the 1940s and 1960s, several comparative studies emphasizing radical differences between the slave-owning system in Brazil (Catholic and paternalist) and in the United States (Protestant and capitalist). See Frank Tannenbaum, *Slave and Citizen: the Negro in the Americas*, New York, Alfred A. Knopf, 1947; Stanley Elkins, *Slavery: a Problem in American Institutional and Intellectual Life*, New York, The Universal Library, 1959. Such comparative schemes, especially the conception of a 'racial democracy' in Brazil, would suffer strong historiographical revisionism from the 1960 and 1970s on. See Florestan Fernandes and Roger Bastide, *Brancos e negros em São Paulo*, São Paulo, Companhia Editora Nacional, 1959; Fernando Henrique Cardoso, *Capitalismo e escravidão no Brasil Meridional*, São Paulo, Difusão Européia do Livro, 1962; Octávio Ianni, *As metamorfoses de escravo*, São Paulo, Difusão Européia do Livro, 1962; Marvin Harris, *Padrões raciais nas Américas*, Rio de Janeiro, Civilização Brasileira, 1967 (original edition, 1964); Carl Degler, *Nem preto nem branco; escravidão e relações raciais no Brasil e nos EUA*, São Paulo, Labor do Brasil, 1976 (original edition, 1971). More recently, since the mid-1970s, *Roll, Jordan, Roll* by Eugene D. Genovese, seems to mark new historiographical reflection, when it discusses precisely the paternalist face of slavery in the United States.

5. Freyre, *Casa-Grande & Senzala*, op. cit.; *Sobrados e Mocambos*, 5th edn, Rio de Janeiro, José Olympio/INL-MEC, 1977, 2v. (original edition, 1936); *Ordem e Progresso*, Rio de Janeiro, José Olympio, 1959, 2v. The series would include *Jazigos e Covas Rasas*, a study on the systems and practices of 'burial and celebration of the dead in patriarcal and semi-patriarcal Brasil', which unfortunately has not been published.

6. Eugene D. Genovese, *Roll, Jordan, Roll; the World the Slaves Made*, New York, Vintage, 1976, p. 5. (original edition, 1972). The idea of paternalism was also taken up by R. W. Fogel and S. L. Engermann, *Time on the Cross, the Economics of American Negro Slavery*, Boston, Little, Brown, 1974. For a conceptual discussion, see Nicholas Abercrombie and Stephen Hill, 'Paternalism and Patronage', *British Journal of Sociology*, 27(4), 413–29, December 1976.

7. Freyre, *Casa-Grande & Senzala*, op. cit., p. lx.

8. Gilberto Freyre, *O escravo nos anúncios de jornais brasileiros do século XIX*, 2nd edn., São Paulo, Companhia Editora Nacional, 1979, p. xii. Also for Graham the benign aspect of Brazilian paternalism had a very relative face. 'No dichotomy existed between force and benevolence: each drew its meaning from the other,' he wrote. In truth, 'the threat of punishment and the promise of benevolence shaped the lives of wives and children, slaves, *agregados*, small landowners, village tradesmen, and other followers of the patron, catching them all in a powerful web of obligations owed and gifts expected.... Everyone was taken up in a constant process of mutual, if unequal, exchange.' See Richard Graham, *Patronage and Politics in Nineteenth-century Brazil*, Stanford, Stanford University Press, 1990, pp. 22–4.

9. Antônio Barros de Castro, 'A Economia Política, o Capitalismo e a Escravidão'. In J. R. do Amaral Lapa (org.), *Modos de produção e realidade brasileira*, Petrópolis, Vozes, 1980.

10. André João Antonil, pseud. João A. Andreoni, *Cultura e opulência do Brasil*, 2nd edition, Introdução e vocabulário de Alice P. Canabrava, São Paulo,

Companhia Editora Nacional, n.d., p. 159.

11. Patricia Mulvey, *The Black Lay Brotherhoods of Colonial Brazil: a History*, PhD Thesis, City University of New York, 1976, p. 109. Besides the brotherhoods linked to professional activities or ethnic groups, there were wider ones such as the 'Brotherhood of Men of Colour', indiscriminately frequented by Africans of different nations, creoles and mulattos. There were also the elite brotherhoods, formed by well-off 'fidalgos and philanthrophists'. See A. J. R. Russel-Wood, *Fidalgos and Philanthropists: the Santa Casa da Misericordia of Bahia, 1550–1755*, London, Macmillan, 1968. Also idem, *The Black Man in Slavery and Freedom in Colonial Brazil*, New York, St Martin's Press, 1982. On Rio de Janeiro, see Ubaldo Soares, *A escravatura na Misericórdia*, Rio de Janeiro, Fundação Romão de Matos Duarte, 1958; Mary C. Karasch, *Slave Life in Rio de Janeiro, 1808–1850*, Princeton, Princeton University Press, 1987, pp. 82–8.

12. Júlio Braga, *Sociedade Protetora dos Desvalidos: uma irmandade de cor*, Salvador, Ianamá, 1987; Pierre F. Verger, *Fluxo e refluxo do tráfico de escravos entre o Golfo de Benin e a Bahia de Todos os Santos dos séculos XVII a XIX*, trad. Tasso Gadzanis, São Paulo, Corrupio, 1987, pp. 517–18 (original in French, 1968).

13. Verger, op. cit., pp. 524–5.

14. Ibid., p. 529.

15. Dom Pedro II, *Conselhos à Regente*, Introdução e notas de João Camillo de Oliveira Torres, Rio de Janeiro, Livraria São José, 1958, p. 62.

16. von Koseritz, op. cit., p. 158. Such event happened, on 11 August 1883, as can be confirmed in the Palace's Visitors' Book.

17. Republican Provisional Government, Decree no. 5 of 19 November 1889.

18. Anonymous, 'Felicitação Oferecida ao Distinto Patriota Monarquista de Família, o Nobre Príncipe Obá II de Africa e Alferes Galvão, no Brasil', *Jornal do Commercio*, 4 May 1884, p. 3.

19. Mello Barreto Filho e Hermeto Lima, *História da Polícia do Rio de Janeiro; aspéctos da cidade e da vida carioca, 1870–1889*, Rio de Janeiro, A Noite, 1944, p. 150.

20. Moraes Filho, op. cit., p. 252.

21. Vicente Reis, 'O Rio de Janeiro no Crepúsculo da Monarquia; Aspéctos de Sua Vida Social e Comercial', *Revista do IHGB*, 345 (1984), 7–83, October/ December 1984. Quotation on p. 71.

22. Lulu Senior, 'Príncipe Obá', *Gazeta de Notícias*, 13 November 1889, p. 1.

23. Dionísio Cerqueira, *Reminiscência da campanha do Paraguai, 1865–1870*, Rio de Janeiro, Biblioteca do Exército, 1980, p. 72.

24. Dom Obá II d'Africa, 'As Vivas Razões da Constituição da Lei que nos Rege e nos faz Respeitá-la', *Jornal do Commercio*, 25 February 1885, p. 5. The idea of provincial fatherland was also supported by certain sectors of the elite. Alberto Sales, an important coffee-grower from São Paulo and one of the mentors of the Republic, defended openly the separation, in 1887, in a book entitled 'A Pátria Paulista'; the guacho Júlio de Castilhos, influenced by the positivist ideal of the 'small fatherlands', would defend the *confederation* instead of *federation*, at the Constituent Assembly of 1891. See Alberto Sales, *A pátria paulista*, Brasília, Editora da Universidade de Brasília, 1993; Francisco de Assis Barbosa, *JK: uma revisão na política brasileira*, Rio de Janeiro, José Olympio, 1960, pp. 107–8.

25. Dom Obá II d'Africa, 'A.S.M. o Imperador e ao e ao País pois Desta Natureza só Aparecem dum Século a Século' (I), *O Carbonário*, 12 July 1886, p. 4.

Much of the historian's knowledge about Abiodun's reign (probably 1770–89) comes from the oral tradition magnificently collected by Rev. Samuel Johnson, around 1897. See *The History of the Yorubas; from the Earliest Times to the Beginning of the British Protectorate*, Lagos, C.S.S. 1976, pp. 182–7. For a current discussion, see Thomas Hodgkin, *Nigerian Perspectives; an Historical Anthology*, 2nd edition, Oxford, Oxford University Press, 1975 (1st edition 1960); Peter Morton-Williams, 'The Oyo Yoruba and the Atlantic Trade, 1670–1830', *Journal of the Historical Society of Nigeria*, 3(1), 25–45, December 1964; Robert S. Smith, *Kingdoms of the Yoruba*, 3rd edition, London, James Currey, 1988 (1st edition 1969); J. A. Atanda, 'The Fall of the Old Oyo Empire: a Re-consideration of its Cause', *Journal of the Historical Society of Nigeria*, 5(4), 477–90, June 1971; idem, *The New Oyo Empire*, London, Longmans, 1973; Robin Law, *The Oyo Empire (c. 1600–c. 1836); a West African Imperialism in the Era of the Atlantic Slave Trade*, Oxford, Clarendon Press, 1977; C. O. Ayodele, *The Traditional Political Institution in Oyo*, M A Thesis, Ibadan University, 1983; Ebiegberi J. Alagoa, 'Oral Tradition and Cultural History in Nigeria', *Storia Della Storiografia*, Milano, Editoriale Jaca Book, no. 5, 1984, pp. 66–76.

26. Dom Obá II d'Africa, 'Ao País e ao respeitável Público' (I), *O Carbonário*, 4 March 1882, p. 4.

27. Linda Lewin, *Politics and Parentela in Paraíba: a Case-study of Family-based Oligarchy in Brazil*, Princeton, Princeton University Press, 1987, p. 10.

28. Dom Obá II d'Africa, 'Questão Diplomática; à S.M. o Imperador' (II), *Jornal do Commercio*, 6 March 1886, p. 4.

29. Idem, 'Plano Maldito dos Adversários; a Inveja e a Razão Convence os Espertalhões dos Direitos de Deus e dos Reis' (I), *O Carbonário*, 18 June 1886, p. 4. On Cotegipe and Junqueira, see 'Questão Diplomática; à S.M. Majestade o Imperador' (I), *Jornal do Commercio*, 3 January 1886, p. 3.

30. Dom Obá II d'Africa, 'A S.M. o Imperador e ao País pois Desta Natureza só Aparecem dum Século a Século', *O Carbonário*, 16 July 1886, p. 4. According to Mello Barreto Filho and Hermeto Lima, 'his superiors respected him and it is said that Duque de Caxias was one of his greatest admirers', op. cit., p. 149.

31. Dom Obá II d'Africa, 'A S.A. Seageríssima o Senhor Príncipe Conde d'Eu' (I), *O Carbonário*, 20 September 1886, p. 4.

32. Conde d'Eu, *Viagem militar ao Rio Grande do Sul*, São Paulo, Companhia Editora Nacional, 1936, p. 135.

33. Letter from Conde d'Eu to the Viscount of Lage, 12 January 1870. Quoted in Oliveira Lima, *O movimento da Independência; o Império Brasileiro, 1821–1889*, 2nd edition, São Paulo, Melhoramentos, pp. 424–5.

34. Dom Pedro II, op. cit., p. 60.

35. Dom Obá II d'Africa, 'A S.A. Sereníssima o Senhor Príncipe Conde d'Eu' (II), *O Carbonário*, 22 September 1886, p. 4; idem, 'A Divindade Manda Não Ser-se Traidor ao Rei' (I), *O Carbonário*, 9 May 1887, p. 4.

36. Robert Levine, *'Valley of Tears'; Canudos as Myth in Brazilian History*, Unpublished, ch. 2, p. 24.

37. *Jornal do Commercio*, 25 April 1887, p. 1.

38. Lulu Senior, op. cit.

39. Moraes Filho, op. cit., p. 252; R. Magalhães Júnior, *O Império em chinelos*, Rio de Janeiro, Civilização Brasileira, 1957, p. 260.

40. Barreto Filho and Lima, op. cit., p. 150.

41. See Nina Rodrigues, *Os Africanos no Brasil*, São Paulo, Companhia Editora

Nacional, 1932, pp. 164–5; Arthur Ramos, *As culturas negras no Novo Mundo*, 4th edition, São Paulo, Companhia Editora Nacional, 1979, pp. 207–8 (1st edition 1935); Octavio da Costa Eduardo, *The Negro in Northern Brazil; a Study in Acculturation*, London, The African Publication Society, 1981, pp. 9–10 (1st edition 1948); Karasch, op. cit., pp. 25–6.

42. *O Paiz*, 9 July 1890, p. 1.

43. *Jornal do Commercio*, 25 April 1887, p. 1.

44. *Diário de Notícias*, 14 July 1890, p. 1; Reis, op. cit., p. 71.

45. Dom Obá II d'Africa, 'Plano Maldito dos Adversários . . .' (I), op. cit.

46. Idem, 'Aos Poderes do Estado', *O Carbonário*, 2 August 1886, p. 4.

47. Diário de Notícias, 14 July 1890, p. 1.

48. *Jornal do Commercio*, 125 April 1887, p. 1.

49. On traditional and charismatic leadership, see Max Weber, *Economia y sociedad; esbozo de sociologia comprensiva*, Mexico, Fondo de Cultura Económica, 1984, pp. 180–204 (1st edition, 1922).

50. *Diário de Notícias*, 14 July 1890, p. 1.

51. Moraes Filho, op. cit., p. 253.

52. *O Paiz*, 13 November 1889, p. 1.

53. *O Paiz*, 9 July 1890, p. 1.

54. Lima Barreto, 'A Matemática não Falha'. In *Bagatelas*, São Paulo, Brasiliense, 1956, p. 182 (article originally published in 1918).

55. von Koseritz, op. cit., p. 160.

56. Barreto Filho and Lima, op. cit., p. 151.

57. Lima Barreto, 'Pela "Secção Livre"'. In *Bagatelas*, op. cit., p. 229 (originally published in 1919).

Chapter 7: Brazilian Questions

1. Dom Obá II d'Africa, 'A Divindade Manda Não Ser-se Traidor do Rei' (III), *O Carbonário*, 23 May 1887, p. 4.

2. Idem, 'A Justiça e a Consciência' (III), *O Carbonário*, 25 April 1887, p. 4.

3. Idem, 'A Justiça e a Consciência' (I), *O Carbonário*, 22 April 1887, p. 4.

4. 1 Samuel 9, 15–18. For the whole process, see ibid., chapters 8–12.

5. Samuel Johnson, *The History of the Yorubas*, Lagos, C.S.S., 1976, p. 40.

6. For a recent analysis of the Oduduwa myth, see Ulli Beier, *Yoruba Beaded Crowns; Sacred Regalia of the Olokuku of Okuku*, London, Ethnographica, 1982, pp. 2–35. Samuel Johnson (1846–1901) recorded another version of the origin myth, where Oduduwa, always a warrior king, did not descend from the heavens to Ile-Ife, but emigrated from Mecca with his idols to escape the persecution of the implacable Islamic monotheists. Johnson, based on this version, thinks there are good reasons for believing that the Yoruba had come, if not from Mecca itself, from the East (words which were virtually synonymous for the people), and more precisely, from Egypt. This version, however, is only found in Oyo, and probably dates from the beginning of the nineteenth century, which was a time of great Islamic penetration. Cf. Johnson. op. cit., chapters I and II. Archaeological evidence seems to indicate that a migration from a north-westerly direction was more probable, following the Rio Niger downstream to what may be the Borgu region.

For a recent survey of the archaeological and historial knowledge available, see Frank Willett, 'Nigeria'. In P.L. Shinnie (ed.), *The African Iron Age*. Oxford, Claredon, 1971, pp. 1–35; Robert S. Smith, *Kingdoms of the Yoruba*, 3rd edition, London, James Currey, 1988, pp. 9–28. For a comprehensive description of the political structure of Oyo and the practical limitations imposed on the absolute power of the Obás, see Peter Morton-Williams, 'The Yoruba Ogboni Cult in Oyo', *Africa*, 30:4 (October 1960), pp. 362–74.

7. Dom Obá II d'Africa, 'A Justiça e a Consciência' (III), op. cit.; idem, 'Plano Maldito dos Adversários; a Inveja e a Razão Convence os Espertalhões dos Direitos de Deus e dos Reis' (II), *O Carbonário*, 21 June 1886, p. 4.

8. Idem, 'A Consciência dos Cantoneiros e os Remorsos dos Quirógrafos Acusa a quem é mal Principiado ser por Castigo de Deus mal Acabado', *O Carbonário*, 20 May 1887, p. 4.

9. Idem, 'Plano Maldito dos Adversários ...' (I), *O Carbonário*, 18 June 1886, p. 4.

10. Idem, 'As Vivas Razões da Constituição da Lei que nos Rege e nos faz Respeitá-la', *Jornal do Commercio*, 25 February 1885, p. 5.

11. Idem, 'Fala a Consciência Universal, que Obriga o Direito Divinal, Interessar-se pelo Bem-estar do Deus da Nação Brasileira', *O Carbonário*, 18 March 1887, p. 4; idem, 'Ao Universo Imploro a Suplicada Saudação' (II), *O Carbonário*, 30 May 1887, p. 4.

12. Idem, 'As Vivas Razões da Constituição...', op. cit.

13. Joaquim Nabuco, *Abolitionism: the Brazilian Antislavery Struggle*, trans. and ed. Robert Conrad, Illinois, University of Illinois Press, 1977, pp. 51–17 (edition, original 1883). According to Oliveira Viana, the parties 'were mere aggregations of clans organised for the common exploitation of the advantages of power'; or, according to Oliveira Lima, displayed labels rather than programmes, 'with no other meaning beyond the labels'. Oliveira Viana, *O Ocaso do Império*, São Paulo, Melhoramentos, 1925, p. 26; Oliveira Lima, *O movimento da Independência; o Império Brasileiro (1821–1889)*, 2nd edition, São Paulo, Melhoramentos, 1921, p. 26.

14. João Dunshee de Abranches, *O cativeiro (Memórias)*, Rio de Janeiro, 1941, p. 226.

15. Senate records, speeches on 18 June 1870. Apud Oliveira Viana, op. cit., p. 26.

16. Lima Barreto, *Bagatelas*, São Paulo, Brasiliense, 1956, p. 182.

17. Dom Obá II d'Africa, 'Ao País e ao Respeitável Público' (V), *O Carbonário*, 1 September 1882, p. 4.

18. Idem, 'Ao País e ao Respeitável Público' (VI), *O Carbonàrio*, 4 September 1882, p. 4. Seven years after the fall of the Conservatives, at the time of the Saraiva cabinet, the prince had been unemployed 'for 7 years'. See Anonymous, "Felicitação Oferecida ao Distinto Patriota Monarquista de Família, o Nobre Príncipe Obá II de Africa e Alferes Galvão, no Brasil', *Jornal do Commercio*, 4 May 1884, p. 3. Two years later, under the Conservative cabinet of the Baron of Cotegipe, the prince was still 'unemployed till this day without the bread of the nation'. See 'O Plano Maldito dos Adversários ...' (II), op. cit. On this point, also 'A S.M. o Imperador e ao País pois Desta Natureza só Aparecem dum Século a Século', *O Carbonário*, 12 July 1886, p. 4; 'A Cruel Inveja ...', *O Carbonário*, 2 May 1887, p. 4; 'A Justiça e à Consciência' (V), *O Carbonário*, 2 May 1887, p. 4.

19. Eduardo Silva (ed.), *Idéias Políticas de Quintino Bocaiúva; cronologia*

introdução, notas bibliográficos e textos selecionados, Brasília, Senado Federal; Rio de Janeiro, FCRB, 1986, v.I, 'Introduction', pp. 55ff. On the position of Dom Pedro as regards elections and the necessary reforms, see Dom Pedro II, *Conselhos à Regente*, Rio de Janeiro, Livraria São José, 1958, pp. 29–30 (original manuscript, 1871).

20. Dom Obá II d'Africa, 'As Vivas Razões da Constituição . . .', op. cit.

21. Idem, 'Untitled' (II and III), *O Carbonário*, 22 and 25 October 1886, p. 4.

22. Idem, 'Plano Maldito dos Adversários . . .' (III), *O Carbonário*, 25 June 1886, p. 4. For the 'evolutionist' and 'revolutionary' currents of thought, see Silva (ed.), *Idéias Políticas de Quintino Bocaiúva*, op. cit., p. 59ff. For the thinking of Silva Jardim, see Antônio da Silva Jardim, *Propaganda Republicana (1888–1889); discursos, opúsculos, manifestos e artigos coligidos, anotados e prefaciados por Barbosa Lima Sobrinho*, Rio de Janeiro, FCRB/Conselho Federal de Cultura, 1978; Idem, *Memórias e Viagens; campanha de um propagandista, 1887–1890*, Lisboa, Typ. da Companhia Nacional Editora, 1891; idem, *Cartas de Silva Jardim a Clóvis Bevilaqua*, Rio de Janeiro, Apollo, 1936; José Leão, *Silva Jardim; apontamentos para a biografia do ilustre propagandista hauridos nas informações paternas e dados particulares oficiais por . . .*, Rio de Janeiro, Imprensa Nacional, 1895.

23. Dom Obá II d'Africa, 'A Justa Palavra Perante Deus, a Majestade e Universidades' (III), *O Carbonário*, 11 June 1883, p. 3. For the complete series, see Appendix C (I, II and III), pp. 165–9.

24. Anonymous, 'Reminiscências de Um do Povo (do meu Diário), *A Imprensa*, Rio de Janeiro, 15 November 1911, p. 2. On the following day, according to Aristides Lobo, one of the conspirators, the people of Rio de Janeiro also 'watched everything dumbstruck, astonished, surprised, without understanding what it meant'. Quoted in José Maria dos Santos, *A política geral do Brasil*, São Paulo, J. Magalhães, 1930, p. 203.

25. Dom Obá II d'Africa, 'As Vivas Razões da Constituição . . .', op. cit. In the same vein, see also 'Questão Diplomática; a S.M. o Imperador' (I), *Jornal do Commercio*, 3 January 1886, p. 3; 'Plano Maldito dos Adversários . . .' (I), op. cit.

26. Idem, 'Fala a Consciência Universal . . .', op. cit. Also, on the same topic, 'Ao Universo Imploro a Suplicada Saudação' (III), *O Carbonário*, 8 June 1887, p. 4.

27. Idem, 'Fala a Consciência Universal . . .', op. cit.

28. Idem, 'A Justiça e a Consciência' (IV), *O Carbonário*, 29 April 1887, p. 4.

29. For a study of these articulations, see Silva (ed.), *Idéias políticas de Quintino Bocaiúva*, op. cit., 'Introduction', pp. 70–76, and other documents in the same collection.

30. Dom Obá II d'Africa, 'A Divindade Manda não Ser-se Traidor ao Rei' (I), *O Carbonário*, 9 May 1887, p. 4. Again on the 'military question', the prince wrote a few days later in support of the Conservative cabinet presided over Cotegipe in its attempt to bring the troops to order, or, as the prince put it, to 'faithful and severe respect, that as soldiers that we are we have sworn to the God or Goddess of the Nation'. See 'Ao Universo Imploro a Suplicada Saudação' (II), op. cit. As for this same state of spirit, it is worth remembering a letter of support to the prince written the previous year. See Anonymous, 'Untitled', *O Carbonário*, 28 June 1886, p. 4.

31. T.H. Marshall, *Cidade, classe social e status*, Rio de Janeiro, Zahar, 1967, ch. III, 'Cidadania e classe social'.

32. Johann Moritz Rugendas, 'Imagens e Notas do Brasil', *Revista do Patrimônio Histórico e Artístico Nacional*, no. 13, 1956, pp. 43–5.

33. Law no. 2,040 of 28 September 1871, Article 4, paragraphs 1,2,3 and 7. *Coleção de Leis do Império do Brasil*, Tome XXXI, Part I, Rio de Janeiro, 1871, pp. 147–51.

34. It is interesting to note that this theoretical opening for citizens' rights, above all after the electoral reform of 1881, would supply the basic arguments for the *abolitionist movement* in the strict sense, in opposition to the *emancipation* process which was then in course. It was because the slaves could be seen as Brazilians and potential citizens (and not just because they were slaves) that the political project of abolition, representing this 'mass without a voice', could be justified. 'We accept this mandate', wrote Joaquim Nabuco, expounding the basic lines of this new movement, 'as political men with political motives, and thus we represent the slaves and the *ingenuous* in the capacity of Brazilians who will regard their own title to citizenship as imperfect as long as there are Brazilians who remain slaves.' See *Abolitionism*, op. cit., pp. 18–22. Quoted from p. 20.

35. In 1846 the minimum income requirement was increased to 200 mil-réis (about US$100) and remained at that level until the end of the Empire. Contemporaries commented that this threshold was so low that only 'beggars' and 'vagabounds' would fail to meet it. See José Antônio Pimenta Bueno, *Direito público brasileiro e análise da Constituição do Império*, Rio de Janeiro, 1857, pp. 194, 472; José de Alencar, *Sistema representativo*, Rio de Janeiro, B.L. Garnier, 1868, p. 93.

36. Dom Obá II d'Africa, 'Ao Universo Imploro a Suplicada Saudação' (III), op. cit.

37. Idem, 'Ao País e ao Respeitável Público' (III and IV), *O Carbonário*, 21 and 28 August 1882, p. 4.

38. Idem, 'Ao País e ao Respeitável Público' (VII), *O Carbonário*, 8 September 1882, p. 4.

39. Ibid.

40. Given the demand that freedom be granted on enlistment and also taking into account the section of the Constitution which guaranteed access to citizenship once freedom had been obtained, it was not slaves who went to war – and this was a key point for men such as Dom Obá II d'Africa – but Brazilian citizens. This is how the Liberal leader, Senator Nabuco, the father of the abolitionist Joaquim Nabuco understood it. 'They will be citizen-soldiers,' he declared in the State Council in November 1866. 'It is the Constitution of the Empire which makes the freedman a citizen, and if there is no dishonour involved in his voting for public officials, how can there be dishonour in being a soldier, in defending the country which freed him and to which he belongs?' See Nabuco, *Abolitionism . . .*, op. cit., p. 48. In support of his argument, Senator Nabuco cited similar procedures both in Bahia, at time of the War of Independence (Provisions of 23 October 1823 and 10 September 1824), and in the United States, where President Lincoln (in proclamations of 22 September 1862 and 1 January 1863) also permitted the enlistment of slaves, in both the army and the navy. See idem, *Um Estadista do Império*, Rio de Janeiro, Nova Aguillar, 1975, pp. 644–5.

41. Dom Obá II d'Africa, 'Ao País e ao Respeitável Público' (VI), *O Carbonário*, 4 September 1882, p. 4.

42. Idem, 'Não há Vitória sem Grande Batalha' (I), *O Carbonário*, 5 October 1886, p. 4.

43. Idem, 'Não há Vitória sem Grande Batalha' (III), *O Carbonário*, 10 October 1986, p. 4.

44. Idem, 'Não há Vitória sem Grande Batalha' (IV), *O Carbonário*, 15 October 1886, p. 4. We will be returning to the question of the saints (or *orixás*) in the next chapter. On the question of the prince's worries about Dom Pedro II and the political fate of the Cotegipe Cabinet, see 'Fala a Consciência Universal . . .' op. cit., p. 4.

45. Idem, 'Plano Maldito dos Adversários . . .' (II), op. cit.

46. Idem, 'A Justa Palavra Perante Deus . . .' (II), *O Carbonário*, 8 June 1883, p. 4.

47. Idem, 'Ao País e ao Respeitável Público' (VII), *O Carbonário*, 8 September 1882, p. 4.

48. Idem, 'A Divindade Manda não Ser-se Traidor do Rei' (I), op. cit.

49. Idem, 'A Justiça e a Consciência' (II), *O Carbonário*, 24 April 1887, p. 4.

50. Idem, 'Não há Vitória sem Grande Batalha' (I), op. cit.

51. Idem, 'Não há Vitória sem Grande Batalha' (II), *O Carbonário*, 8 October 1886, p. 4; idem, 'Untitled' (I), *O Carbonário*, 18 October 1886, p. 4.

52. Idem, 'Ao Universo Imploro a Suplicada Saudação' (I), *O Carbonário*, 27 May 1887, p. 4. In the discussions in the Chamber, some Deputies tried to hold up the progress of the project (Revocation of Art. 60 of the Criminal Code) extending its effects, besides the civil right, to the internal regulations of the navy, where corporal punishment remained part of the disciplinary penalties. Others, such as Lourenço de Albuquerque, deputy for Alagoas, remembered that such penalties continued to exist in civilized England. 'England, where nerves are not so delicate', he said ironically, 'has maintained corporal punishment in its armada and frequently uses it for other crimes.' See Brazil: Congresso Nacional, Câmara dos Depudados, *Anais do Parlamento Brasileiro*, 1886, v.V, pp. 452–3, 470, 479–83. For a debate on the question of public whipping in Brazil, see José Bonifácio de Andrada e Silva, aliás o Moço, *Discursos Parlamentares*, selection and introduction by Francisco de Assis Barbosa, Brasília, Câmara dos Deputados, 1979 (Perfis parlamentares, 13); Carolina Nabuco, *A vida de Joaquim Nabuco*, 2nd edn, São Paulo, Companhia Editora Nacional, 1929, pp. 204–5; Joaquim Nabuco, *Abolitionism*, op. cit., pp. 85–96; Evaristo de Morais, *A campanha abolicionista (1879–1888)*, 2nd edition, Brasília, Editora Universidade de Brasília, 1986, p. 179; Jean Baptiste Debret, *Viagem pitoresca e histórica ao Brasil*, Notes by Sérgio Milliet. 3rd edition, São Paulo, Martins, 2 vols.; Johann Moritz Rugendas, *Voyage Pittoresque dans Bresil*, Paris, Engelmenn, 1835.

53. Joaquim Nabuco, *Abolitionism*, op. cit., pp. 49 and 51–2.

54. Dom Obá II d'Africa, 'As Vivas Razões da Constituição . . .', op. cit.

55. Joaquim Nabuco, *Abolitionism*, op. cit., p. 19.

56. See Antônio Paim, *História das Idéias Filosóficas no Brasil*, São Paulo, Grijalbo, 1967; idem, *A Filosofia da Escola do Recife*, Rio de Janeiro, Saga, 1966.

57. Joaquim Nabuco, *Abolitionism*, op. cit., p. 22.

58. Raymundo Nina Rodrigues, *Os Africanos no Brasil*, São Paulo, Companhia Editora Nacional, 1945, pp. 24–6; idem, *O animismo fetichista dos negros baianos*, Rio de Janeiro, Civilização Brasileira, 1935. For a more recent view of the author, see also Thomas E. Skidmore, *Preto no branco: raça e nacionalidade no pensamento brasileiro*, Rio de Janeiro, Paz e Terra, 1976 (original in English, 1974); Abdias Nascimento, *O genocídio do negro brasileiro*, Rio de Janeiro, Paz e Terra, 1978; Roque de Barros Laraia, 'Relações Entre Negros e Brancos no Brasil', *BIB*, Rio de Janeiro, (7), 11–21, 1979; João Batista Borges Pereira, *Estudos antropológicos e sociológicos sobre o negro no Brasil; aspectos históricos e*

tendências atuais, São Paulo, Universidade de São Paulo, 1981.

59. Sílvio Romero, *A literatura brasileira e a crítica moderna; ensaio de generalização*, Rio de Janeiro, Imprensa Industrial de João Paulo Ferreira Dias, 1880, p. 53. Also Antônio Cândido, *O método crítico de Sílvio Romero*, São Paulo, 1963; Skidmore, op. cit., pp. 48–53; Marshall C. Eakin, 'Race and Identity: Sílvio Romero, Science, and Social Thought in Late 19th Century Brazil', *Luso-Brazilian Review* 22(2), 1985, p. 152.

60. Dom Obá II d'Africa, 'A S.A. Sereníssima o Senhor Príncipe Conde d'Eu' (I), *O Carbonário*, 20 September 1886, p. 4.

61. Idem, 'Plano Maldito dos Adversarios . . .' (III), op. cit.

62. Anonymous, 'Ao País' (III), *O Carbonário*, 20 December 1886, p. 4.

63. A friend of His Highness, Principe Obá II d'Africa, pseudonym. 'O Dedo de Deus Chama a Atenção do Globo Civilizado para ver a Verdade', *O Carbonário*, 23 February 1887, p. 4. For similar letters of support, see Anonymous, 'Ao País' (I and II), *O Carbonário*, 13 and 17 December 1886, p. 4; Anonymous, 'A pedidos', *Jornal do Commercio*, 4 May 1884, p. 3.

64. Dom Obá II d'Africa, 'Questão Diplomática; à S.M. o Imperador' (II), *Jornal do Commercio*, 6 March 1886, p. 4.

65. Idem, 'Ao Universo Imploro a Suplicada Saudação' (II), op. cit.

66. Idem, 'A Justiça e a Consciência' (V), op. cit.

67. Idem, 'Untitled' (I), op. cit.

68. Anonymous, 'Untitled', *O Carbonário*, 28 June 1886, p. 4.

69. Dom Obá II d'Africa, 'Untitled', *O Carbonário*, 25 March 1887, p. 4.

70. Idem, 'A Consciência dos Cantoneiros e os Remorsos dos Quirógrafos Acusa a quem é Mal Principiado ser por Castigo de Deus mal Acabado', *O Carbonário*, 20 May 1887, p. 4.

71. Idem, 'A Divindade Manda não Ser-se Traidor do Rei' (III), op. cit.

72. In the time of Dom Obá II d'Africa, the Imperial capital was feeling the first impact of this immigration policy. It was having a profound effect not just on the living standards of the poor, as we have already noted, but also on the cultural composition of the city. According to available data, between 1864 and 1872 a total 88,823 immigrants disembarked in Rio de Janeiro, or an average of 9,869 per year. The majority (56,315) were Portuguese, followed by Italians (9,307), French (5,862), English (5,252), Spanish (3,229), North Americans (3,515), Germans (3,119) and others (2,188). In the early stages of the abolitionist process, between 1873 and 1880, the yearly average rose to 21,771 immigrants, to total 304,796 new inhabitants in 14 years. In this phase, the majority were Italians (112,279), Portuguese (110,891), Germans (23,467), Spanish (15,684), Austrian (9,022), French (3,475), English (2,215) besides Swiss, Russians, North Americans and others. On the eve of final Abolition, in 1887 alone, 31,310 foreigners arrived. See Eduardo Prado, 'Immigration'. In M.F. de Sant'Anna Nery (ed.), *Le Bresil*, Paris, Charles Delagrave, 1889, p. 495. The process continued, above all, in post-abolition period and in the Republic. With a decree passed on 28 June 1890, the young Republic made it possible for all those able to work to immigrate without bureaucratic formalities, 'except' Asians and Africans who needed special authorization from Congress. As a result, around 2.7 million Europeans emigrated to Brazil between 1887 and 1914. In the country as a whole, the white population increased from around two-fifths to two-thirds of the population between 1890 and 1940. See *Censos Demográficos* (Demographic Censuses) from 1950 and 1980. On the subject of 'whitening' and immigration, see Skidmore, op. cit., pp. 142–62.

73. Dom Obá II d'Africa, 'Untitled', *O Carbonário*, 4 September 1882, p. 4.

74. Idem, 'A S.M. o Imperador e ao País pois Desta Natureza só Aparece dum Século a Século' (II), *O Carbonário*, 16 July 1886, p. 4.

75. Idem, 'A S.A. Sereníssima o Senhor Príncipe Conde d'Eu' (III), *O Carbonário*, 24 September 1886, p. 4.

76. Idem, 'Untitled', *O Carbonário*, 4 September 1882, p. 4.

77. Idem, 'Ao País e ao Respeitável Público' (V), *O Carbonário*, 1 September 1882, p. 4.

78. Idem, 'A S.M. o Imperador e ao País ...' (II), op. cit.

79. Idem, 'Não há Vitória sem Grande Batalha' (I), op. cit.

Chapter 8: Sources, Presuppositions and Symbolic Power

1. Dom Obá II d'Africa, 'A Cruel Inveja Contra o Príncipe Dom Obá II d'Africa, Apesar que Contra a Força há Resistência, o Certo é que o Diabo não Pode mais que Deus' (II and III). *O Carbonário*, 19 and 22 November 1886, p. 4. The social role of *paraty* (sugarcane rum) within the ranks of slaves, freedmen and free men of colour in Rio de Janeiro at the time of Dom Obá can be evaluated by its various nicknames. Many of these names were a recognition of the spirit's role as an instrument of inspiration or of consolation in hard times (as the prince himself thought of it). It could be called the '*abrideira*' (opener), '*branquinha*' (little white lady), '*água-benta*' (holy water), '*capote-de-pobre*' (poor man's overcoat) and even 'sete-virtudes' (seven virtues). But when drunk in excess, it could be transformed from holy water to '*agua-de-briga*' (fight water), '*tira-teima*' (score-settler) and even '*desmancha*-samba' (samba party breaker-upper).

2. Lulu Senior, 'Príncipe Obá', *Gazeta de Notícias*, 13 November 1889, p. 1.

3. Dom Obá II d'Africa, 'Ao País e ao Respeitável Público' (III), *O Carbonário*, 21 August 1882, p. 4.

4. Idem, 'A Cruel Inveja ...' (III and IV), *O Carbonário*, 22 and 26 November 1886, p. 4. It was not possible to locate this 'volume of poetry' titled *Infernal Intrigas*, in the public archives of Rio de Janeiro, Salvador or Lençóis. It was probably a small, handprinted booklet of the type known as '*cordel*'.

5. Idem, 'Questão Diplomática; a S.M. o Imperador' (I), *Jornal do Commercio*, 3 January 1886, p. 3; idem, 'Plano Maldito ...' (I), *O Carbonário*, 21 June 1886, p. 4. The prince apparently quotes this from heart. Cf. Luís de Camões (*c.* 1525–80), *Os Lusíadas*, Lisbon, Biblioteca Nacional, 1921, I Canto. The prestige in which the intellectuals of the age held the Portuguese bard can be gauged by the various items in the highly detailed study carried out by Osvaldo Melo Braga, *Bibliografia de Joaquim Nabuco*, Rio de Janeiro, Imprensa Nacional, 1952. On the same subject, see Hamilton Elia, *Camões e a literatura brasileira*, Rio de Janeiro, FCRB, 1973; Gilberto Mendonça Teles, *Camões e a poesia brasileira*, Rio de Janeiro, FCRB, 1973. About Antônio de Castro Alves (1847–71) a poet of the romantic school, author of lyrical, republican and abolitionist compositions, see Castro Alves, *Obra Completa*, Rio de Janeiro, Aguilar, 1960 (introductory study by Eugênio Gomes); Nelson Werneck Sodré, *História da literatura brasileira*, 2nd edition, Rio de Janeiro, José Olympio, 1940, pp. 141–51; Antônio Cândido, *Formação da literatura brasileira; momentos decisivos*, 2nd edition, São Paulo,

Martins, 1964; José Guilherme Merquior, 'O Navio Negreiro', *Cadernos Brasileiros*, Rio de Janeiro, no. 35, May–June 1966; idem, *De Anchieta a Euclides; breve história da literatura brasileira*, Rio de Janeiro, José Olympio, 1977, pp. 91–6.

6. Dom Obá II d'Africa, 'Não há Vitória sem Grande Batalha' (II), *O Carbonário*, 8 October 1886, p. 4.

7. Idem, 'A Cruel Inveja ...' (IV), op. cit. The prince's affirmation seems to bear no relationship to the biography of his contemporary, King Humbert of Italy (1844–1900), the son of, and successor to, Victor Emmanuel II, who had never been in exile but, nevertheless, was known as 'Re buono e generozo' and even 'Padre del popolo'.

8. Idem, 'Plano Maldito ...' (I and II), *O Carbonário*, 21 and 25 June 1886, p. 4.

9. Idem, 'Ao País e ao Respeitável Público' (II), *O Carbonário*, 18 August 1882, p. 4.

10. Idem, 'A Cruel Inveja ...' (III), op. cit. On 2 July 1823, the Brazilians invaded Salvador in a festive manner, taking it from the Portuguese troops. There are well-documented studies on the entire episode: Braz do Amaral, *História da Independencia na Bahia*, 2nd edition, Salvador, Progresso, 1957; Luís Henrique Dias Tavares, *A Independência do Brasil na Bahia*, 2nd edition, Rio de Janeiro, Civilizacão Brasileira/MEC, 1977; F.W.O. Morton, *The Conservative Revolution of Independence*, D Phil thesis, Oxford University, 1974. For a comprehensive vision of the whole period, see Wanderley Pinho, 'A Bahia (1808–1856)'. In Sérgio Buarque de Holanda (ed.), *História Geral da Civilização Brasileira*, São Paulo, Difusão Européia do Livro, 1964, tomo II, vol. II, pp. 242–311.

11. José Bonifácio de Andrada e Silva, *Memoir Addressed to the General Constituent and Legislative Assembly of the Empire of Brazil, on Slavery*, trans. William Walton, London, 1826, p. 16; Octavio Tarquinio de Sousa (org.), *O pensamento vivo de José Bonifácio*, São Paulo, 1944; Vicente Barreto, *Ideologia e política no pensamento de José Bonifácio de Andrada e Silva*, Rio de Janeiro, Zahar, 1977, p. 71ff; Emília Viotti da Costa, 'A Consciência Liberal nos Primórdios do Império'. In *Da Monarquia a República*, São Paulo, Ciências Humanas, 1979, pp. 109ff.

12. Dom Obá II d'Africa, 'Não há Vitória sem Grande Batalha' (II), op. cit.

13. Cf. Joaquim Nabuco, *Abolitionism: the Brazilian Antislavery Struggle*, trans. and ed. Robert Conrad, Illinois, University of Illinois Press, 1977 (1st edition: London, 1883).

14. See above, note 5.

15. Dom Obá II d'Africa. 'Ao País e ao Respeitável Público' (III), *O Carbonário*, 21 August 1882, p. 4.

16. Idem, 'Ao País e ao Respeitável Público' (IV), *O Carbonário*, 28 August 1882, p. 4.

17. Rev. Samuel Johnson, *The History of the Yorubas: from the Earliest Times to the Beginning of the British Protectorate*, Lagos, C.S.S., 1976 (1st edition 1921), Part I, ch. VIII.

18. N.A. Fadipe (1893–1944), *The Sociology of the Yoruba*, Ibadan, Ibadan University Press, 1970, pp. 302–3 and 311. More recently Elechi Amadi dedicated an entire chapter to the study of the concept of goodness and ethic philosophy contained in the proverbs of the Yoruba and Nigeria in general. See *Ethics in Nigerian Culture*, Ibadan, Heinemann, 1982, ch. 7. Continuing in the modern world, proverbial expressions, often of African origin, play a major part both in

Rastafarian thinking and in the rhetorical style of black preachers in Jamaica, the United States and Great Britain. See David Sutcliffe and Carol Tomlin, 'The Black Churches'; and Pastor L. A. Jackson, 'Proverbs of Jamaica'. In David Sutcliffe and Ansel Wong (eds.), *The Language of the Black Experience: Cultural Expression through Word and Sound in the Caribbean and Black Britain*, Oxford, Basil Blackwell, 1986, pp. 15–31 and 32–6.

19. See, respectively, letter to Miss C. Darwin (Maldonado, 22 May 1833) and to J. M. Herbert (2 June, 1833). In Francis Darwin (ed.), *The Life and Letters of Charles Darwin*, 3rd edition, London, John Murray, 1887, vol. I, pp. 246 and 248.

20. Dom Obá II d'Africa. 'Não há Vitória sem Grande Batalha' (II), op. cit.; Idem, 'A Cruel Inveja . . .' (II), op. cit.

21. Idem, 'A Justa Palavra Perante Deus, a Majestade e as Universidades' (III), *O Carbonário*, 11 June 1883, p. 3.

22. Amadi, op. cit., pp. 55–6.

23. Dom Obá II d'Africa, 'Ao País e ao Respeitável Público' (III), op. cit.

24. Idem, 'Não há Vitória sem Grande Batalha' (II), op. cit.

25. Idem, 'Ao País e ao Respeitável Público' (VI), *O Carbonário*, 4 September 1882, p. 4. The expression came into being between 1830 and 1850, a period in which the African traffic continued openly even though a law had been passed against it. The law was, therefore, 'just for an Englishman's eyes', the English being opposed to the slave trade.

26. Idem, 'Plano Maldito . . .' (II), op. cit. This idea – one that cannot have been considered 'natural' within the slave system – was one of the instructions given by Jesus to his disciples. Cf. Matthew 10, 10.

27. Idem, 'Ao País e ao Respeitável Público' (III), op. cit.

28. Idem, 'Ao País e ao Respeitável Público' (II), op. cit. It is interesting to see in some of the *jongos* (improvised verses) sung both in the Corte and in the surrounding rural regions that slaves, freedmen and free men of colour often refer to themselves, allegorically, as 'monkeys' or 'old monkeys'. The expression 'Macaco velho não mete a mão em cumbuca' derives from the image of intelligence and sagacity attributed to primates in popular lore. ('An old monkey does not put his hand in the "cumbuca".' A 'cumbuca' was a hollowed-out, dried gourd used to trap monkeys which had one smallish opening and contained some tempting morsel of food. An inexperienced monkey would put his hand inside but, once he had clutched the food, be unable to get it out again.) The same comparison can be found not only in Sudanese culture but also in Jamaica, 'follow-fashion monkey broke him neck' (see Jackson, op. cit., p. 32) and in the Bantu cultures. A good example in this instance is the *jisabu* of Angola, 'o kima Katale o mukila ue', an invitation to moderation and self-criticism that came into Brazilian tradition in a virtually literal translation: 'monkey, watch your tail!' Quoted in Arthur Ramos, *O folclore negro do Brasil; demopsicologia e psicanálise*, 2nd edition, Rio de Janeiro, Casa do Estudante do Brasil, 1954, pp. 224–6.

29. Johnson, op. cit., p. 102; Fadipe, op. cit., p. 307.

30. Dom Obá II d'Africa, 'A Cruel Inveja . . .' (III), op. cit.; idem, 'Ao País e ao Respeitável Público' (II), op. cit.

31. The title of the ten-page booklet is a comprehensive summary of its argument. See J.J. do C.M., *Carta do compadre do Rio S. Francisco do norte, ao filho do compadre do Rio de Janeiro, qual se lhe queixa do paralelo, que faz dos índios com os cavalos, de não conceder aos homens pretos maior dignidade, que a de reis do Rozário, e de asseverar, que o Brasil ainda agora esta engatinhando.*

E crê provar o contrário de tudo isso por ... (Letter from a comrade in the north of the São Francisco River, to the son of a comrade in Rio de Janeiro, which complains of the parallel which likens Indians to horses, of not conceding black men greater dignity than acting as fancydress kings for Nossa Senhora do Rozario, and to ascertain that Brazil is still in its infancy. And to prove the opposite of all this by ...), Rio de Janeiro, Impressão Nacional, 1821, pp. 4–5. This is the oldest example I was able to find of popular writing on the subject. The historical argument, the accumulated experience of daily living, which was fundamental here, is clearly distinguished, perhaps for the first time in a written work: the *slave* on one hand, the *black race* on the other. This work embodies the crux of this argument about race as it stood at the end of the colonial period: 'if there have not been many blacks who have emerged as great men', wrote the dark-skinned J.J. do C.M., 'it is because the servile condition in which they have been placed amongst us does not permit it ... but despite this, how many heroes could they recount, if they knew the prodigious Art of transmitting their names to posterity? ... without going further than Brazil, there is Henrique Dias, whom we all admire; was he not black? Did the accident of his colour stop him from carrying out the great acts of fidelity, valour and heroism during the restoration of Pernambuco? ... Is the bold and valiant Corps of the King's Loyal Freedmen not made up of blacks? Did they, because of this, not conduct themselves with honour and bravery in the southern war? Amongst those awarded military medals, do you not find black colonels and officers who carried out their duty and behaved with dignity? Do you not see very dignified sacerdotes and canons? Are the blacks less able and apt for the Letters, Arts and Officialdom? With certainty, no; we have proof to spare, both here amongst us and over there in Lisbon.'

32. Leonardo Mota, *Violeiros do Norte*, São Paulo, Editora Monteiro Lobato, 1925, pp. 93–4.

33. Dom Obá II d'Africa, 'Ao País e ao Respeitável Público' (VI), *O Carbonário*, 4 September 1882, p. 4. The influence of biblical quotations is also evident here. Concerning the last quotation in particular, see Luke 23, 34: 'Father, forgive them; for they know not what they do.'

34. Idem, 'A Justiça e a Consciência' (I), *O Carbonário*, 22 April 1887, p. 4.

35. Idem, 'Untitled' (III), *O Carbonário*, 25 October 1886, p. 4.

36. Idem, 'A Justa Palavra Perante Deus, a Majestade e Universidades' (III), op. cit.

37. Cândido da Fonseca Galvão, handwritten request. See Appendix A, p. 162.

38. Dom Obá II d'Africa, letter to Dom Pedro II, Rio de Janeiro, 31 January 1882. See Appendix B, p. 164.

39. Idem, 'Raiza-me de Abiodun', *O Carbonário*, 30 November 1888, pp. 3 and 4.

40. Idem, 'Ao Exmo. Sr. Conselheiro Ernesto Ferreira França', *O Carbonário*, 13 March 1889, p. 4.

41. Idem, 'A Justa Palavra Perante Deus, a Majestade e as Universidades' (II), *O Carbonário*, 8 June 1883, p. 4.

42. Idem, 'A Paixão de N.S. Jesus Cristo', *O Carbonário*, 26 April 1886, p. 4.

43. Idem, 'A S.A. Serreníssima o Senhor Principe Conde d'Eu' (II), *O Carbonário*, 22 September 1886, p. 4.

44. Field research, February 1987.

45. Dom Obá II d'Africa, 'Questão Diplomática; a S.M. o Imperador' (I), op. cit. In his novel Afrânio Peixoto mentions the three rival musical bands in Lençóis

198 PRINCE OF THE PEOPLE

in the nineteenth century. There was the 'Banda Oito de Dezembro', dedicated to Nossa Senhora da Conceição; the 'Dois de Fevereiro', dedicated to Senhor dos Passos; and the 'Primeiro de Janeiro', dedicated to Saint Benedict and made up exclusively of blacks. See *Bugrinha*, 10th edition Rio de Janeiro, Conquista; Brasília, INL, 1972. Basic historical data on Benedict the Black can be found in Donald Attwater, *Dictionary of Saints*, Harmondsworth, Penguin, 1970, pp. 62–3.

46. Dom Obá II d'Africa, 'A S.A. Sereníssima o Senhor Príncipe Conde d'Eu' (II), op. cit.

47. Idem, 'A Cruel Inveja . . .' (I), *O Carbonário*, 17 November 1886, p. 4.

48. Raimundo Nina Rodrigues, *Os africanos no Brasil*, São Paulo, Companhia Editora Nacional, 1977; Manuel Querino, *Costumes africanos no Brasil*, Rio de Janeiro, Civilização Brasileira, 1938; Arthur Ramos, *Introdução à antropologia brasileira*, 3 vols, Rio de Janeiro, Casa do Estudante do Brasil, 1947; Edison Carneiro, *Candomblés da Bahia*, Rio de Janeiro, Ouro, 1968.

49. For Xangô and other Yoruba founding fathers, see Johnson, op. cit., pp. 143–54. For the cult of Xangô in Africa and Brazil, see Pierre Fatumbi Verger's very well-documented *Orixás; deuses iorubás na África e no Novo Mundo*, São Paulo, Corrupio/Circulo do Livro, 1981, pp. 134–41.

50. Dom Obá II d'Africa, 'A Divindade Manda não Ser-se Traidor do Rei' (I and II), *O Carbonário*, 9 and 16 May 1887, p. 4.

51. Cf. Johnson, op. cit., pp. 85–6. On the symbolism of left and right, see Fadipe, op. cit., pp. 311–12; Juana Elbein dos Santos, *Os nagô e a morte*, 4th edition, Petrópolis, Vozes, 1986, pp. 72ff.

52. On the Yoruba mythological period, see Johnson, op. cit., pp. 143–54. An excellent photograph of 'Ogum's staff' wrought in iron and shaped almost identically to the prince's abstract representation, can be found in Verger, op. cit., p. 109. The historical syncretism of the Holy Ghost with *Oxum* was registered here, probably for the first time. For a systematization of syncretic identification from the pioneering studies of Nina Rodrigues onwards, see Waldemar Valente, *Sincretismo religioso Afro-brasileiro*, 3rd edn., São Paulo, Companhia Editora Nacional, 1977, pp. 98–106.

53. Câmara Cascudo attributed the idea (in truth, a magnificent analysis of the applied cultural history) to José Bonifácio de Andrada e Silva. Cf. *Dicionário do folclore brasileiro*, Brasília, INL, 1972, pp. 338–9 and 384–5.

54. Melo Morais Filho, *Festas e tradições populares do Brasil*, 3rd edition, Rio de Janeiro, Briguiet, 1946, ch. 'A Festa do Divino'.

55. Peixoto, op. cit., p. 31.

56. Eduardo Silva, *As queixas do povo*, Rio de Janeiro, Paz e Terra, 1988, pp. 75–7.

57. Morais Filho. op. cit., p. 546.

58. Cf. Gilberto Freyre, *Ordem e Progresso*, Rio de Janeiro, José Olympio, 1959, 1 Tomo, 'Nota Metodológica', p. XXXI. It is interesting to note that the author arrives at this conclusion after getting 183 Brazilians born between 1850 and 1900 to answer intimate and highly detailed questionnaires that he calls 'provoked autobiographies' and 'a retrospective anthropological and sociological inquiry'. In truth, not just the canes, but all the 'rigour' and symbolism of the fashion for Brazilian plantation masters' dress has been one of the recurring themes and one of the most important contributions (though one that has been little noted) of Freyre's 'Proustian sociology'. See *Vida Social no Brasil nos meados do século*

XIX, trans. Waldemar Valente, 2nd edition, Rio de Janeiro, Artenova; Recife, Instituto Joaquim Nabuco de Pesquisas Sociais, 1977, pp. 92, 112 and passim (original in English 1922); *Cassa-grande & Senzala*, 25th edition, Rio de Janeiro, José Olympio, 1987, p. 416 and passim.

    59. *O Paiz*, 15 November, 1886, p. 1; *Diário de Notícias*, 14 July 1890, p. 1.

    60. Johnson, op. cit., p. 52 (original, 1897; 1st edition, 1921).

    61. Fadipe, op. cit., p. 307.

    62. Peter B. Clarke, 'Charismatic Authority and the Creation of a New Order; the Case of the Mahdiyyat Movement in South-western Nigeria'. In Donal B. Cruise O'Brien and Christian Coulon (eds.), *Charisma and Brotherhood in African Islam*, Oxford, Clarendon Press, 1988, pp. 157–82. Quotations on p. 175.

    63. James Wetherell, *Brazil: Stray Notes from Bahia: Being Extracts from Letters, etc. during a Residence of Fifteen Years*, ed. William Hadfield. Liverpool, Webb and Hunt, 1860, p. 77.

    64. Field research, 1986 and 1987.

Conclusion

    1. *Revista Illustrada*, 2 and 9 June 1888, pp. 2–6.

    2. Quoted in Stanley J. Stein, *Vassouras, a Brazilian Coffee County, 1850–1900*, Princeton, Princeton University Press, 1985, p. 257.

    3. *Revista Illustrada*, 15 September 1888, p. 3.

    4. Roberto da Matta, *Carnavais, malandros e heróis; para uma sociologia do dilema brasileiro*, 3rd edition, Rio de Janeiro, Zahar, 1981, ch. IV.

    5. Visconde de São Boaventura, *A Revolução no Brasil*, 1894, p. 18. Apud Gilberto Freyre, *Ordem e progresso*, Rio de Janeiro, José Olympio, 1959, p. CXIX.

    6. *Revista Illustrada*, 2 July 1888, p. 4.

    7. Julio Verim, 'Pela Política, *Revista Illustrada*, 18 May 1889, p. 2.

    8. *O Paiz*, 13 November 1889, p. 1; *Jornal do Commercio*, 13 November 1889, p. 1.

    9. *Diário de Notícias*, 9 July 1890, p. 1.

Bibliography

1. Manuscript Sources

1.1 *Arquivo Seletivo do Exército* (Rio de Janeiro)

'Oficiais dos Corpos de Voluntários da Pátria em Sua Organização', 1865 (manuscript book).
Companhia de Zuavos, Pasta 9, 'Voluntários de Diversos Estados que Marcharam para a Guerra do Paraguai'.
Pasta 539, Maço 17.
Pasta 'Cândido da Fonseca Galvão'.
'Papéis que Serviram de Base ao Decreto de 25 set. 1872, Concedendo Honras do Posto de Alferes a Cândido da Fonseca Galvão'.
Ministério da Guerra, 2a. Secção. Repartição do Ajudante General, Doc. 1.602.
Ministério da Guerra, la. Secção. Repartição Fiscal, Doc. 1.184.

1.2 *Museu Histórico Nacional* (Rio de Janeiro)

Livro de Assinaturas do Palácio Imperial da Quinta da Boa Vista, 1882–5. Arquivo Histórico, IMr2.
'O Príncipe Obá'. Arquivo Histórico, Doc. 72A.
Coleção Uniformes Militares. Arquivo Histórica, Um 188.

1.3 *Arquivo da Instituto Histórico e Geografico Brasileiro* (Rio de Janeiro)

Lata 416. Booklet by J.J. do C.M., 1821.

1.4 *Arquivo Geral da Secretaria do Patrimônio Histórico e Artístico Nacional* (Rio de Janeiro)

Pasta de Tombamento: 'Casa dos 7 Candeeiros'.

1.5 *Museu Imperial de Petrópolis* (Petrópolis)

Arquivo de Manuscritos, Maço 187, doc. 8473.

1.6 Arquivo Público do Estado da Bahia (Salvador)

Atos do Governo, Maço 976.
Presidência da Província. Governo Câmara de Lençóis, 1858–81.
Presidência da Província. Governo Câmara de Lençóis, 1859–89.
Seção Histórica. Correspondência, Livro 689.
Assembléia Legislativa. Abaixo Assinados, 1835–6.
Guerra do Paraguai, Maço 3668.
Avisos Recebidos. Ministro da Guerra, Maço 828.

1.7 Coleção Particular de Mestre Oswaldo (Lençóis, BA)

Manuscritos do Farmacêutico João de Miranda Neves. 'Livro I' (c.1908–1912); 'Livro II' (c.1916–17); 'Livro III' (1917).

2. Printed Sources

2.1 Articles by Dom Obá II d'Africa

Dom Oba II d'Africa, 'Ao País e ao Respeitável Público' (I), *O Carbonário*, 4 March 1882, p. 4.
—— 'Ao País e ao Respeitável Público' (II), *O Carbonário*, 18 August 1882, p. 4.
—— 'Ao País e ao Respeitável Público' (III), *O Carbonário*, 21 August 1882, p. 4.
—— 'Ao País e ao Respeitável Público' (IV), *O Carbonário*, 28 August 1882, p. 4.
—— 'Ao País e ao Respeitável Público' (V), *O Carbonário*, 1 September 1882, p. 4.
—— 'Ao País e ao Respeitável Público' (VI), *O Carbonário*, 4 September 1882, p. 4.
—— 'Ao País e ao Respeitável Público' (VII), *O Carbonário*, 8 September 1882, p. 4.
—— 'Untitled', *O Carbonário*, 4 September 1882, p. 4.
—— 'A Justa Palavra Perante Deus, a Majestade e Universidades' (I), *O Carbonário*, 4 June 1883, p. 4.
—— 'A Justa Palavra Perante Deus ...' (II), *O Carbonário*, 8 June 1883, p. 4.
—— 'A Justa Palavra Perante Deus ...' (III), *O Carbonário*, 11 June 1883, p. 3.
—— 'As Vivas Razões da Constituição da Lei que nos Rege e nos faz Respeitá-la', *Jornal do Commércio*, 25 February 1885, p. 5.
—— 'A S.M. Imperador', *Jornal do Commércio*, 28 February 1885, p. 5.
—— 'Questão Diplomática; a S.M. o Imperador' (I), *Jornal do Commércio*, 3 January 1886, p. 3.
—— 'Questão Diplomática; a S.M. o Imperador' (II), *Jornal do Commércio*, 6 March 1886, p. 4.
—— 'Protesto', *O Carbonário*, 26 March 1886, p. 4.
—— 'A Paixão de N.S. Jesus Cristo', *O Carbonário*, 26 April 1886, p. 4.
—— 'Plano Maldito dos Adversários; a Inveja e a Razão Convencem os

Espertalhões dos Direitos de Deus e dos Reis' (I), *O Carbonário*, 18 June 1886, p. 4.

—— 'Plano Maldito dos Adversários...' (II), *O Carbonário*, 21 June 1886, p. 4.

—— 'Plano Maldito dos Adversários...' (III), *O Carbonário*, 25 June 1886, p. 4.

—— 'A S.M. o Imperador e ao País pois Desta Natureza só Aparece dum Século a Século' (I), *O Carbonário*, 12 July 1886, p. 4.

—— 'A S.M. o Imperador e ao País...' (II), *O Carbonário*, 16 July 1886, p. 4.

—— 'Aos Poderes do Estado', *O Carbonário*, 2 August 1886, p. 4.

—— 'A S. A. Sereníssima o Senhor Príncipe Conde d'Eu' (I), *O Carbonário*, 20 September 1886, p. 4.

—— 'A S.A. Sereníssima o Senhor Príncipe Conde d'Eu' (II), *O Carbonário*, 22 September 1886, p. 4.

—— 'A S.A. Sereníssima o Senhor Príncipe Conde d'Eu' (III), *O Carbonário*, 24 September 1886, p. 4.

—— 'Não há Vitória sem Grande Batalha' (I), *O Carbonário*, 5 October 1886, p. 4.

—— 'Não há Vitória sem Grande Batalha' (II), *O Carbonário*, 8 October 1886, p. 4.

—— 'Não há Vitória sem Grande Batalha' (III), *O Carbonário*, 10 October 1886, p. 4.

—— 'Não há Vitória sem Grande Batalha' (IV), *O Carbonário*, 15 October 1886, p. 4.

—— Untitled (I), *O Carbonário*, 18 October 1886, p. 4.

—— Untitled (II), *O Carbonário*, 22 October 1886, p. 4.

—— Untitled (III), *O Carbonário*, 25 October 1886, p. 4.

—— Untitled (IV), *O Carbonário*, 1 November 1886, p. 4.

—— 'A Cruel Inveja contra o Príncipe D. Obá II d'Africa, Apesar que Contra a Força há resistência, o Certo é que o Diabo não Pode mais que Deus', (I) *O Carbonário*, 17 November 1886, p. 4.

—— 'A Cruel Inveja...' (II), *O Carbonário*, 19 November 1886, p. 4.

—— 'A Cruel Inveja...' (III), *O Carbonário*, 22 November 1886, p. 4.

—— 'A Cruel Inveja...' (IV), *O Carbonário*, 26 November 1886, p. 4.

—— 'Cruel Intriga...', *O Carbonário*, 29 November 1886, p. 4.

—— 'Fala a Consciência Universal, que Obriga o Direito Divinal, Interessar-se pelo Bem-estar do deus da Nação Brasileira', *O Carbonário*, 18 March 1887, p. 4.

—— Untitled, *O Carbonário*, 25 March 1887, p. 4.

—— 'A Justiça e a Consciência', (I) *O Carbonário*, 22 April 1887, p. 4.

—— 'A Justiça e a Consciência', (II) *O Carbonário*, 24 April 1887, p. 4.

—— 'A Justiça e a Consciência', (III) *O Carbonário*, 25 April 1887, p. 4.

—— 'A Justiça e a Consciência', (IV) *O Carbonário*, 29 April 1887, p. 4.

—— 'A Justiça e a Consciência', (V) *O Carbonário*, 2 May 1887, p. 4.

—— 'A Cruel Inveja...', *O Carbonário*, 2 May 1887, p. 4.

—— 'A Divindade Manda não Ser-se Traidor do Rei', (I) *O Carbonário*, 9 May 1887, p. 4.

—— 'A Divindade Manda não Ser-se Traidor do Rei', (II) *O Carbonário*, 16 May 1887, p. 4.

—— 'A Divindade Manda não Ser-se Traidor do Rei', (III) *O Carbonário*, 23 May 1887, p. 4.

——— 'A Consciência dos Cantoneiros e os Remorsos dos Quirógrafos Acusa a quem é mal Principado ser por Castigo de Deus mal Acabados', *O Carbonário*, 20 May 1887.

——— 'Ao Universo Imploro a Suplicada Saudação', (I) *O Carbonário*, 30 May 1887, p. 4.

——— 'Ao Universo Imploro a Suplicada Saudação', (II) *O Carbonário*, 30 May 1887, p. 4.

——— 'Ao Universo Imploro a Suplicada Saudação', (III) *O Carbonário*, 8 June 1887, p. 4.

——— 'Raiza-me de Abiodun', *O Carbonário*, 30 November 1888, p. 3.

——— 'Ao Exmo. Sr. Conselheiro Ernesto Ferreira França', *O Carbonário*, 13 March 1889, p. 4.

2.2 Letters of support for Dom Obá II d'Africa

Anonymous, 'Manifestação de Apreço', *Jornal do Commercio*, 16 January 1880, p. 2.

Anonymous, 'Felicitação Oferecida ao Distinto Patriota Monarquista de Família, o Nobre Príncipe Obá II de África e Alferes Galvão, no Brasil', *Jornaldo Commercio*, 4 May 1884, p. 3.

Anonymous, Untitled, *O Carbonário*, 28 June 1886, p. 4.

Anonymous, 'Ao País', (I) *O Carbonário*, 13 December 1886, p. 4.

Anonymous, 'Ao País', (II) *O Carbonário*, 17 December 1886, p. 4.

Anonymous, 'Ao País', (III) *O Carbonário*, 20 December 1886, p. 4.

Um Amigo de S.A., Príncipe Obá II d'Africa, pseud., 'O Dedo de Deus Chama a Atenção do Globo Civilizado para ver a Verdade', (I) *O Carbonário*, 18 February 1887, p. 4.

——— 'O Dedo de Deus Chama a Atenção do Globo Civilizado para ver a Verdade', (II) *O Carbonário*, 23 February 1887, p. 4.

2.3 Published documents and contemporary works

Abranches, João Dunshee de, *O Cativeiro (Memórias)*, Rio de Janeiro, 1941.

Albuquerque, Medeiros e, *Quando eu era vivo, 1867–1934*, 2nd edition, Rio de Janeiro, Livraria Globo, 1945.

Alencar, José de, *Sistema representativo*, Rio de Janeiro, B. L. Garnier, 1868.

——— *Obra Completa*, 4 vols, M. Cavalcanti Proença, Rio de Janeiro, Aguilar, 1959.

Almeida, Caetano Furquim de, 'Carestia dos Gêneros Alimentícios'. In *Relatório do Presidente da Província do Rio de Janeiro*, Rio de Janeiro, 1858, Anexo K.

Alves, Castro, *Obra completa*, ed. Eugênio Gomes, Rio de Janeiro, Aguilar, 1960.

Andrada e Silva, José Bonifácio de, *Memoir Addressed to the Constituent and Legislative Assembly of the Empire of Brazil, on Slavery*, trans. William Walton, London, 1826.

——— *Discursos Parlamentares*, selection and introduction by Francisco de Assis Barbosa, Brasília, Câmara dos Deputados, 1979 (col. Perfis parlamentares, 13).

Antonil, André João, *Cultura e Opulência do Brasil*, 2nd edition, Introdução e vocabulário de Alice P. Canabrava, São Paulo, Companhia Editora Nacional, s.d.

Anonymous, 'Reminiscências de Um do Povo (do meu Diário)', *A Imprensa*, Rio de Janeiro, 15 November 1911, p. 2.

Azevedo, Aluísio de, *O cortiço*, São Paulo, Martins, 1965.

Barreto, Filho, Mello et Lima, Hermeto, *História da Polícia do Rio de Janeiro; aspéctos da cidade e da vida carioca 1870–1889*, Rio de Janeiro, A Noite, 1944.

Barreto, Lima, *Bagatelas*, São Paulo, Brasiliense, 1956.

Brasil, Congresso Nacional, Câmara dos Deputados, *Anais do Parlamento Brasileiro*, Rio de Janeiro, 1854.

—— Câmara dos Deputados, *Annais do Parlamento Brasileiro*, Rio de Janeiro, 1886–8.

—— *Coleção de Leis do Império do Brasil*, Tomo XXXI, Rio de Janeiro, 1871.

—— *Coleção das Ordens do Dia da Repartição de Ajudância General Publicadas no Ano de 1872*, Rio de Janeiro, Typ. do Diário do Rio de Janeiro, 1874.

—— Repartição de Ajudante General, *Coleção das Ordens do Dia*, Rio de Janeiro, Typ. de G. Leuzinger & Filhos, 1889.

—— *Recenseamento da população do Império do Brasil a que se procedeu no dia 1 de agosto de 1872*, Vol. 21, Rio de Janeiro, Oficina de Estatística, 1873–6.

—— *Recenseamento do Distrito Federal de 1890*, Rio de Janeiro, Oficina de Estatística, 1901.

—— *Recenseamento do Rio de Janeiro (Distrito Federal) realizado em 20 de setembro de 1906*, Rio de Janeiro, Oficina de Estatística, 1907.

Bueno, José Antônio Pimenta, *Direito público brasileiro e análise da Constituição do Império*, Rio de Janeiro, 1857.

Camões, Luís de, *Os lusíadas*, Lisboa, Biblioteca Nacional, 1921.

Cerqueira, Dionísio, *Reminiscências da campanha do Paraguai, 1865–1870*, Rio de Janeiro, Biblioteca do Exército, 1980.

Couty, Louis, *L'Esclavage au Brésil*, Paris, Librairie de Guillaumin, 1881.

—— *Le Brésil en 1884*, Rio de Janeiro, Faro e Lino, 1884.

Darwin, Francis (ed.), *The Life and letters of Charles Darwin*, 3rd edition, London, John Murray, 1887, vol. I.

Davatz, Thomas, *Memória de um colono no Brasil*, tradução, introdução e notas de Sérgio Buarque de Holanda, 2nd edition, São Paulo, Martins, 1951.

Debret, Jean Baptiste, *Viagem pitoresca e histórica ao Brasil*, notes by Sérgio Milliet, 3rd edition, São Paulo, Martins, 2 vols, 1972.

D'Eu, Conde, *Viagem militar ao Rio Grande do Sul*, São Paulo, Companhia Editora Nacional, 1936.

Dias, Antônio Gonçalves, *Polsias Completas e Prosa Escolhida*, ed. Manuel Bandeira and Antonio Houaiss, Rio de Janeiro, Aguilar, 1959.

Dom Pedro II, *Conselhos à Regente*, introdução e notas de João Camillo de Oliveira Torres, Rio de Janeiro, Livraria São José, 1958.

Galvão, Rodolpho, *Das concepções delirantes; seu valor diagnóstico*, Rio de Janeiro, Typ. de G. Leuzinger & Filhos, 1886.

Gomes, A Carlos, *O Guarani: ópera baile em quatro atos. Versão e adaptacão brasileiras de C. Paula Barros segundo o original italiano de Antonio Scalvini extraído do romance O Guarani de José de Alencar*, Rio de Janeiro, MEC, 1936.

Great Britain, Parliamentary Papers, 1878, vol. 75; 1881, vol. 89; 1882, vol. 70; 1886, vol. 65.

Hartt, Charles Frederick, *Geology and Physical Geography of Brazil*, London, Trübner, 1870.

Jardim, Antônio da Silva, *Memórias e viagens; campanha de um propagandista, 1887–1890*, Lisboa, Typ. da Companhia Nacional Editora, 1891.

—— *Cartas de Silva Jardim a Clóvis Bevilaqua*, Rio de Janeiro, Apollo, 1936.

—— *Propaganda Republicana (1888–1889); discursos, opúsculos, manifestos e artigos coligidos, anotados e prefaciados por Barbosa Lima Sobrinho*, Rio de Janeiro, FCRB/Conselho Federal de Cultura, 1978.

J. J. do C. M., pseud., *Carta do compadre do Rio São Francisco do norte, ao filho do compadre do Rio de Janeiro qual se lhe queixa do paralelo, que faz dos índios com os cavalos, de não conceder aos homens pretos maior dignidade, que a de reis do Rozário, e de asseverar, que o Brasil ainda agora esta engatinhando. E crê provar o contrário de tudo isso por ...* Rio de Janeiro, Impressão Nacional, 1821.

João do Rio, pseud. Paulo Barreto, *As religiões no Rio*, Rio de Janeiro, H. Garnier, s.d.

—— *A alma encantadora das ruas*, Rio de Janeiro, Organização Simões, 1951.

—— Koseritz, Carl von, *Imagens do Brasil*, tradução Afonso Arinos de Melo Franco, São Paulo, Martins, 1943.

Leclerc, Max, *Cartas do Brasil*, trad. prefácio e notas de Sérgio Milliet, São Paulo, Companhia Editora Nacional, 1942.

Lima, Hermeto, *A identidade do homem pela impressão digital*, Rio de Janeiro, Imprensa Nacional, 1913.

—— *O alcoolismo no Rio de Janeiro*, Rio de Janeiro, Imprensa Nacional, 1914.

—— *A infâmia alcoólatra*, Rio de Janeiro, Imprensa Nacional, 1916.

—— *Os crimes célebres do Rio de Janeiro*, Rio de Janeiro, Empresa de Romances Populares, 1921.

—— 'O Príncipe Obá', *Revista da Semana*, Rio de Janeiro, 21 February 1925, p. 30.

Lulu Senior, pseud., 'Príncipe Obá', *Gazeta de Notícias*, Rio de Janeiro, 13 November 1889, p. 1.

Moraes Filho, Mello, *Quadros e Crônicas*, Rio de Janeiro, Garnier, s.d.

—— *Festas e tradições populares do Brasil*, 3rd edition, Rio de Janeiro, Briguiet, 1946 (1st edition, 1895).

Nabuco, Joaquim, *Um estadista do Império*, Rio de Janeiro, Nova Aguillar, 1975.

—— *Abolitionism: the Brazilian Antislavery Struggle*, trans. and ed. Robert Conrad, Illinois, University of Illinois Press, 1977.

—— *Cartas aos abolicionistas ingleses*, ed. José Thomaz Nabuco, Recife, Fundação Joaquim Nabuco/Massangana, 1985.

Peixoto, Afrânio, *Bugrinha*, 10th edition, Rio de Janeiro, Conquista; Brasília, INL, 1972.

Pompéia, Raul, *Obras* (VI), org. e notas de Afrânio Coutinho, Rio de Janeiro, Civilização Brasileira, 1982.

Prado, Eduardo, 'Immigration'. In M.F. de Sant'Anna Nery (ed.), *Le Brésil*, Paris, Charles Delagrave, 1889.

Querino, Manuel, *Costumes africanos no Brasil*, Rio de Janeiro, Civilização Brasileira, 1938.

Reis, Vicente, 'O Rio de Janeiro no Crepúsculo da Monarquia; Aspéctos de Sua Vida Social e Comercial', *Revista do IHGB*, no. 345, oct./dez. 1984.

Rugendas, Johann Moritz, *Voyage pittoresque dans Brésil*, Paris, Engelmenn, 1835.

206   PRINCE OF THE PEOPLE

—— 'Imagens e Notas do Brasil', *Revista do Patrimônio Histórico e Artístico Nacional*, 13 (1956): 17–84.

Sales, Alberto, *A pátria paulista*, Brasília, Editora da Universidade de Brasília, 1983.

Sales, Campos, *Da propaganda à presidência*, São Paulo, s. ed. 1908.

Soares, Sebastião Ferreira, *Notas estatísticas sobre a produção agrícola e carestia dos gêneros alimentícios no Império do Brasil*, Rio de Janeiro, Typ. Imp. e Const. de J. Villeneuve, 1860.

Spix, Johann von and Karl von Martius, *Viagem pelo Brasil, 1817–1820*, São Paulo, 3 vols, Melhoramentos, 1976.

Verim, Julio, 'Pela política', *Revista Illustrada*, 18 May 1889, p. 2.

Wehrs, C. Carlos J., *O Rio Antigo: Pitoresco e musical; memórias e diário*. Rio de Janeiro, Organização Tipográficca Brasileira, 1980.

Werneck, Francisco Peixoto de Lacerda, Barão de Pati do Alferes, *Memória sobre a fundação de uma fazenda na província do Rio de Janeiro*, edição original de 1847 e edição modificada e acrescida de 1878, ed. Eduardo Silva, Brasília, Senado Federal; Rio de Janeiro, FCRB, 1985.

Werneck, Luís Peixoto de Lacerda, *Idéias sobre colonização precedidas de uma sucinta exposição dos princípios gerais que regem a população*, Rio de Janeiro, E & H Laemmert, 1855.

—— 'Breves Considerações Sobre a Posição Atual da Lavoura do Café', *Almanack Administrativo Mercantil e Industrial da Corte e da Província do Rio de Janeiro*, Rio de Janeiro, 12, 2a. serie (7): 93–109, 1855.

Wetherell, James, *Brazil: Stray Notes from Bahia: being Extracts from Letters, etc. during a Residence of Fifteen Years*, ed. William Hadfield, Liverpool, Webb and Hunt, 1860.

2.4 Newspapers and periodicals

O Carbonário, Rio de Janeiro, 1881–9.
O Corsário, Rio de Janeiro, 1881–3.
Diário de Notícias, Rio de Janeiro, 1890.
Distracção, Rio de Janeiro, 1886.
Gazeta da Tarde, Rio de Janeiro, 1881.
Gazeta de Notícias, Rio de Janeiro, 1889–90.
A Imprensa, Rio de Janeiro, 1911.
Jornal do Commercio, Rio de Janeiro, 1865 and 1882–7.
O Paiz, Rio de Janeiro, 1886–90.
Revista da Semana, Rio de Janeiro, 1925.
Revista do IHGB, Rio de Janeiro, 1838–1984.
Revista Illustrada, Rio de Janeiro, 1888–90.
A Tarde, Salvador, 1917.

3. Secondary Sources

Abercrombie, Nicholas and Hill, Stephen, 'Paternalism and Patronage', *British Journal of Sociology*, 27(4): 413–29, 1976.

Abreu, Sílvio Fróes, *A riqueza mineral do Brasil*, 2nd edition, São Paulo, Companhia Editora Nacional, 1975.

Adamo, Sam C., *The Broken Promise; Race, Health, and Justice in Rio de Janeiro, 1890–1940*, PhD Thesis, University of New Mexico, 1983.

Alagoa, Ebiegberi J., 'Oral Traditôn and Cultural History in Nigeria', *Storia Della Storiografia*, Milano, Editoriale Jaca Book, n.5, 1984, pp. 66–76.

Algranti, Leila Mezan, *O feitor ausente; estudo sobre a escravidão urbana no Rio de Janeiro*, Petropolis, Vozes, 1988.

Amadi, Elechi, *Ethics in Nigerian Culture*, Ibadan, Heinemann, 1982.

Amaral, Braz do, *História da Independência na Bahia*, 2nd edition, Salvador, Progresso, 1957.

Atanda, J.A. 'The Fall of the Old Oyo Empire: A Re-Consideration of its Cause'. *Journal of the Historical Society of Nigeria*, 5(4): 477–90, 1971.

—— *The New Oyo Empire*, London, Longmans, 1973.

Attwater, Donald, *Dictionary of Saints*, Hardmondsworth, Penguin, 1970.

Augel, Moema Parente, *Visitantes estrangeiros na Bahia oitocentista*, São Paulo: Cultrix; Brasília: INL, 1980.

Ayódelé, C.O., *The Traditional Political Institutions in Oyo*, MA Thesis, Ibadan University, 1983.

Azevedo, Eliane S., *Análise antropológica e cultural dos nomes de família na Bahia*, Salvador, Centro de Estudos Afro-Orientais/UFBA, 1981.

Barber, Karin, 'How Man Makes God in West Africa: Yoruba Attitudes Towards the Orisa', *Africa* 51(3), pp. 724–45, 1981.

Barbosa, Francisco de Assis, *JK: uma revisão na política brasileira*, Rio de Janeiro, José Olympio, 1960.

—— (org.), 'Cadernos do IV Centenário', *Jornal do Brasil*, jan.–dez. 1965.

Barreto, Vicente, *Ideologia e política no pensamento de José Bonifácio de Andrada e Silva*, Rio de Janeiro, Zahar, 1977.

Beier, Ulli, *Yoruba Beaded Crowns; Sacred Regalia of the Olokutu of Okuku*, London, Ethnographica, 1982.

Bento, Cláudio Moreira, 'O Exército e a abolição'. In Arno Wehling (org.), *Abolição do cativeiro*, Rio de Janeiro, IHGB, 1988.

Bergstresser, Rebecca Baird, *The Movement for the Abolition of Slavery in Rio de Janeiro; Brazil, 1880–1889*, PhD Thesis Stanford University, 1973.

Bethell, Leslie, *The Abolition of the Brazilian Slave Trade; Britain, Brazil and the Slave Trade Question, 1807–1869*, Cambridge, Cambridge University Press, 1970.

Bocaiúva, Quintino, *Idéias políticas de Quintino Bacaiúva*, ed. Eduardo Silva, Brasília, Senado Federal, Rio de Janeiro, FCRB, 1986.

Bourdieu, Pierre, Darnton, Robert and Chartier, Roger, 'Dialogue à propos de l'histoire culturelle', *Actes de la Recherche en Sciences Sociales*, no. 59, September 1985, pp. 86–93.

Braga, Júlio, *Sociedade Protetora dos desvalidos: uma irmandade de cor*, Salvador, Ianamá, 1987.

Braga, Osvaldo Melo, *Bibliografia de Joaquim Nabuco*, Rio de Janeiro, Imprensa Nacional, 1952.

Branner, John C., 'The Tombador Escarpment in the State of Bahia, Brazil', *American Journal of Science*, New Haven, 30 (179): 335–43, 1910.

Buesco, Mircea, 'Aspectos Econômicos do Processo Abolicionista', *Revista de Informação Legislativa*, Brasília, 25 (98): 71–86, 1988.

Cabral, Sérgio, *As escolas de samba*, Rio de Janeiro, Fontana, 1974.

Calmon, Pedro, *História Social do Brasil*, 2 tomo, Espírito da Sociedade Imperial, 3rd edition, São Paulo, Companhia Editora Nacional, 1937.

Cândido, Antônio, O método de Sílvio Romero, São Paulo, Martins, 1963.
—— Formação da literatura brasileira; momentos decisivos, 2nd edition, São Paulo, Martins, 1964.
Cardoso, Ciro F.S., Escravo ou camponês? São Paulo, Brasiliense, 1987.
Cardoso, Fernando Henrique, Capitalismo e escravidão no Brasil meridional, São Paulo, Difusão Européia do Livro, 1962.
Carneiro, Edson, A sabedoria popular, Rio de Janeiro, MEC/INL, 1957.
—— Candomblés da Bahia, Rio de Janeiro, Ouro, 1968.
Carvalho, Delgado de, História da cidade do Rio de Janeiro, Rio de Janeiro, Secretaria Municipal de Cultura, 1988.
Carvalho, José Murilo de, Os bestializados; o Rio de Janeiro e a República que não foi, São Paulo, Companhia das Letras, 1987.
—— and Silva, Eduardo, 'Entre a Enxada e o Voto', Acervo: Revista do Arquivo Nacional, Rio de Janeiro, 2 (1): 23–8, 1987.
Cascudo, Luís da Câmara, Dicionário do folclore brasileiro, 4th edition rev. e aum, São Paulo, Melhoramentos, Brasília: INL, 1976.
Castro, Antônio Barros de, 'A Economia Política, o Capitalismo e a Escravidão'. In J. R. do Amaral Lapa (org.), Modos de produção e realidade brasileira, Petrópolis, Vozes, 1980.
Centro Integrado de Estudos Geológicos, Morro do Chapéu, Bahia, Brasília, Departamento Nacional da Produção Mineral, 1987.
Chalhoub, Sidney, Visões da liberdade; uma história das últimas décadas da escravidão na Corte, São Paulo, Companhia das Letras, 1990.
Chartier, Roger, Cultural History; between Practices and Representations, trans. Lydia G. Cochrane, Cambridge, Polity Press, 1988.
Clarke, Peter B., 'Charismatic Authority and the Creation of a New Order; the Case of the Mahdiyyat Movement in South-western Nigeria'. In Donal B. Cruise O'Brien and Christian Coulon (eds.), Charisma and Brotherhood in African Islam, Oxford, Clarendon Press, 1988, pp. 157–82.
Colson, Frank, 'On Expectations – Perspectives on the Crisis of 1889 in Brazil', Journal of Latin American Studies. Cambridge, 13(2): 265–92, 1981.
Conrad, Robert Edgar, Os últimos anos da escravatura no Brasil, 1850–1888, Rio de Janeiro, Civilização Brasileira; Brasília, INL, 1975.
—— Tumbeiros, São Paulo, Brasiliense, 1985.
Costa, Emília Viotti da, Da senzala à colonia, São Paulo, Difel, 1966.
—— Da Monarquia à República: Momentos decisivos, São Paulo, Grijalbo, 1977.
Costa, Wilma Peres, 'Notas Sobre o Jacobinismo Brasileiro'. Trabalho apresentado no Seminário Rio Republicano, FCRB, 1984.
Cunha, Manuela Carneiro da, Negros, estrangeiros; os escravos libertos e sua volta à Africa, São Paulo, Brasiliense, 1985.
Da Matta, Roberto, Carnavais, malandros e heróis; para uma sociologia do dilema brasileiro, 3rd edition, Rio de Janeiro, Zahar, 1981.
Darnton, Robert, O grande massacre de gatos, Rio de Janeiro, Graal, 1986 (original edition 1984).
Davidson, Basil, Black Mother; African and Atlantic Slave Trade, 3rd edition, Middlesex, Penguin, 1980.
Davis, David Brion, Slavery and Human Progress, New York, Oxford University Press, 1984.
—— The Problem of Slavery in Western Culture, New York, Oxford University Press, 1988.

Dean, Warren, *Rio Claro: um sistema brasileiro de grande lavoura, 1820–1920*, São Paulo, Paz e Terra, 1977.

Degler, Carl, *Nem preto nem branco; escravidão e relações raciais no Brasil e nos EUA*, São Paulo, Labor do Brasil, 1976.

Drescher, Seymour, *Capitalism and Antislavery; British Mobilization in Comparative Perspective*, London, Macmillan, 1986.

Duarte, Paulo de Queiroz, *Os Voluntários da Pátria na Guerra do Paraguai*, Rio de Janeiro, Bibioteca do Exército, 2 vols, 1981–4.

Eakin, Marshall C., 'Race and Identity: Sílvio Romero, Science, and Social Thought in Late 19th Century Brazil', *Luso-Brazilian Review*, 22(2): 151–74, 1985.

Eduardo, Octavio da Costa, *The Negro in Northern Brazil; a Study in Acculturation*, London, The African Publication Society, 1981.

Efegê, Jota, *Ameno Resedá, o rancho que foi escola*, Rio de Janeiro, Letras e Artes, 1975.

Elia, Hamilton, *Camões e a literatura Brasileira*, Rio de Janeiro, FCRB, 1973.

Elkins, Stanley, *Slavery; a Problem in American Institutional and Intellectual Life*, New York, The Universal Library, 1959.

Eneida, *História do carnaval carioca*, Rio de Janeiro, Civilização Brasileira, 1958.

Fadipe, N. A., *The Sociology of the Yoruba*, Ibadan, Ibadan University Press, 1970.

Faoro, Raimundo, *Os donos do poder*, Porto Alegre, Globo, 1958.

Fernandes, Florestan and Bastide, Roger, *Brancos e negros em São Paulo*, São Paulo, Companhia Editora Nacional, 1959.

Fogel, R. W. and Engermann, S. L. *Time on the Cross, the Economics of American Negro Slavery*, Boston, Little, Brown, 1974.

Fonseca, Walter, *Fonseca, uma família e uma história*, São Paulo, Obelisco, 1982.

Freyre, Gilberto, *Ordem e progresso*, Rio de Janeiro, José Olympio, 2 vols, 1959.

———— *Sobrados e Mocambos*, 5th edition, Rio de Janeiro, José Olympio/INL-MEC, 2 vols, 1977.

———— *Vida social no Brasil nos meados do século XIX*, trans. Waldemar Valente, 2nd edition, Rio de Janeiro, Artenova, Recife, Instituto Joaquim Nabuco de Pesquisas Sociais, 1977.

———— *O escravo nos anúncios de Jornais brasileiros do século XIX*, 2nd edition, São Paulo, Companhia Editora Nacional, 1979.

———— *Casa-Grande & Senzala*, 25th edition, Rio de Janeiro, José Olympio, 1987.

Ganem, Nadir, *Lençóis de outras eras*, Brasília, Thesaurus, 1984.

Gebara, Ademir, *O mercado de trabalho livre no Brasil*, São Paulo, Brasiliense, 1986.

Genovese, Eugene D., *Roll, Jordan, Roll; the World the Slaves Made*, New York, Vintage, 1976.

Ginzburg, Carlo, *O queijo e os vermes; o cotidiano e as idéias de um moleiro perseguido pela inquisição*, tradução Betânia Amoroso, São Paulo, Companhia das Letras, 1987 (1st edition, 1976).

Goncalves, Aureliano Restier, 'Carnes Verdes em São Sebastião do Rio de Janeiro, 1500–1900', *Revista de Documentos Para a História do Rio de Janeiro*, vol. III, Rio de Janeiro, Arquivo do Distrito Federal, 1952.

Gordon, Jacob U., 'Yoruba Cosmology and Culture in Brazil; a Study of African Survivals in the New World', *Journal of Black Studies*, 10(2): 231–44, 1979.

Gorender, Jacob, *O escravismo colonial*, São Paulo, Atica, 1978.

Graham, Richard, 'Os fundamentos da ruptura de relações diplomáticas entre o Brasil e a Grã-Bretanha em 1863: "Aquestão Christie"', *Revista de História*, 24(49), 117–38, 379–402, 1962.

—— 'Landowners and the Overthrow of the Empire', *Luso-Brazilian Review*, 7(2): 44–56, 1970.

—— 'Government Expenditures and Political Change in Brazil, 1880–1899', *Journal of Interamerican Studies and World Affairs*, 19(3): 339–68, 1970.

—— 'Escravidão e Desenvolvimento Econômico: Brasil e Sul dos Estados Unidos no Século XIX', *Estudos Econômicos*, 13(1): 223–57, 1983.

—— *Patronage and Politics in Nineteenth-century Brazil*, Stanford, Stanford University Press, 1990.

Graham, Sandra Landerdale, 'The Vintém Riot and Political Culture; Rio de Janeiro, 1880', *Hispanic American Historical Review*, 60(3): 432–49, 1980.

—— *House and Street: the Domestic World of Servants and Masters in Nineteenth-century Rio de Janeiro*, Cambridge, Cambridge University Press, 1988.

Hahner, June, 'Jacobinos versus Galegos: Urban Radicals versus Portuguese Immigrants in Rio de Janeiro in the 1890's', *Journal of Interamerican Studies and World Affairs*, 18(2): 125–54, May 1976.

Harris, Marvin, *Padrões raciais nas Américas*, Rio de Janeiro, Civilização Brasileira, 1967.

Hodgkin, Thomas, *Nigerian Perspectives; an Historical Anthology*, 2nd edition, Oxford, Oxford Unversity Press, 1975 (1st edition, 1960).

Holanda, Sérgio Buarque de, 'As Colônias de Parceria'. In Sérgio B. de Holanda (org.), *História geral da civilização brasileira*, Tomo V, São Paulo, Difel, 1960, pp. 245–60.

Ianni, Octávio, *As metamorfoses do escravo*, São Paulo, Difusão Européia do Livro, 1962.

Instituto Brasileiro de Geografia e Estatística, *Enciclopédia dos municipios Brasileiros*, Rio de Janeiro, 1959, vol. xx.

Johnson, Samuel, *The History of the Yorubas: from the Earliest Times to the Beginning of the British Protectorate*, Lagos, C.S.S., 1976.

Karash, Mary C., *Slave Life in Rio de Janeiro, 1808–1850*, Princeton, Princeton University Press, 1987.

Lacombe, Américo Jacobina, 'A Cultura Africana no Brasil', *Jornal do Brasil*, 27 November 1988, p. 7. Caderno B/Especial.

—— , Silva, Eduardo and Barbosa, Francisco de Assis, *Rui Barbosa e a queima dos arquivos*, Brasília, Ministério da Justiça; Rio de Janeiro, FCRB, 1988.

Lanna, Ana Lúcia Duarte, *A transformação do trabalho: a passagem para o trabalho livre na Zona da Mata mineira, 1870–1920*, 2nd edition, Campinas, Editora da UNICAMP, 1989.

Lamounier, Maria Lúcia, *Da escravidão ao trabalho livre*, Campinas, Papirus, 1988.

Laraia, Roque de Barros, 'Relações Entre Negros e Brancos no Brasil', *BIB; Boletim Informativo e Bibliográfico de Ciências Sociais*, Rio de Janeiro (7): 11–21, 1979.

Law, Robin, *The Oyo Empire (c. 1600–1836); a West African Imperialism in the Era of the Atlantic Slave Trade*, Oxford, Clarendon Press, 1977.

Leal, Victor Nunes, *Coronelismo, enxada e voto*, 2nd edition, São Paulo, Alfa-Omega, 1975.

Leão, José, *Silva Jardim; apontamentos para a biografia do ilustre propagandista hauridos nas informações paternas e dados particulares oficiais por* ... Rio de Janeiro, Imprensa Nacional, 1895.

Le Goff, J., 'As Mentalidades, uma História Ambigua'. In J. LeGoff e P. Nora (orgs), *História: novos objetos*, Rio de Janeiro, Francisco Alves, 1976.

Levine, Robert, *'Valley of Tears': Canudos as Myth in Brazilian History*, Unpublished.

Lévi-Strauss, Claude, *O pensamento selvagem*, 2nd edition, São Paulo, Companhia Editora Nacional, 1976.

Lewin, Linda, *Politics and Parentela in Paraíba: a Case-study of Family-based Oligarchy in Brazil*, Princeton, Princeton University Press, 1987.

Lima, Oliveira, *O movimento da Independência; o ImpérioBrasileiro, 1821–1889*, 2nd edition, São Paulo, Melhoramentos, s.d.

Luz, Nícia Vilela, *A luta pela industrialização do Brasil*, São Paulo, Difusão Européia do Livro, 1961.

Machado Neto, Zahidé et al., *O coronelismo na Bahia*, Salvador, Universidade Federal da Bahia, 1972.

Magalhães, João Batista, *A erolução militar do Brasil: anotações para a História*, Rio de Janeiro, Biblioteca do Exercito, 1958.

Magalhães Júnior, R., *Arthur Azevedo e sua época*, São Paulo, Saraiva, 1953.

—— *O Império em chinelos*, Rio de Janeiro, Civilização Brasieira, 1957.

Maia, Tom and Maia, Teresa Regina de Camargo, *Velha Bahia de hoje*, Rio de Janeiro, Expressão e cultura, 1985.

Mariz, Vasco, *A canção brasileira*, Rio de Janeiro, MEC, 1959.

Marshall, T. H., *Cidade, classe social e status*, Rio de Janeiro, Zahar, 1967.

Mattoso, Kátia M. de Queirós, 'A Propósito das Cartas de Alforria; Bahia, 1779–1850', *Anais de História*, Assis (SP), 4 (1972): 23–52.

——, Klein, Herbert S., and Engerman, Stanley L., 'Notas Sobre as Tendências e Padrões dos Preços de Alforrias na Bahia, 1819–1888'. In J. J. Reis (org.), *Escravidão e invenção da liberdade; estudos sobre o negro no Brasil*, São Paulo, brasiliense; Brasília: CNPq, 1988, pp. 60–72.

Menezes, Raimundo de, *Emílio de Menezes, o último boêmio*, São Paulo, Saraiva, 1949.

Merquior, José Guilherme, 'O Navio Negreiro', *Cadernos Brasileiros*, Rio de Janeiro, no. 35, May–June 1966.

—— *De Anchieta a Euclides; breve história da literatura brasileira*, Rio de Janeiro, José Olympio, 1977.

Morais, Evaristo de, *A campanha abolicionista, 1879–1888*, 2nd edition, Brasília, Editora da Universidade de Brasília, 1986.

Morton, F.W.O., *The Conservative Revolution of Independence*, DPhil Thesis, Oxford University, 1974.

Morton-Williams, Peter, 'The Yoruba Ogboni Cult in Oyo', *Africa*, 30(4): 362–74, 1960.

—— 'The Oyo Yoruba and the Atlantic Trade, 1670–1830', *Journal of the Historical Society of Nigeria*, 3(1): 25–45, 1964.

Mota, Leonardo, *Violeiros do Norte*, São Paulo, Editora Monteiro Lobato, 1925.

Moura, Roberto, *Tia Ciata e a pequena África no Rio de Janeiro*, Rio de Janeiro, FUNARTE, 1983.

Mulvey, Patricia, *The Black Lay Brotherhoods of Colonial Brazil: a History*, PhD Thesis, City University of New York, 1976.

212   PRINCE OF THE PEOPLE

Murad, Abid, *A batalha de Tuiuti e uma lição de civismo*, Rio de Janeiro, Biblioteca do Exército, 1957.

Nabuco, Carolina, *A vida de Joaquim Nabuco*, 2nd edition, São Paulo, Companhia Editora Nacional, 1929.

Nascimento, Abdias, *O genocídio do negro brasileiro*, Rio de Janeiro, Paz e Terra, 1978.

Nequete, Lenine, *Escravos & Magistrados no segundo Reinado*, Brasília, Fundação Petrônio Portella, 1988.

Oliveira, Maria Inês de, *O liberto: o seu mundo e os outros; Salvador, 1790–1890*, São Paulo: Corrupio; Brasília, CNPq, 1988.

Paim, Antônio, *A filosofia da Escola do Recife*, Rio de Janeiro, Saga, 1966.

—— *História das idéias filosóficas no Brasil*, São Paulo, Grijalbo, 1967.

Pang, Eul-soo, *Bahia in the First Brazilian Republic; coronelism and oligarchies, 1889–1933*, Gainesville, University Press of Florida, 1979.

Peixoto, Afrânio, *Bugrinha*, 10th edition, Rio de Janeiro, Conquista; Brasília, INL, 1972.

Pereira, João Batista Borges, *Estudos antropológicos e sociológicos sobre o negro no Brasil; aspéctos históricos e tendências atuais*, São Paulo, Universidade de São Paulo, 1981.

Pinho, Wanderley, 'A Bahia (1808–1856)'. In Sérgio Buarquede Holanda (ed.), *História Geral da Civilização Brasileira*, São Paulo, Difusão Européia do Livro, 1964, Tomo II, 2 vol., pp. 242–311.

Pinto, Egon Prates, *Armorial brasileiro*; iluminuras de Luís Gomes Loureiro, Rio de Janeiro, Revista da Semana, 1936.

Pinto, L.A. Costa, *O negro no Rio de Janeiro*, São Paulo, Companhia Editora Nacional, 1953.

Planella, João José, *Índice por assuntos gerais da Revista do IHGB, 1838–1983*, Porto Alegre, mimeo., 1983.

Pontes, Eloy, *A vida exuberante de Olavo Bilac*, 2 vols, Rio de Janeiro, José Olympio, 1944.

Queiroz, Maria Isaura Pereira de, *O mandonismo local na vida política brasileira*, São Paulo, I.E.B., 1969.

Ramos, Arthur, *Introdução à antropologia brasileira*, 3 vols. Rio de Janeiro, Casa do Estudante do Brasil, 1947.

—— *O folclore negro do Brasil; demopsicologia e psicanálise*, 2nd edition ilustrada e revista, Rio de Janeiro, Casa do Estudante do Brasil, 1954.

—— *As culturas negras no Novo Mundo*, 4th edition. São Paulo, Companhia Editora Nacional, 1979.

Reis, Elisa Maria da Conceição Pereira, *The Agrarian Roots of Authoritarian Modernization in Brazil, 1880–1930*, PhD Thesis, Massachusetts Institute of Technology, 1979.

Ribeiro, Gladys Sabina, *'Cabras' e 'pés-de-chumbo': os rolos do tempo; o antilusitanismo na cidade do Rio de Janeiro, 1890–1930*, Tese de Mestrado, Universidade Federal Fluminense, 1987.

Richardson, David (ed.), *Abolition and its Aftermath*, London, Frank Cass, 1985.

Rodrigues, E. Martins, Falcon, Francisco José Calazans and Neves, Margarida de Souza, *A Guarda Nacional no Rio de Janeiro, 1831–1918*, Rio de Janeiro, PUC, 1981.

Rodrigues, Raymundo Nina, *O animismo fetichista dos negros baianos*. Rio de Janeiro, Civilização Brasileira, 1935.

———— Os africanos no Brasil, São Paulo, Companhia Editora Nacional, 1945.

Romero, Sílvio, A literatura brasileira e a crítica moderna; ensaio de generalização, Rio de Janeiro, Imprensa Industrial de João Paulo Ferreira Dias, 1880.

Russel-Wood, A. J. R., Fidalgos and Philanthropists: the Santa Casa da Misericórdia of Bahia, 1550–1755, Londres, Macmillan, 1968.

———— The Black Man in Slavery and Freedom in Colonial Brazil, New York, St Martin's Press, 1982.

Sales, Fernando, Lençóis, coração diamantino da Bahia, Salvador, s. ed., 1973.

Santos, Francisco Agenor de Noronha, As freguesias do Rio antigo, Rio de Janeiro, Cruzeiro, 1965.

Santos, José Maria dos, A política geral do Brasil, São Paulo, J. Magalhães, 1930.

Santos, Juana Elbein dos, Os nagô e a morte, 4th edition, Petrópolis, Vozes, 1986.

Schwartz, Stuart B., 'The Manumission of Slaves in Colonial Brazil; Bahia, 1684–1745', Hispanic American Historical Review, 54 (4): 603–35, 1974.

———— 'Resistance and Accommodation in Eighteenth-century Brazil: the Slaves' View of Slavery', Hispanic American Historical Review, 57(1): 69–81, 1977.

———— Sugar Plantations in the Formation of Brazilian Society; Bahia, 1850–1935, Cambridge, Cambridge University Press, 1985.

Schwarz, Roberto (org.), Os pobres na literatura brasileira, São Paulo, Brasiliense, 1983.

Senna, Ronaldo de Salles, Garimpo e religião na Chapada Diamantina: um estudo do Jarê, variante regional do sincretismo candomblé de caboclo – umbanda, Tese de Mestrado, Universidade Federal da Bahia, 1973.

Shinnie, P. L. (ed.), The African Iron Age, Oxford, Clarendon, 1971.

Silva, Eduardo, Barões e escravidão; três gerações de fazendeiros e a crise da estrutura escravista, Rio de Janeiro, Nova Fronteira; Brasília, INL, 1984.

———— (org.), Idéias políticas de Quintino Bocaiúva, 2 vols, Brasília, Senado Federal, Rio de Janeiro, FCRB, 1986.

———— As queixas do povo, Rio de Janeiro, Paz e Terra, 1988.

———— and Reis, João J., Negociação e conflito; a resistência negra no Brasil escravista, São Paulo, Companhia das Letras, 1989.

Silva, José Luis F. Werneck da, Isto é o que me parece: a Sociedade Auxiliadora da Indústria Nacional na formação social brasileira, 1827–1904, 2 vols., Tese de Mestrado, Universidade Federal Fluminense, 1979.

Simonsen, Roberto, 'Aspéctos da História Econômica do Café', Anais do 3o. Congresso de História Nacional, Rio de Janeiro, IHGB, 1941, vol. IV, pp. 211–99.

Skidmore, Thomas E., O preto no branco; raça e nacionalidade no pensamento brasileiro, Rio de Janeiro, Paz e Terra, 1976.

Slenes, Robert, The Demography and Economics of Brazilian Slavery, 1850–1888, PhD Thesis, Stanford University, 1976.

Smith, Robert S., Kingdoms of the Yoruba, 3rd edition, London, James Currey, 1988.

Soares, Luís Carlos, Urban Slavery in Nineteenth-century Rio de Janeiro, PhD Thesis, University of London, 1988.

Soares, Ubaldo, A escravatura na Misericórdia, Rio de Janeiro, Fundação Romão de Matos Duarte, 1958.

Sodré, Nelson Werneck, História da literatura brasileira, 2nd edition, Rio de Janeiro, José Olympio, 1940.

————História da Imprensa no Brasil, Rio de Janeiro, Civilização Brasileira, 1966.

Sousa, Octávio Tarquinio de (ed.), *O pensamento vivo de José Bonifácio*, São Paulo, 1944.

Stein, Stanley J., *Vassouras, a Brazilian coffee county, 1850–1900*, Princeton, Princeton University Press, 1985.

Sutcliffe, David and Wong, Ansel (eds.), *The Language of the Black Experience: Cultural Expression through Word and Sound in the Caribbean and Black Britain*, Oxford, Basil Blackwell, 1986.

Tannenbaum, Frank, *Slave and Citizen: the Negro in the Americas*, New York, Alfred A. Knopf, 1947.

Tavares, Luís Henrique Dias, *A Independência do Brasil na Bahia*, 2nd edition, Rio de Janeiro, Civilização Brasileira/MEC, 1977.

Tavares-Neto, J. and Azevedo, E. S., 'Racial Origin and Historical Aspects of Family Names in Bahia, Brazil', *Human Biology*, 49 (1977): 287–99.

Taunaey, Afonso d'Escragnolle, *Pequena história do café no Brasil*, Rio de Janeiro, DNC, 1945.

Teles, Gilberto Mendonça, *Camões e a Poesia Brasileira*, Rio de Janeiro, FCRB, 1973.

Tolipan, Heloísa, 'Sambista Centenária', *Jornal do Brasil*, 28 February 1987, Caderno Cidade, p. 5.

Valente, Waldemar, *Sincretismo religioso Afro-brasileiro*, 3rd edition, São Paulo, Companhia Editora Nacional, 1977.

Vasconcelos, Ary, *Panorama da música popular brasileira*, 2 vols, São Paulo, Martins, 1964.

Vaz, Lílian Fessler, 'Notas Sobre o Cabeça de Porco', *Revista do Rio de Janeiro*, 1(2): 29–35, 1986.

Verger, Pierre Fatumbi, *Orixás; deuses iorubás na África e no Novo Mundo*, São Paulo, Corrupio/Circulo do Livro, 1981.

——— *Fluxo e refluxo do tráfico de escravos entre o Golfo de Benin e a Bahia de Todos os santos dos séculos XVII a XIX*, trad. Tasso Gadzanis, São Paulo, Corrupio, 1987.

Viana, Oliveira, *O Ocaso do Império*, São Paulo, Melhoramentos, 1925.

Vilaça, Marcos Vinicius and Albuquerque, Roberto de, *Coronel, Coronéis*, Rio de Janeiro, Tempo Brasileiro, 1965.

Weber, Max, *Economia y sociedad; esbozo de sociologia compreensiva*, México, Fondo de Cultura Económica, 1984.

Witter, José Sebastião, *Ibicaba, uma esperiência pioneira*, 2nd edition, São Paulo, Arquivo do Estado de São Paulo, 1982.

Index